The Invitation

"Blessed are those who are invited to the marriage supper of the Lamb."

The Role of Intimacy in Life, Judgment and Eternal Inheritance

Michael Davidson

Acknowledgments

I would like to extend my heartfelt thanks to my wife, Irene, for her selfless work in the production of this book. It was a special joy to discover that my life partner had the skills that I lacked but desperately needed. Without her expertise in editing, this book would never have made it to print.

I would like to thank my son, Paul, for his graphic design work on the cover as well as his other valuable input. I have also appreciated the support and assistance of my daughter, Debbie. I am grateful, as well, to the many friends and relatives whose prayers and encouragement have given me much needed support.

I thank the Lord for His unspeakable mercy. *"No man can receive anything except it be given him from heaven."* At a time when I desperately needed to hear from God, He spoke so much more than I could ever have imagined. To Him be the glory.

Table of Contents

Introduction

We all know the importance of passion. A passionless marriage is sterile. An athlete or musician who lacks passion won't excel. A motivational speaker without passion will inspire no one. And yet we can live out the bulk of our lives without passion for God. The reason is simple: We can get along without it. But in doing so we also sacrifice intimacy, for the two go hand in hand. The result is costly — in both time and eternity.

I don't believe the vast majority of us have ever understood life, let alone the afterlife. I believe that most people are ambitious and self-centered. That's OK, even normal. God can work with that. A truly self-centered person would pursue God because only He offers true riches. A truly ambitious person would want only the best for himself, and he would make God his priority. But for many, all that ambition and self-centeredness is wasted on other pursuits because passion for God is absent. We have failed to understand what God has to offer.

Some people are just naturally passionate for God, and will seek Him no matter how intense the struggles and temptations of life. These people are rare. For most of us, there needs to be insight. We need to know what we're missing. We need a revelation of the world to come as well as an understanding of what is at stake at the Judgment Seat of Christ. That understanding doesn't come easily. It can't be imparted with a few upbeat quips and a smattering of feel-good anecdotes.

One author, commenting on this book's length, asked, "Who is going to read a book this long? Books are getting shorter, not longer, because people don't read anymore." My answer to him was simple: Would you fear a judgment that could be explained in fifty pages? Would you give your life for an inheritance that could be summarized in thirty? Would you forsake all for a God whose glory could be described in ten? If there is one subject we need to take time with, it is this one.

We live in the "just give me the jist of it" generation. For booksellers, this is the day of dummies and fakers. I recall, with humble clarity, the day I bought DOS for Dummies. My first in the faker's series was "The Fakers Guide to Classical Music", and I wasn't disappointed. With those thirty pages under my belt, I could fake classical music with the best of them. But this book is neither for dummies nor fakers; it is for those who care about their souls. It is an investment.

I never intended to write a book; it was the furthest thing from my mind. I was in my mid-fifties when I was beset with a serious bout of insomnia. So serious and prolonged, in fact, that I had to take early retirement. That was a difficult time. God was faithful, but in many ways my life, including my ministry, ground to a halt. I struggled and sought the Lord for a year. During this period He spoke many things, but there was no breakthrough — at least not the kind I was seeking.

One day I woke up to what I expected would be just another dreary day of fatigue and boredom. Instead, there was a definite change in the "atmosphere". My mind was flooded with inspired thoughts, so I took a pen to record them, expecting a few pages at most. When my wife returned four hours later, I was still frantically scribbling, and I announced to her that I was writing a book. I had gone from total dryness to an open heaven. As a Bible teacher, this experience was not unfamiliar, but now it was occurring on a scale that I had never encountered before.

I had two such "visitations", totaling a period of over six months. The book that you are now reading is the result. From start to finish, the book took three years: two years of writing and one of editing. Strangely, the most difficult thing to nail down was the core theme of the book. Because I hadn't planned to write a book, I didn't start with a theme in mind. It was obvious early on what the core elements would be, but how they would mesh and which one would emerge as the unifying factor, eluded me.

When God finally did speak, He was very clear: This book is about passion. More precisely, it is about the goal of passion, which is intimacy with God. Eternal life was our Lord's preoccupation and it needs to be ours as well. So while this book addresses intimacy in time, our focus is really intimacy in eternity.

That being the case, why is a large section of the book devoted to the Judgment Seat of Christ? I asked God the same question and the answer was readily apparent: How we live our lives will determine our rank in the eternal kingdom, and our rank determines our intimacy with God. It is through the process of judgment that God assesses our lives.

It is possible to read the entire Bible and never even notice the theme of Judgment. You have probably never heard a sermon on it unless your pastor is actually a prophet, and even then it is doubtful. But in His grace, God gives us insight into this seminal event that will determine our activities, assignments, and access in the ages to come.

People buy books based on their "felt need". If you bought this book because you feel a need to draw closer to God, then you made a wise choice. God gives gifts to those who seek Him, the chief gift being Himself. But you won't truly understand the dimension of God's gift to you until you have finished the section on Judgment. In your search for intimacy, the unexpected discovery of the believer's judgment will impart truth that will forever change the way you look at life. If that truth changes the way you live, then it will also change your rank in eternity.

One of the great tensions in Scripture is between truth and love. "Mercy and truth have met together (in Jesus)" (Ps. 85:10). "Do not let kindness and truth leave you; bind them around your neck" (Prov. 3:3). "Speaking the truth in love, we are to grow up..." (Eph. 4:15). I tried to write this book while keeping these two things in balance, but it wasn't easy. It would have been far easier to strive for a "soft landing" by accenting mercy, kindness, and love at the expense of truth.

Intimacy with God, in time and eternity, is the theme of this book. But intimacy is impossible without truth, according to Jesus in John chapter 4. For those who love truth and have a passion for Jesus, I believe this book will be easy reading although easy doesn't mean unchallenging. God "has set eternity in our hearts", but, with few exceptions, we need to be challenged to the core before we can accept the eternal goals that God has for us. Life on earth is often just too comfortable and engaging.

And so, dear reader, you are about to embark on an adventure. This book begins and ends with the Marriage Feast of the Lamb, and you are invited. "The Four Pillars of Judgment" form the core of this book because it is this that establishes our inheritance. God Himself is our chief inheritance and, as we grow in this revelation, both judgment and eternity become less obscure and threatening. They are seen for what they truly are: the pathway to intimacy.

Everything in this book, as in life, moves us relentlessly to the final section and the final chapter. At the wedding feast, judgment is a distant memory, as death is swallowed up in life, and we enjoy our inheritance among those who worship before the throne. May this book bring you closer to the throne, both now and in the ages to come.

SECTION ONE

Orientation to the Eternal

ONE

The Meaning of Life

"Jesus Saves!"

As a catchy one-liner, it lacked a certain punch, but you couldn't fault the simplicity. I was at a famous resort, staring at the sign outside a church. Sprawled on the grass beneath it was a young man who definitely needed saving. I didn't know the fellow or any of his companions, but I smiled at the irony. Their backpacks, scruffy beards, and ragged denims spoke volumes about their mission.

The year was 1975, and they were part of an army of hitchhiking college kids. In that age of innocence, thumbing the highways meant adventure, not death at the hands of a psycho. They were trying to "find themselves", or discover the meaning of life, or unearth some lofty ideal that would answer the cry of their hearts.

I've been there, and it's a hard place.

But I wish I'd taken a photo of those weary seekers, pausing in the shade of a "Jesus Saves" sign before continuing their quest for truth. The caption would have read "Right under their noses - so near and yet so far!" For they would circle the globe and scour every back alley before they would even consider such a prosaic answer as "Jesus saves". And maybe some of us did too. But for those of us who have discovered that Jesus saves and have found Life, the search is over.

So now what?

Have we reached the end, or is it really a new beginning? We are born again children of God and new creatures in Christ, so it is a beginning. We arrive at the meaning of life only to discover that we are immediately on another journey. This second journey is just as compelling as the first one. And, as with any journey, it is important to start well. For the Christian, life has literally taken on new meaning and it is this meaning that we must grasp. If we do, it will keep us on course in our journey to the City of God. With this in mind, let us move to an event from the recent past.

The Great Aspiration

It was a beautiful June morning. At the graveside eulogy for his father, the former President Regan, Ron Jr. stood before the gathering and declared with finality, "Our concerns are no longer his." With that brief statement, Ron captured the essence of death: the spirit's blessed release from the physical life described by Moses as "labor and sorrow" (Ps. 90:10).

But though death taunts us with its impenetrable shroud, it is life that mystifies us. Without doubt, the age-old question as to its meaning has haunted mankind like no other. But for a Christian, the meaning of life was never meant to be a mystery. It is best explained by something I call "the great aspiration".

What is the greatest thing you can aspire to in this lifetime? To be granted the honor demanded of Jesus by the mother of James and John. That woman's request stood protocol on its ear. She wanted her sons to sit next to Jesus in the coming Kingdom — one on the left and one on the right. The impudence! The raw ambition! At least that's the way the others saw it. Maybe that's how you saw it too, not realizing that in this short passage lay a jewel.

This is, after all, the crux of everything: "seating", if you will, in the Kingdom. The woman erred only in believing that it was hers for the asking, whereas all rank in the Kingdom is earned. Plus, her timing was a bit off, because the seating isn't established until the invitations go out. That can't happen until the Judgment and the proclamation of Revelation 19:9: *"Blessed are those who are invited to the marriage supper of the Lamb."*

The Meaning of Life

The meaning of life, then, is best framed with a question. The question is simply this: How can I live my life so that I will gain the greatest possible proximity to the Lord Jesus Christ throughout the ages to come? That thought hasn't even occurred to most people, let alone been the focus of their life. But that is the overriding issue of life, and the one that is settled at the believers' judgment.

If that question doesn't inspire us, then our dreams are too small. Plus, we are at a disadvantage, because where there is no inspiration, there will seldom be aspiration. Aspiration is the tidal wave that carries us over the debris and discouragement of life to our appointed place in God. That is why our Lord's response to the mother of James and John is very telling.

Jesus gave her no rebuke, so we know that the request did not displease Him. He treated it with the seriousness it deserved. But with an intensity that was predictive of His own suffering, He spoke of the cup they would have to drink and the baptism they would have to undergo. To the loud assertions of James and John that they were ready, Jesus added His agreement. But He closed the discussion with the observation that these seats were not His to give. And then, ever the teacher, Jesus seized the moment to clarify this most important issue: greatness in the Kingdom.

As the consummate observer, Jesus knew the vanity of men. He saw their values and their willingness to wager their souls for the trifles of life. He had only praise and esteem for those who invested in the eternal, but scorn and derision for those who didn't. The disciples had been arguing earlier about which of them was the greatest. Now with the sons of Zebedee making an outright appeal for position, it seemed an apt time for discussion.

So He called a meeting.

Greatness in the Kingdom

It sounds carnal, doesn't it, God calling a meeting to discuss how to become great? Something in that scene doesn't fit our distorted view of God. As if that wouldn't be important to Him; as if He wouldn't be interested in revealing the source and course of greatness, an all-consuming passion of the human race.

No, the absorption with true greatness is not strange or misguided. It's the lack of it that is so appalling. So many squander their lives on foolish passions, yet have a pie-in-the-sky disdain for the glories of heaven. They seek the very "greatness" Jesus condemned — the gathering of objects and accolades all for the sake of earthly prestige. One cynic commented wryly on this pointless exercise with the words: "I spend money I don't have, to buy things I don't need, to impress people I don't like."

So what is this greatness that Our Lord gave so much time to in His various discourses? Not what you'd expect. As usual, He turns everything on its head. He tells them to aim for greatness by behaving the opposite of great. Greatness in the world is measured, as Jesus pointed out, by authority and control. "Not so with you," He told them, but rather "*he who would be greatest, must be servant of all.*"

Servanthood

How deflating. What's the point of being great if you can't be great? Anyone could be a servant. Or could they? He had to break their hearts before they could begin to intuit, or even desire, what He was suggesting. His moment would

18

come. In one of the most poignant scenes in history, God would wash the dirty feet of His own creation.

We are all familiar with this scene; it evokes many emotions. Yes, the humility is stunning, but on the other hand, this is God. We have our leaders, our idols, and our great men on pedestals. It's disturbing to the soul to have them wait on us. Plus it threatens our dignity and our fragile psyches to witness God doing something that is beneath the pride of man.

But a greater shock is coming. Speaking of the second advent, our Lord makes this statement: "*Blessed are those slaves whom the master shall find on the alert when he comes; truly I say to you, that he will gird himself to serve, and have them recline at table, and will come up and wait on them*" (Luke 12:37).

Hold it now!

A master waiting on his slaves? A master serving supper to his slaves?

The Master?

Yes indeed. This is a clear reference to the Marriage Supper of the Lamb when God Himself will be our waiter. Truly, nobody could have invented the God of the Bible. The gods that men invent are always vain and pompous like their master, Satan. But the Son of Man came not to be served, but to serve. He took that attitude back with Him to heaven where He now waits *for* us, to wait *on* us.

The humility is mind-boggling, but the message is clear: servant leadership is not an oxymoron. He has acted out the contradiction and shown us that it is attainable for those who would be great on earth, and mandatory for those who would be great in heaven. As it turns out, the term *greatness* is "code", and involves more than just serving. Wherever we see it in scripture we are touching the eternal, and are eminently closer to the heartbeat of God.

Jesus used it often.

The Heartbeat of God

Jesus told one individual to sell all he had and give to the poor, and he would be great in the Kingdom of Heaven. In another discourse, Jesus stood a child in their midst and declared that this was greatness — to be childlike. To the persecuted, He gave the exhortation: *"Rejoice, for **great** is your reward in heaven."* But all of these statements were mere appetizers to a subject that Our Lord seemed to obsess on — eternal inheritance, or greatness in the Kingdom. The Spirit would later add many of the details.

We have urgent commands to seek the kingdom and to enter by the narrow gate. We are told that there is an inheritance awaiting us in heaven, pure and undefiled. We hear of crowns and new names and people who reign with Christ for a thousand years. We hear of thrones and dominions and everlasting praise. We have parables and the visions of those who are caught up. We have lofty descriptions of a celestial city. We hear frequent mention of a judgment and a heavenly fire and the need to bear fruit that lasts. We see creatures, we see a tree, we see pearly gates and streets of gold, all with the overriding atmosphere of peace. We are told of a great cloud of witnesses, the church of the firstborn whose names are written in heaven. We are given details of the consummation of the age in all of its apocalyptic fury. We witness the final victory and the casting of death into the lake of fire. And at long last, the wiping away of all tears. The Judgment is complete, and every man receives his due from God.

Rank in the Kingdom is established.

Stepping Back

Let's back up a bit. Once we're saved we join a church and tackle this tome called the Bible. We hear about the sanctification process that changes us into the likeness of Christ. Sounds farfetched, but OK, we're on board. We discover that we're now battling the sin that we formerly embraced, so that's good. It makes life a struggle, but the Christian life is so fulfilling that we'd never go back.

But we soon learn that we must seek first the Kingdom of God, go into all the world and preach the gospel, and visit the sick and imprisoned. We need to find our ministry in the church, join a small group, get involved in prayer, but above all, worship God and put Him first. And still there is more. Sounds a bit much when we already work forty hours a week plus commuting. We're also trying to get ahead in life, raise a family, do home repairs, befriend our neighbors and still find time for leisure. And now this: greatness in the Kingdom!

Who has time for the kingdom? Or better yet, what is the kingdom? Are we actually supposed to care about the after-life when we can barely manage life itself?

Yes.

Everything we do in life, while having temporal meaning, forms a permanent record that God uses to evaluate us for our most important role of all. That role is assigned after death and is eternal in nature. While it's not impossible to enter into your eternal destiny without understanding the big picture, it is much harder. The big picture is the kingdom, and not surprisingly, that was our Lord's favorite topic.

Some people have a chaotic approach to life and just muddle through, making progress in a seemingly random fashion. Others appear to have a high spiritual IQ and, with little guidance, make right choices and grow in God. And still others, like myself, can't do the Christian life well if they don't understand how it works. And because we are seldom taught the big picture, most of us are mesmerized by the minutia. We major on the minors and are transfixed by the trivial.

One visiting prophet could never get far into his message without quoting his favorite poem: "Some men die in shrapnel, others die in flames, but most men die one day at a time, playing silly games." Something in the force of that man's personality shook us up every time he said it. "No," our hearts cried in unison, " don't let me waste my life playing silly games. I want to play in the big leagues. I want to do things that will resonate a million years from now." He aroused passion. And none of us will get very far without it.

But it is passion for Jesus that is most important of all.

If you have it, you will find in this book a satisfying way to achieve the ultimate goal of that passion: intimacy with God in the City of Light. Muddling through will get you to heaven, but it takes passion and wisdom to inherit all things. It takes passion to even care. Cry out for passion!

Implications of Greatness

At first glance, the word *greatness* may seem vain and frivolous, or even worse, grandiose and unattainable. But let us personalize the term. Whereas on earth it may mean serving, in heaven it means intimacy. If intimacy with God goes hand-in-hand with greatness, then isn't greatness a goal worth seeking? Doesn't that qualify as the ultimate aspiration? Doesn't that erase the argument that pursuing greatness is vain? David tells us plainly in Psalm 16, *"The Lord...is my inheritance."* Though our works result in praise, glory and honor, these are simply the benefits that go with the true inheritance — the Lord Himself.

When Jesus talked about inheritance, He never mentioned intimacy. He took the opposite tack, perhaps because He knew the heart of man. He focused instead on greatness and glory. Many of us still don't get it. We're far too polite. Jesus *encouraged* self-interest! He fostered it! He appealed to it!

He told us in the most forceful Greek tense to seek treasure in heaven, not on earth. Period. It was a command. If your motivation is simply to barter a better deal for yourself in the world to come, then good for you. You're a wise man! Go for it! That was His attitude. That was His main point in the parable of the shrewd steward. But there is so much more to consider.

The pure in heart can join the dots.

They know that greatness equals intimacy.

God Speaks

Greatness equals intimacy.

I don't know how or when I first discovered that fact. I do know that early in my Christian life I began to develop a very clear goal. There are people who know from their first day on the job what position they hope to achieve before retirement — be it President or CEO. We applaud this kind of ambition and generally esteem people who set long-term goals and achieve them through diligence and sacrifice. I never had such a secular goal; mine was spiritual in nature and related to my eternal position in God.

My life has been fraught with difficulty, but not with failure. My biggest failure was having to repeat first year university. Though fear of failure never marred my life, that incident clearly affected me. When I got saved at twenty-eight, I realized that there was only one supreme failure and I feared it immensely. That was the failure to achieve God's eternal purposes, and to enter the Kingdom having fallen short. Although years would pass before I would study the Judgment in detail, one thing I realized early on was that not every Christian would inherit a throne. In my simple understanding, this was the great dividing line. A throne was like the ultimate prize in the "Christian game of life". Gaining one, in a sense, became my goal.

While this was always in the back of my mind, I don't recall the circumstances that led to an evening that was strange, to say the least. On the night in question, I found myself on my face before God, crying out to Him with one simple question: "Lord, will I have a throne in heaven?" In anguish, I repeated that question over and over again. That cry didn't issue from a heart of selfish ambition, but from one that desperately wanted to pass the great test **of** life. I'm not referring to a test **in** life, but to life itself. Passing that test meant a throne and intimacy with God.

The next day Wayne, a pastor from a nearby town, was passing through and called me for lunch. We had been good friends for years, and I considered him a mentor in the Lord and a man of God. I readily agreed, and at noon we found ourselves at a quiet Greek restaurant where we shared a delicious souvlaki.

Wayne is now an apostle to the nations, and at that time his prophetic mantle was already apparent. But still it took me by surprise when half way through the meal he stopped, put down his fork and, looking me straight in the eye, made a bold declaration: "Mike, the real reason I called you for lunch is because on the way into town God told me to call you and give you a message. The message is: 'You *will* have a throne'."

To say that I was stunned would be putting it mildly. That was the strongest word God had given me up to that point in my life. But the implications were profound. While my prayer the previous night might seem bizarre to many, to God it obviously wasn't. Not only did He receive it, He went out of His way to answer it in the quickest and most miraculous way possible. That speaks volumes about what pleases the heart of God.

But this story is not just about me because you have the same promise. However, all of God's promises are conditional. Jesus says in Revelation 3 that *"He who **overcomes**, I will grant to sit down with Me on My throne"* (verse 21). It would take years of refining before I could be assured that God had dealt with the character flaws that could have cost me that throne. My purpose in telling the story is to emphasize how powerfully God cares about this issue. It's one thing to read about thrones in scripture; it is quite another to have God speak to you about them personally.

Let the force of it hit you. God cares if you have a throne!

Forget false humility and misplaced meekness. Ask Him for one!

The Tyranny of the Urgent

How can we respond to such a mystical exhortation? Thrones?! It seems so irrelevant. Seeking one is scarcely a thought that intrudes itself into a mind that has "a thousand more important things to deal with". Many of these "important" things are actually mundane distractions, but yes, they have to be dealt with. We call it the tyranny of the urgent.

And that is the deception.

Look up the word "throne" in a concordance and you'll see that it appears hundreds of times, and many of the references relate to the saints in the afterlife. It certainly appears more times in the Bible than the things we routinely worry and fantasize about. The deception is that our fantasies are real and that the thrones aren't, when the opposite is true. By "real", I mean lasting. The Bible says this world is passing away, but the unseen spiritual world is forever. Thrones are forever; shiny new cars aren't.

In the next chapter we'll see that a wrong attitude towards heaven puts you at a serious disadvantage in the race of life. Paul alludes to this very clearly. Let us consider the words of this spiritual giant and observe the crass and almost simplistic way in which he views the Christian life.

Running the Race

Paul says something very curious in one of his letters: "*Do you not know that those who run in a race all run, but only one receives the prize? Run in such a way that you may win*" (*1 Cor. 9:24*). Strange words. Paul taught against competition in the Body; he taught against comparing ourselves with one another. Instead he emphasized the value and uniqueness of each member of the Body. So what is his point here?

Paul is railing against mediocrity. In the race of life, we are to have the same tenacity as a runner in a real race where there is only one prize. It's unacceptable to simply finish, which is the marathoner's mindset. We are to run as if it is all or nothing. That is how athletes did it in Paul's day. They trained to win — second place was no better than last. And they did it for a perishable wreath. By implication, how can we run the race of life half-heartedly when our reward is so vastly superior — an imperishable wreath?

Every Christian alive today is in a race. Everyone reading this book is in a race. One of the greatest men who ever lived has just told us it will take everything to win the race. He has told us the consequences of not winning this race. What is at stake is an imperishable wreath. This wreath represents Jesus, though with Him comes glory and honor.

We can appreciate Paul's intensity, but we may have trouble sharing it. After all, "running so as to win" is not a phrase that we are overly familiar with. In practical terms, what does it mean with respect to our faith?

The Question We Must Ask

Ask yourself this question: If Jesus walked into my church next Sunday and offered just one prize for the most faithful, committed person there, would I be the winner? A typical response would be, "No, my pastor would be the winner." Why? Pastors *should* be faithful and committed, but there is no suggestion in the scripture that any less will be required of us. Even though the present church structure might suggest that that is the case, it certainly is not. We will be judged with Christ as our standard, not some cultural tradition that allows "lay people" to be less spiritual.

A better answer would be that you and I can't possibly *know* if we would, in fact, win. All we can know is this: are we running **so** as to win? This we must be able to answer. If indeed there was only one winner, am I running **so** as to win? Based on my life, do I have as much chance as the next person?

Being in a position to win is not something that will just happen. It will take our best effort and all of God's grace. That is Paul's message. That is **running** "so as to win". But what about this whole matter of winning? What does winning mean? Paul is already saved, yet he talks about "winning Christ". *"I have suffered the loss of all things...that I might win Christ"* (Phil.3:8).

The Bottom Line

Let me say it in such a way that there can be no misunderstanding: If you don't hear, "Well done!" on Judgment Day, you didn't win. If you don't receive a throne, you didn't win. If you don't rule and reign with Christ, you didn't win. If you weren't an overcomer, you didn't win. You may be saved, but in the language of the Pauline epistle, you didn't "win Christ".

This is not about going to heaven, because Paul had assurance of that. Anyone with an ounce of ambition can see something more in this man's fervor — a prize. *The* Prize. He had seen the third heaven. He had seen the Lord and the reward of the righteous. He knew what was at stake, and it made him a driven man.

Paul's journey has ended. I believe it ended in greatness. How about ours? How will it end?

This book is about the journey to greatness, which is the journey to God. To successfully travel this journey, we have to raise our sights a little higher; we have to cast our glance a little further; we have to set our mind on *"things above where Christ is seated"*. But most important of all, we have to set our desire on Christ Himself.

Most of us have failed to understand the links between suffering and glory, faithfulness and inheritance, temporal loss and eternal gain, greatness and intimacy. It is time to make those connections. Those are the things that will resonate at the believers' judgment. But before we look at the judgment, we must look deeper into the connection between the temporal and the eternal. The sport of orienteering will help us in this regard.

TWO

The Role of Heaven

Orienteering is the sport of traversing unknown territory using only a map and a compass. The most basic principle is that you must fix your eyes on a distant landmark or you'll be lost. That is a perfect picture of the Christian life. With the Spirit as our guide, there are really two things that prevent us from losing our way: the map and the compass — the Bible and the eternal. We traverse life with the Word as a roadmap and heaven as the goal. If we take our eyes off either one, we can become as lost and disoriented as the unbelievers around us.

If you are only fixing on something ten feet or ten days in front of you, for sure you'll be lost. Temporal goals are necessary, but that is all some people have. Following God requires more than focus and zeal. It takes vision. People stumble when they lose sight of the goal, and lesser things begin to look attractive. They lose their compass; some even their moral compass. They begin to fail the treasure test. Jesus told us heart and treasure can't be separated. Where the one is, there you will find the other. If you're not storing up treasure in heaven, your heart is in this world, though you may deny it with every breath.

Jesus wants your heart, but so does heaven.

Seeking the Lord with all your heart should be the desire of every Christian. And if finding God *only* caused us to live better, more fruitful lives, then that's not a bad thing. But

finding God and following Him in this life will have repercussions a thousand years from now. It is important to know
that. If we teach and believe anything less, then we miss the
big picture of why we pursue Him: to establish something in
time that will have its full expression *and benefit* in eternity.

Life Without Heaven

When I was a young Christian, Evie Tournquist was one
of my favorite artists. She recorded a song where the dominant lyric went something like this: "If heaven had never
been promised, it would be worth it just having the Lord." I
know what she meant, and I've had moments when I've felt
the same. Walking with God in this life is its own reward.
Heaven is like a bonus, the icing on the cake. That is a nice
sentiment, but a little naïve and patently unscriptural.

The apostle Paul said if there is no resurrection from the
dead, we may as well eat, drink, and be merry, for tomorrow
we die. He said something even more puzzling: *"If we have
only hoped in Christ in this life, we are of all men most to be
pitied"* (I Cor.15:19). Pitied! What an odd choice of words.
Odd perhaps, but very accurate.

Here is where growing up as a unbeliever gives me an
advantage. I know how unbelievers think, because I once
thought the same way. I used to pity religious people. There
was only one overtly religious guy in the high school I
attended, and I had two major responses to him — admiration and pity. But the dominant feeling was pity, for I did not
want to be like him.

Why do most unbelievers pity Christians? *Because unbelievers have no concept of the eternal.* To them it's a myth.
They can't see heaven but they *can* see our lives, and that is
the problem. Watching our lives without knowing where we
are headed can lead them to a wrong conclusion. They may
admire us, but what we have, most of them don't want. They
pity our lot.

To them Christians are guilt-ridden, sin-obsessed, narrow-minded people. Christians *have* to be good. They lead boring lives. They can't think for themselves. They spend their weekends in dull meetings. They have to tithe. They can't have *real* fun. They carry big black Bibles. And in a world that dreads the label "uncool", Christians are the epitome of uncool.

That's a little extreme, but in many ways our critics are right. If it wasn't for heaven, the Christian life wouldn't make a lot of sense. Paul was one of the greatest men who ever lived, and possibly the most fervent of all Christians, but even he said it wouldn't be worth it without heaven. Would you follow God if it all ended with this life? Probably not, unless you're greater than the apostle Paul. I, for sure, wouldn't. We are not supposed to admit that, as if it is somehow wrong to do so. But it is not.

The Bible says Abraham wouldn't have *"lived as an alien"* if he wasn't seeking the eternal city whose *"architect and builder is God"*. Are we greater than Abraham? The saints in Hebrews 11 suffered torture in order to *"attain to a better resurrection"*. Are our motives more righteous than theirs? Like Paul, these people loved the Lord, but love wasn't enough. They needed heaven. Indeed, there is only one great motive for finding God, living right, and enduring suffering: the next world.

A Reason to Seek God

To try to teach passion for Jesus apart from the eternal is somewhat pointless, and yet we do it all the time. In fact, that is pretty much all we do. We somehow expect people to have such pure motives, that they will sacrifice all to pursue a relationship with God that has unseen benefits.

The scripture says, *"He who comes to God must believe… that He is a rewarder of those who diligently seek Him"* (Heb. 11:6). There, in a nutshell, is the problem. To pursue God, you almost have to be selfish. You have to believe there's a benefit. You have to believe that it's worth the work. In large part, we don't, and to a certain extent, it really isn't, if all we have is this life. It's the effect it has on the next life that gives seeking Him its real import. If we start with the eternal, then we will discover that there are some temporal benefits as well. But they pale by comparison.

We struggle with these statements largely because we have not been properly taught. We must ask ourselves one simple question: "Am I seeking the Lord with all my heart right now?" The answer is probably "No". It is certainly the right thing to do, but that is not incentive enough. There is only one reason we don't seek God with all our hearts: the cost. There is only one thing that will make us pay the cost: a greater benefit. That is the way God made us. We can dress it up any way we want, but it's really that simple.

Godly Constraints on Earthly Intimacy

Finding God in this life is good, but at best, we experience Him through a veil. The real aim is to experience Him intimately, face to face, on the other side. But how we meet Him here will determine how we experience Him there. Intimacy in time will determine intimacy in eternity.

So the constraints put on following Him here are simply roadblocks set up to determine who will know Him more intimately *there*. If knowing Him here was such a big issue, He certainly could have made it easier. But He didn't. Quite the opposite, *He made it very hard*. So hard, that many people have given up; they have stopped pursuing God; they are content with their lives. Over time, the hunger dissipates and apathy feels quite normal.

The fact is, it is very possible to live a godly life and yet never experience God in a deep way here on this earth. He will bless you for your godliness, and you'll die the death of the righteous, but you will pay a price. As in everything, you either pay now or you pay later. You will receive back in direct proportion to how you gave.

At one point in Mark's gospel, Jesus gave his famous camel illustration describing the difficulty of a rich man being saved. Peter, with a note of concern in his voice, reminded the Lord of something: *"Peter began to say to Him, 'Behold, we have left everything and followed You.' "* Jesus replied with a list of benefits that will follow this decision.

Benefits of Service: Three Plus One

In summary, Jesus promised three things: fellowship, persecutions and eternal life. It doesn't seem all that attractive until we hear the next verse: *"But many who are first, will be last, and the last, first."* This is a direct reference to the eternal kingdom where bedraggled itinerant preachers, while low on the pecking order here, will have great status there.

It will be the same for us. We are not greater than Peter. If we follow God, we will have fellowship with Him and each other. We will have persecutions and eternal life. But if that is where it ended, it wouldn't be all that tantalizing. But it doesn't. If we serve well, we will also have prominence in the eternal kingdom. With prominence comes intimacy. With intimacy comes glory and honor. Jesus never expected us to work for nothing. He pays very well, and He goes to great lengths to explain what the wages are.

Unless we are greater than Abraham, Peter, and Paul, it's a safe bet that none us would serve God without heaven — payday. To tell ourselves otherwise is foolishly pompous. But with so little teaching on the eternal, the practical effect of heaven and inheritance is negligible. To most people it is no longer the goal. It is something we teach in Sunday School, but it is not a subject for mature adults. That takes its toll. It tends to root us in the physical.

But think of life motivated by the eternal. We would "give what we cannot keep, to gain what we cannot lose".

We would have an undivided heart. We would work for the food that doesn't perish. We would make temporal decisions based on eternal goals.

Our lives would look very different, but so would our afterlives.

Judgment and Glory

Physical life has one unique characteristic: it is the only chance we have to offer ourselves to God. In a sin-ridden world where we must walk by faith, this offering comes at great cost. Faith, sin, and suffering have no part in the ages to come. Caught as we are between eternity past and a kingdom without end, our brief seventy years are but a moment in time.

But what a special moment, indeed.

Once we cross spiritual Jordan, the word "sacrifice" will have no relevance. Once we enter the eternal city, "resisting sin" will be a meaningless term. Once we see Him face to face, the "struggle to worship" will seem like a curious oddity. It is only now in this age that the angels peer with wonder at the race of men of whom the scripture says: *"Though they have not seen Him, yet they love Him."*

God is constantly making a statement to the unseen galleries about our love for Him, and the words He uses are our lives. And by His grace, we share in the reward of our passion, because life has one other critical dimension. Whether we realize it or not, the exchange of service here, for glory there, is a "limited time offering". At death, the record ends, the book is sealed, the die is cast, and the assignments are given. Then comes to pass that which is spoken of in Ecclesiastes:

"Wherever the tree falls, there it lies" (Ecc.11:3).

THREE

The Purpose of Judgment

In the last chapter we alluded to the eternal bliss that will one day be ours as children of God. But the quality of that bliss can't be established until our lives are judged. And while I can think of nothing more profound and sobering than our encounter with God, it is but one facet of a much larger event. Indeed the scripture records three separate judgments.

Remember, as well, that judgment is as much for God as it is for us. According to Psalm 89, the foundation of His throne is righteousness and justice, and justice has to be dispensed lest God violate His own nature.

In Isaiah 42 we find unusual language to describe God's commitment to justice: *"Behold My Servant (Jesus) whom I uphold...He will faithfully bring forth justice. He will not be disheartened or crushed, until He has established justice in the earth."* What is God saying? In the vernacular, something like the following: "If it's the last thing He does, Jesus is going to bring justice to the earth." There will be no short cuts or oversights, no compromises or convenience. Those who have longed for justice will not be disappointed.

God, you see, keeps a daybook. And your name is in it. So is mine.

We all have an appointment with God, for *"It is appointed unto man once to die and after this the judgment"* (Heb. 9:27). It's the one appointment we can't break, defer or reschedule. *"For He has fixed a day on which He will judge the world,"* and *"He will judge the world in righteousness."* Though this scripture says "world", all of us go to this appointment individually and alone. As in death, no one can go with us. No matter how much we've depended on people all our lives, we must make the journey through death alone and stand before Him in judgment alone.

In life there are really only three critical days — the day we are born, the day we are born again, and the day we are judged. The day of our death is merely a point of transition and has importance only in that certain things are fixed for all eternity. After death they can never be altered. These "things" are very important because it is *they* that come under judgment. It is *they* that decide our eternal future.

For most of us, the word "judgment" has negative connotations, so we'd rather not think about it. In that sense, even Christians can be fatalistic. Why worry about what you can't change? Do the best you can and let the chips fall where they may. But of course, what you know about judgment and how you prepare for it will dramatically effect how you experience it. With this as a guiding principle, let us look more closely at the judgments. There are three recorded in scripture.

The Great White Throne Judgment

The Great White Throne Judgment is our starting point.

"And I saw the dead, the great and the small, standing before the throne, and books were opened; and another book was opened, which is the book of life; and the dead were judged from the things which were written in the books, according to their deeds... And if anyone's name was not found written in the book of life, he was thrown into the lake of fire." *(Rev. 20:12,15)*

Is there any more chilling passage of scripture? Some day that event will take place exactly as described. This is the judgment of all the people who have died outside of Christ throughout the ages. Their destination is hell, and here they are judged for their deeds, to determine the severity of their punishment. Where are these people now? They are in the temporary abode of the wicked. *"Then the Lord knows how to rescue the godly from temptation, and to keep the unrighteous under punishment for the Day of Judgment" (II Pet. 2:9).* This judgment takes place after the final battle, at the end of time.

Two Problems

There are two main arguments that many people have with the Great White Throne Judgment. First, they believe that those who have never heard the gospel should not be there. I understand this thinking. The mind recoils at the thought of people in hell who never had the chance to make a decision for Christ.

But there's one problem with this argument: it makes a mockery of the great commission. If not hearing the gospel protects a person from hell, then the kindest thing we can do is not preach it. For in almost every gathering where the gospel is preached, there are those who reject it. Unfortunately, this argument fails the test of logic. God is not always fair, but He's always right. We will have to wait for eternity to see the rightness of this.

The second argument goes something like this: I can see God sending evil people to hell, but why good people? Hitler in hell I can understand, but my next-door neighbor wouldn't hurt a fly. It just seems so unfair. The problem with this argument is that *"there is no one who does good, not even one" (Psalm 53:3).* That is the clear teaching of scripture. There are no good people in hell because there are no good people.

We tend to picture a mass of humanity heading to heaven and God picking out the evil ones and sending them to hell; but, in fact, it is just the opposite. Like lemmings running towards a cliff, we are all heading for hell. God rescues some, not based on any innate goodness, but based on their response to the gospel and the enigmatic concept known as election.

A Profound Experience for Believers

Those of us who died in Christ will be more than interested spectators. In I Corinthians 6 we are told with emphasis, *"Do you not know that the saints will judge the world?"* We are told elsewhere that *"I saw thrones, and **they** sat upon them and judgment was given to **them**"* (Rev. 20: 4). As hard as it may be to assimilate, we have an important role to play in the judgment of the world. But it is more than just our role in judgment that should hold our fascination; it is the solving of so many puzzles that have baffled researchers for eons. Those of us who are more politically aware will see the uncovering of the cryptic events we have wondered about all our lives.

It is often said in the case of war, that it is the victors who write the history books. To the victors go the spoils and the high moral ground. The vanquished, on the other hand, are tried for war crimes. We will be very surprised on that day to see who the true villains are.

Every honest student of history has found villains amongst many of our most celebrated leaders. For trying to set the record straight, these people are called conspiracy nuts or revisionists. But judgment will be a day of vindication. A final history of the world will be written before the eyes of every living creature. And better yet, your story is being woven into this epic journal, even to the details of the past twenty-four hours.

There is currently a great interest in Bible codes. It is postulated by some serious investigators that, if we could plumb the depths of the scriptures, we would find an amazing thing. By applying the correct codes, we would find, concealed in its pages, the details of every human life and every human event. This should not be surprising, for if God has not already written these details in His book, they will yet be written.

At a time of great fixation with Hollywood's latest special-effects blockbuster, I find the lack of interest in judgment a curious thing. Nothing in human history or human creation can rival the drama of the great judgments, let alone the mammoth revelations that unfold from there.

The Judgment of the Nations

The second judgment is the Judgment of the Nations pictured in Matthew 25 and mentioned in Joel 3:1,2. This judgment involves the sheep and the goat "nations" and is prefaced with the following scripture:

> *"But when the Son of Man comes in His glory, and all the angels with Him, then He will sit on His glorious throne.*
> *And all the nations will be gathered before Him and He will separate them from one another, as the shepherd separates the sheep from the goats."(Matt. 25:31,32)*

It's a bit confusing because the word "ethnos" translated "nations" occurs 158 times in the New Testament. In 92 cases it is translated "gentiles", in 61 cases it is translated "nations", and in five cases it is translated "heathen". So the choice of the word "nations" doesn't convey the best meaning.

The bottom line is that, though there may be nations at this judgment, the judgments themselves are still of individuals. What is this judgment based on? As referred to in

Joel 3, it is based on how these individuals treated the Jews during the great tribulation. Matthew 25 indicates the issues: *"I was hungry and you gave Me something to eat; I was thirsty and you gave Me drink... ."* So those that helped the Jews are the sheep and those that didn't are the goats.

We should also say that this judgment, like the others, is based strictly on grace and faith, not works. There is no works-based salvation presented in the Bible, and to teach that a nation of people can inherit the kingdom because of works, is heresy. The reason the sheep nations helped the Jews wasn't just because they were generous people, but because they were born again.

This judgment also answers the question of who goes into the millennium. At the time of this judgment, there will be a sizeable portion of the earth's population still alive. The millennial kingdom is set up and, according to Matthew 25, the sheep enter the kingdom.

The Judgment Seat of Christ

This brings us to the third judgment — the Judgment Seat of Christ. This judgment takes place at the resurrection of the righteous and everyone in attendance has the same destination — heaven. This is the judgment of believers, and it is here that our works are judged. This judgment is pictured for us in I Corinthians 3.

> *"For no man can lay a foundation other than the one which is laid, which is Jesus Christ.*
>
> *For if any man builds upon the foundation with gold, silver, precious stones, wood, hay, straw,*
>
> *each man's work will become evident; for the day will show it, because it is to be revealed with fire; and the fire itself will test the quality of each man's work.*

> *If any man's work which he has built upon it remains he shall receive a reward.*
> *If any man's work is burned up, he shall suffer loss, but he himself shall be saved, yet so as through fire."* (*1Cor. 3:11-15*)

God gives us this powerful metaphor to burn an impression into our minds. The words employed are very emotive; they are designed to evoke a response. The picture of a life riddled with hay, wood, and stubble, burning up with great loss, is graphic and appalling. Conversely, the reward for a life with works akin to gold, silver, and precious stones, is gripping and wondrous.

And then we have one of the most poignant and profoundly distressing statements in all of scripture: *"If any man's work is burned up, he shall suffer loss, but he himself shall be saved, yet so as through fire."* Here in one sentence we have the greatest gift a believer can receive, followed by the greatest loss a believer can experience. Both are eternal.

Think about that.

Think about it the next time you meet a believer with a "just saved" mentality whose excuse for indifference is the famous one liner: "You don't have to go to church to be a Christian." Think about it as you go about your daily routine. Think about it, and as you do, cry out for the wisdom to distinguish straw from gold.

Then get on your knees and ask God for one more thing: the power to choose — the power to choose jewels over junk, God over Satan, and your Savior over yourself. Many will make bad choices; some will even be disinherited. They will come through the judgment bearing the ignominious distinction: "Saved, yet so as through fire."

41

Clarifying the Greek Word *Bema*

The Greek word for the judgment seat is *bema*, which means "a judge's stand or throne". It occurs twelve times in the New Testament. In every case except one, it refers to the Judgment Seat of Christ or the judgment seat of an official such as Herod. The exception is Acts 7:5 where the word refers to a portion of the promised land. The strange use of *bema* in this verse is unimportant to our discussion.

In the other eleven cases, appearing at the judgment seat was a sober event. It was the equivalent of standing before a judge in a modern day courtroom. This is an important point. I have never heard a Christian author or speaker use the word *bema* as the Bible does. They have always used it in one of its secular applications, primarily as the judge's booth at an athletic event. Why is that?

There are a couple of reasons that I can think of to explain this. The first reason would simply be ignorance: repeating what others have said without checking the facts. I have been guilty of that. The other reason has its roots in faulty doctrine. We have been taught that the Judgment Seat of Christ is a place where rewards are handed out, and nothing more. That fits much better with the athletic event analogy than the courtroom analogy.

Many have likened this event to a contemporary track-and-field day. With the current emphasis on making sure that every child "succeeds", many schools give prizes to every participant. There are no disappointments, everything is positive, everyone wins. This is how Judgment Day is portrayed. Cheering crowds, beautiful weather, all of us standing before God receiving prizes and awards. There is truth in this, of course, but that is a very incomplete picture.

I Corinthians 3 tells us that before there is reward, there is fire.

And after the fire, there is loss.

Anyone who doesn't think it will be sobering to stand before God's throne and give an account of his life needs a reality check. Forget the sports analogies. It is God our Judge who will be there, not the Chairman of the Olympic Committee.

Consequences

Whenever we teach about consequences, people tend to respond in their spirits: "But how about grace?" Grace certainly protects us from the eternal consequence of sin, which is hell. It ensures that we will enjoy eternity forever despite our failures. But grace does not extend to rewards for at least one obvious reason: If grace can nullify every command to forsake the temporal for the eternal, then I would choose the temporal. If grace says that "the good life" has equal merit with "the crucified life", then I choose the good life. If grace says you can miss God, waste years of your life, and in the end it doesn't matter, then obviously we make far too much of finding God's will. But grace doesn't say that. Grace and rewards don't mix very well.

Some have pointed to the Parable of the Laborers in Matthew chapter 20 as an example of grace being extended. In the parable, laborers who worked differing hours were paid the same wage. But the fact that they all worked destroys this argument because grace and works are in opposition to each other. God tells us the motive of the landowner in the following words: *"Or is your eye envious because I am **generous?**"* The landowner was being generous, not gracious. Will God be generous to some on Judgment Day? I believe so; but if He is, it won't be on a whim. He tells us the criterion in the parable.

When asked by the landowner why they were standing idle so late in the day, the laborers replied, *"Because no one hired us."* In other words, it wasn't their fault. The parallel to the gospel narrative is that some get saved late in life because "no one hired them." There are people who, for whatever reason, hear the gospel long after their youth has been spent. But sometimes their response is amazing. After accepting Christ, they make up for lost time by being totally passionate. I believe people like this qualify for God's generosity.

But generosity is not God's response to the person whose faith has been shipwrecked by the troubles of life. That is why we must be wary of the sentiment: "All's well that ends well." When I look at people who have wasted years on disappointment or bitterness, I feel a great sadness. When, later in life, they make their peace with God, it is wonderful. The natural human tendency is to say that because they finished well, that is really all that counts; at Judgment Day, everything will be fine.

Finishing well *does* count, especially in the area of repentance. But the years cannot be reclaimed. We must steadfastly resist the idea that there is a ditch of disappointment or dissipation where we can spend decades without consequence, as long as we return to the road of faith before we die. It is simply not true. This will become apparent when we study the Judgment in greater detail.

Preparation for the Afterlife

I have always had a fascination with the believers' judgment. To some it may appear morbid, a bit like preferring funerals to weddings. But, in fact, I find funerals to be the more moving experience, perhaps because of the judgment that follows. On the matter of funerals, Solomon had very firm views. In Ecclesiastes 7, he makes this rather cynical statement: "*It is better to go to a house of mourning, than to go to a house of feasting, for this is the end of all men and the living should take it to heart.*"

Many people credit statements like this to Solomon's backslidden and depressive mindset. But in the finality of a funeral there is something starkly honest. It is a reminder: someday that will be you in that casket; someday that will be me. Funerals confront us with our own mortality, and as such are a gift from God.

I see in the elaborate preparations made for the afterlife by Egyptian kings something both compelling and unnerving. I find it compelling because they *knew*. They knew that the passage into the afterlife was momentous and required great preparation. Their tombs are astonishing because they recognized death to be the apocryphal event that it is.

In many ways these tombs rivaled their palaces, and there is something fitting in this. They made a huge investment in that final journey, and that is the part that is unnerving. All of their gods, all of their pomp, and all of their journey preparations couldn't change one thing: their final destination. How insufferably sad and, by comparison with some of us, how terribly unfair.

To be sure, grace has nothing to do with fairness, or it wouldn't be grace. But how strange that some Christians treat the matter of life and death in such a cavalier fashion. The medieval potentate knew there was a "great divide", and that crossing over required preparation. The modern cultist embraces death and its promise of seventy virgins or a place in the godhead, and he governs his life accordingly. Pathetic, except on one point: they live for the inevitable, they invest in the inevitable, and they prepare for the inevitable. Death is the inevitable.

And for the Christian there is so much more to prepare for.

We meet the eternal God, our Blessed Savior, and our heavenly Bridegroom. We enter a kingdom prepared for us from the foundations of the world. We pass through a judgment that evaluates every moment of our lives. We are assigned rank based on our works. We should be the most prepared people on earth. But are we? The experiences of four godly men will help us in our attempt to understand why this preparation is so important.

Four Prophetic Voices

For me, the subject of the judgment has been an anchor, an incentive for diligent living in time of great trial. It is something God has deposited in my life for which I am grateful. Having such a preoccupation, I've read everything I could find on the subject and collected the few books, tapes, and videos that are available. Some of these authors and speakers have had life-changing encounters with God.

When it comes to the dreams, visions, and divine encounters of godly men, we must not be too hasty in our acceptance or endorsement. We must judge all things and hold fast to that which is true. The four men I'm about to mention are unimpeachable from the standpoint of both character and reputation. For this reason I do not hesitate to share their revelations because, as we shall see, the whole point of their encounter with God was that it be shared as a warning to us.

The first individual is Brian Bailey, a Bible teacher and international board member for World MAP. On one of his tapes he relates his experience of dying. He saw himself being lifted out of his body, and he knew he was being taken to heaven. He was a pastor who had served the Lord faithfully; yet the closer he got to heaven, the more anxious he became. He could see heaven very clearly, but he had a sense of dread.

"Before you get to heaven," he related, "you have to cross a river that separates the living from the dead. You're shown your life on a screen, and where you have repented the screen is blank. You're also shown what your life would have been like if you'd lived on." He then saw the things God had intended for his life that had been cut short because of his untimely death. What he witnessed threw him into anguish and torment.

Commenting on this experience, he said that no matter how difficult your trials on earth are, never ask God to take you home before the time. He said the agony of seeing what God had intended for your life and that you have fallen short, is worse than any pain on earth. Think about that — worse than any pain on earth.

He asked God if he could go back, and obviously God granted that wish, for he is still alive today. But God gave him a message: "Warn my people. Tell them about the judgment so that they won't be slack. Tell them to cry out for mercy, that they might finish their race, no matter how great their trials. Tell them to look after their bodies so that premature death won't rob them of fruitful years. Tell them that it matters.

" How and when you go home matters."

The second person is Howard Pittman. His name is known to many because in the last thirty years he has preached to thousands of audiences spanning the globe. He only has one message, the one given to him by God outside the gates of heaven when he died about thirty-five years ago. God had a word for Pittman and a message for the Laodicean church. That word was "repent!" Repent, for we shall all stand before God to give an account of our lives.

For those who have sin in their lives he had a terse message. Regardless of how much sin you have in your life, God's got enough fire. Better the fire now than the judgment then. I have never heard anyone challenge the veracity of Pittman's experience or the validity of his ministry.

We need to heed this word.

The topic of judgment is not an easy one to teach or receive if one is faithful to the facts as presented in scripture. It is tempting to think that the message would come out very differently if presented by a man with a mantle for teaching God's love. But we have such a man, and his teaching contains the same elements as the men previously discussed. His name is Mike Bickle, and he is a well-known pastor and the founder of the International House of Prayer (IHOP).

He, perhaps more than any man of his generation, is associated with a passion for Jesus. In fact, he's the author of a book bearing that title. His teachings on the Song of Solomon are some of the deepest I've heard. He understands the Lord's passion for His bride, and thus his commentary on the believers' judgment is of particular note. His series on this subject is extremely detailed and runs to seven audio-tapes. It is excellent material, but comes with some familiar warnings.

Shortly after his father died in 1974, Mike had a divine encounter while in a trance. He was told that judgment was more serious than he and others had been led to believe.

Later, in 1978, he had a vision in which he was standing before God. In the vision God was pronouncing judgment on Mike's life using words like "wasted" and "futile". It was actually a preview of what Judgment Day would be like for him if he was *only* a "good pastor", preaching "good sermons". God called him to something higher, and failure to achieve it would have harsh consequences. It changed his life, and out of that stern warning came much fruit. God left him with this message: "Tell your friends about Judgment Day. They're under a misconception; it's not what they think.

"Warn my people about the judgment."

The name most closely associated with the teaching of the Judgment Seat of Christ is Rick Howard. In a vision he was actually taken to the I Corinthians 3 judgment scene himself. He was privy to the joy and blessing that people received as their just reward for a life of faith and service unto God. But he also saw the judgment fire burn up the empty works of others. He witnessed first hand the weeping and despair that resulted as a lifetime of work, so to speak, went up in smoke.

He observed a man he knew that had refused a call on his life to the nation of India.

The loss this man experienced was beyond words.

These four teachers may differ from each other in many respects, but their message is the same. They all speak with great sobriety of a day when God will judge His people. Each is like a voice from the future, warning us that there is so much at stake. These warnings are God's mercy to those who hear and heed them. At stake is glory beyond anything we could imagine.

A News Blackout

The news media must choose from thousands of stories daily to fill the brief space that is allotted to them. We all know that this is selective coverage, and that some critical events go unreported while we are fed an endless diet of trivia. This has at least one parallel in Biblical truth.

Most of us have never heard a sermon on the Judgment Seat of Christ and would be hard pressed to quote even one scripture that relates to it. We could easily assume, from the lack of coverage, that it is "not big news". That is why the message of the four prophets just mentioned may seem inexplicable to many. It is totally outside our frame of reference. Surely God doesn't feel that strongly about a subject that we've never even been taught on.

Yes, He does.

We will leave the prophesies without further explanation. By the end of this book they will cease to be just the arcane experiences of those who have "gone beyond", but the heart of God that we somehow managed to miss. In missing God's heart, we have missed opportunities that were meant to shape our destiny. Let us thank the Lord there is still time.

Time to listen; time to heed.

The Determinants of Reward

We have looked at the "great aspiration". We have discussed briefly the effect that our earthly lives will have on our eternal state. But we still lack the definition and detail that will tell us how to properly live our lives. We lack, as well, a clear picture of what is at stake. We need to know *how* to live, but we also need to know *why* right living matters. For this we need the teaching of the Judgment Seat of Christ in greater detail.

The Word of God reveals that four things will be under consideration at the Judgment Seat of Christ. They are sin, stewardship, character and good works. Since there is only one judgment but four elements, how these elements mesh or play out, is not entirely clear. Nevertheless, it behooves us to consider all four aspects as we prepare for that day.

While it may be hard to separate good deeds from stewardship, were we to focus solely on deeds, we would be in danger of missing the big picture — our accountability for our gifts, resources, relationships, etc. But alternatively, were we to focus only on stewardship, we might miss the little picture — prayer, fasting, self-denial, acts of kindness, etc.

In treating the judgment of our deeds and that of our stewardship, God gives us two separate pictures in scripture. Clearly this is for our instruction. Therefore to treat the judgment as a homogenous event is to close ourselves off from revelation that God makes freely available.

Secondly, the issue of character being judged comes up frequently in the scriptures. What God does *in* us is separate and distinct from what God does *through* us. Both are important, and the one certainly impacts the other. But we must recognize that good works can be very separate from character qualities like humility. Sometimes God will even limit the one to develop the other.

God takes many of us through suffering that for a time reduces our output, but is pivotal to the development of our character. It has been said that God is more interested in winning all of *us*, than in winning all of the world *through* us. Regardless of whether or not that is true, it highlights the distinction between character and deeds. Both are important and will be dealt with separately at the judgment.

Lastly, we come to the subject of sin. Most of the books written on the Judgment Seat of Christ never even mention sin. In this book, however, I will spend more time on this area than any other. The reason is simple — so does the Bible. The lack of teaching on sin is a classic case of reading the Bible through a filter. Our theology on the atonement and the oft-repeated phrase that "only our works are judged", have blinded us to the many scriptures that speak about the judgment of our sin.

The section on sin may be radical to many, but it is much needed. There is a huge disconnect between the Christian life as pictured in scripture, and what we see lived out in western culture. That is the inevitable outcome of teaching judgment as a benign event where sin is never mentioned.

It is curious how most of us can excuse the most blatant sin — until it is committed against *us*. When it is us that is defiled and despoiled, it is quite different. When *we* are the target of abuse, betrayal, exploitation, malicious gossip, or financial ruin, suddenly we begin to look at grace in a new way. We are required to forgive, and hopefully we do so, but we also want justice. And when the perpetrator is a believer, the offence isn't less onerous, but quite the opposite — it is actually *more* onerous, and justifiably so. We want assurance that God will one day bring justice to bear on every situation, and that everything that is hidden will be revealed.

On that we have His solemn promise.

Timeless Measures of the Christian Faith

The four areas of judgment, together with the believer's inheritance, form the major content of this book. However, examining the fruit of the Christian life without looking at the life itself, can cause some major oversights. Watching a figure skater practice certain techniques is informative, but it's the performance that gives them full expression. Knowing the melody and harmony to a piece by Bach is instructive, but we gain more from hearing the full orchestral work.

Likewise, it's good to separate out the elements of judgment, but we also need to integrate them back into the Christian life lest we miss the forest for the trees. Revisiting some major Bible themes like "the cross" and the "army of God" will help us in this regard.

Inheritance in the Eternal Kingdom

Most students in the modern era understand the concept of an open-book exam. If by analogy the believer's judgment is an exam or examination, then it is indeed open-Book. God hides nothing concerning our judgment because His Word reveals clearly the life that is rewarding and fruitful. There are religions where there is no assurance of salvation or blessing in the afterlife until one's life is weighed in the balance after death. Happily, every born-again child of God has assurance of salvation. The next two sections explore the basis on which our eternal reward is established.

But it is in the final section that we discover what God has prepared for those who love Him. It is here that we explore the blessing and reward that will be the companion of every believer for eternity. There are many books written about heaven, but heaven, as we shall see, is a Kingdom, not a democracy. A Kingdom by definition is a pyramid structure with King Jesus forming the apex and positions accorded below Him based on service. To teach on heaven without teaching on Judgment is somewhat incomplete. It ignores the great variance in the way that we will experience heaven. It ignores the great variance in the way we will experience God.

The consistent thread that runs throughout this book is that the ultimate goal for the Christian is intimacy with God. The underlying truth of judgment is that each of the four pillars is a test of our passion and intimacy on earth. Take the matter of sin. If we have intimacy with God we keep short accounts, we walk in the light as He is in the light, and we are holy as He is holy. Underlying good stewardship, good character, and good works, we find the same constant: intimacy. Our heavenly inheritance is proportional to our earthly intimacy.

God's Eternal Love

Before we move on to the Four Pillars of Judgment we need a bridging chapter. We need a better understanding of God, His love and His grace. There are misimpressions that need to be corrected, and the result, I believe, will be glorious. In the end we have to trust our Lord's statement that the truth will set us free. So let us look at the love of God to gain strength and insight for the chapters that lie ahead.

FOUR

The Eternal Love of God

The love of God.

Many years ago I heard a tape by a teacher named Dennis Cramer. On it he described an incident where he was caught up to heaven and met the resurrected Christ. During this encounter, the Lord put his arm around Dennis and, looking deep into his eyes, exclaimed, "Dennis, I've always believed in you." That statement pushes every button. It touches the longing that is in every heart to be loved, affirmed, trusted, and treasured — especially by an authority figure and, above all, by God. When I described Cramer's experience to a church group, I saw the emotion of all of those longings sweep across their faces.

Once while addressing a congregation I told them to repeat the following phrase: "God will never love me more in the future than He loves me right now." Then I said, "Do it again." And I continued, making them say it over and over. Eventually people began to weep. For some it was cathartic. As the message finally got from their head to their heart, the revelation set them free. But some wept for a very different reason.

The repetition by their mouths of something their hearts told them was false, eventually caused a dissonant meltdown. Everything they had learned in life told them that love was earned and that you never really measured up. Love was conditional, and the better you were, the more you would be loved. They had projected that belief onto God. To repeatedly declare that God could never love them more no matter how much they improved, was too much for their programming. They went into default mode. They broke down.

This is one of life's great tragedies.

I have known people who could not pray to God the Father. The word "father" itself was an offence because of their mistreatment at the hands of an earthly father. Ask any group of a hundred people to raise their hands if they've never had a hug or a simple "I love you" from their dad, and half of the hands will go up. One of them would be mine. It hurts. It's a hurt that never really goes away. In a subtle way it can affect everything.

Thankfully I *do* believe that God loves me, but initially this assurance was a gift. I had a dramatic conversion that literally changed me overnight. Otherwise I would have had as many reasons as the next person to doubt God's love. And, as often as not, the next person does doubt it. I know this to be true based on hundreds of conversations over the years. How difficult this makes the Lord's job! How difficult it makes the job of the teacher! How do we communicate the righteous demands of the gospel to a fragile person who will take every correction as a rejection? It's hard. We need to convinced of God's love in order to mature.

"The just shall live by faith," but that faith is more than believing that salvation is through the shed blood of Christ. It is believing that nothing can separate us from the love of God. It is believing that despite every failure, every accusation from the enemy, and every evidence of God's indifference, He will never leave us nor forsake us.

In Ephesians we are told to put on the shield of faith. But how does one put on this particular faith shield — the faith that God loves me? Without that shield we won't get far in life. Memorizing certain verses will help. Marrying a person who loves you unconditionally is a bonus. Immersing yourself in the Bible so that you understand God's character, covenant, and commitment, is important.

But the surest way is both the most difficult and the most rewarding. You cannot learn to trust God's love by sitting in a pew any more than you can learn how to swim by reading a book. When you set aside your fears and doubts and begin to respond in obedience to what God is calling you to do, amazing things begin to happen. When you partner with God in the great work of the gospel, and His love and power flows through you to others, you experience a fulfillment that has no equal on earth. But you experience something else as well: God. When you see Him using you, you experience the unavoidable truth that He loves you.

We are fond of saying that we should base our doctrine on truth, not experience. Yes, to be sure. If it's not in Scripture, don't look for it in life. But if it is in Scripture, then it is important that we experience it. It's when "faith" moves from the latent *logos* of Scripture, to the *rhema* reality in our lives that we are changed. And the biggest change occurs when God ministers through us to others. Initially my faith in God's love was a gift, but no longer. God has used me to touch the lives of so many people, that I could never doubt His love again.

God loves you with an everlasting love. If you are plagued with doubts, set out to prove His love. Go and do the things that you are commanded to do, and see if He doesn't show up. Are you worried that you're not a Christian because you don't feel His love? Fast, pray and worship as you're commanded to do in Scripture. Tell God you won't let Him go until He blesses you. God loves that attitude. He is scouring the whole earth to *"show Himself strong on behalf of those whose heart is perfect towards Him."*

God's Character

Maybe you've heard the story of the Christian air traveler who asked the passenger seated next to him if he believed in God. The man responds in the negative. The witness then asked him to describe the God he didn't believe in. Upon hearing the description, our witness replied that he didn't believe in that kind of God either. He then went on to describe the God of the Bible. Well, not exactly. He gave a brief description of God's love and mercy in sending His Son to die for us. It's a good story with an important message, but as a commentary on God, it is woefully inadequate.

There have been an enormous number of books that have sought to explain God and His relationship to His people. There are books that have taken the names of God in Scripture and expanded on them to explain facets of His character. I have one that explores seventy, but another author expounds on 365. These names reveal a more complete picture of the God who, in an absolute sense, is unknowable. It may take a million years to truly understand His love and all of eternity to know Him completely. But it is essential to our growth that we study the self-portraits that He does provide us. So what do we need to know about God that will help us to really understand His love?

A Jealous God

Firstly, God is a jealous God. He says that about Himself. He was jealous when Israel, His "wife", went after strange gods. His constant expressions of anger over their idolatry in the Old Testament initially disturbed me. It wasn't the fact that He was angry; this I could accept. It was the constant tireless expression of His anger that bothered me. Part of my dismay was the way He constantly allowed Himself to be portrayed as a jilted lover.

The teen years taught us that when someone we are dating dumps us, we are very humiliated, and we don't broadcast the fact. But concerning His feelings of rejection, God holds nothing back. And somehow His lovesick tirades embarrassed me. His lack of composure bothered me. Why is the God of the universe constantly "losing it"? I thought self-control and temperance in all things was a virtue. As a recently converted twentieth century heathen, I somehow expected God's major self-portrait to be that of sophisticated, erudite, philosopher King; not jilted lover.

My only answer is that God's love and humility are completely beyond our comprehension. He wants us to know exactly how He feels about infidelity, and He uses the force of repetition to drive home the point. Repetition is the mother of learning. Certainly, with the deletion of these passages the Bible would have been a much shorter, user-friendly book. But this is not wasted space. It reveals His heart perhaps more than we want to see it revealed.

But with so much of the Bible committed to these rants, isn't it curious that our focus is "God's love for us" and not our need to be faithful to God? The implication is that many of us have a man-centered gospel. We are chosen out of the world and betrothed to Christ, Paul tells us. While God's love is wondrous, at some point our love for Him needs to be a driving force in our life. If this doesn't happen, we will inevitably leave our first love and spend our affections elsewhere.

God's chief competition is the world system, and that is why *"friendship with the world is enmity with God."* That's in the New Testament. The dictionary defines the word *enmity* as "the feelings that enemies have for each other; hostility or hatred." So by definition, people who fawn over the world are out of favor with God. Ask yourself if you have an unhealthy infatuation with the world and, if so, try to see it from God's point of view. Try to understand His response.

None of our whoring would evoke an emotional response from God if He didn't love us. People want a God who loves them but without the passion that breeds jealousy. They want a Father that only pampers but doesn't discipline. That is not our God. Jealousy is the inevitable response when those whom you love are also the object of your affections.

You can love your boss and be somewhat detached if he is unfaithful to his wife. But you have a totally different response to infidelity that comes from the one who has your affections — YOUR spouse. Your response to *your* spouse ignoring you, or, choosing others over you, or committing outright adultery is the same as Gods: anger, jealousy, disappointment, and action. God doesn't raise up an army to punish us the way He did when Israel sinned, but to assume that He doesn't rebuke and resist us, flies in the face of scripture.

The Goodness of God

With reference to God's character we often misunderstand the word "good". We confuse God's goodness with His blessing. God is always good, and He is good to everyone. He tells us:

> *"But love your enemies, and do good, and lend, expecting nothing in return; and your reward will be great, and you will be sons of the Most High*; **for He Himself is good to ungrateful and evil men.**"
> (Luke 6:35)

The reason God can tell us to love our enemies and do good to them is because He does the same.

God loves everyone and is good to everyone, but what He cannot do is bless everyone for the simple reason that He cannot bless unrighteousness. There are dozens of proverbs that talk about the blessing of the righteous and the evil that befalls the unrighteous. Deuteronomy 28 is a comprehensive list of the things that bring blessings and the things that bring curses. It is written to God's people, but the moral principles apply to all. Even unbelievers who discover godly principles and live by them, will enjoy greater prosperity in the broadest sense of the word.

God loves all believers and is good to even those who commit sins like adultery, but He cannot bless them. When God takes His blessing off a person's life, that person encounters all the promises for the unrighteous. He also reaps what he sows, as do we all. This is still the goodness of God, because the wages of sin is death. When people experience enough death in their health, finances, relationships, etc., they frequently repent and return to God.

One of the greatest ways God's goodness is manifest is through discipline. God outlines His role as disciplinarian in many scriptures such as Hebrews 12, Proverbs 3, and Revelation 3. This has a parallel in the human family. Everyone knows that a good parent is one who disciplines a child in an atmosphere of love. To shower a child with blessing and favor when he disobeys, hoping he will repent, is usually misguided and is what we term "permissive".

Nevertheless, every child is different, and all children go through stages. Sometimes blessing a child at a critical point can turn his heart, and we need to be aware of that. Sometimes God does the same with us. He blesses us despite our attitude or behavior, and sometimes it turns our hearts. When this happens, we call it *"the goodness of God that leads to repentance"* (Rom. 2:2-5). But, of course, God didn't decide to be good for a change; He's always good. This time however, we receive blessing instead of discipline, and we are overwhelmed with God's mercy, although we call it His goodness.

Unfortunately, God's blessing can have the opposite effect on people. It is supposed to produce gratitude, but pride is often the result. God brings Israel a warning in Deuteronomy 28:

"Beware lest you forget the Lord your God by not keeping His commandments and His ordinances and His statutes which I am commanding you today; lest,

when you have eaten and are satisfied, and have built good houses and lived in them, and when your herds and your flocks multiply, and your silver and gold multiply, and all that you have multiplies, then your heart becomes proud, and you forget the Lord your God who brought you out from the land of Egypt, out of the house of slavery....Otherwise, you may say in your heart: 'My power and the strength of my hand made me this wealth.'" (Deut. 8:11-14,17)

We find the equivalent situation in our Lord's letter to the church at Laodicea. They said they were rich and had need of nothing. No doubt they were talking about their wealth, creature comforts, and perceived spiritual state. Like Israel, they were right about the material wealth, but they had ceased to give God credit and serve Him with passion. Jesus said they were lukewarm, and therefore spiritually they were miserable, poor, blind and naked.

But it is not just pride and lukewarmness that can result from God's blessing. In times of great license, people can treat God's grace as a license to sin. In Ezekeil 33:13 God has to sound this warning: *"When I say to the righteous, he will surely live, and he so trusts in his righteousness that he commits iniquity, none of his righteous deeds will be remembered; but in that same iniquity of his which he has committed he will die."*

So what is the application today? We live in perilous times. Men are indeed lovers of self. The most shocking thing about the Barna polls, especially where standards and morality are concerned, is that there is no discernable difference between the church and the world. Obviously we live in a time of great material blessing, but righteousness and gratitude are not the result. We can only assume that there is something wrong with the message Christians are receiving.

It is always important to teach the love and goodness of God, as long as we understand the term "goodness". To never tell people about the consequences of sin in this life and the life to come is misguided. An overemphasis on trying to encourage righteousness through various types of positive messages is akin to being a permissive parent. It may work for the eager-to-please, committed Christian, but lacks the balance that most of us need.

The Anger of God

At a service I was present at recently, the pastor exhorted the flock to accept that God loves them. He went so far as to say, "I know many of you don't believe it, but it's true." It *is* true and, yes, many do not believe it. We have covered some of the reasons why, but there is another reason people often feel abandoned by God that is never discussed. It is the anger of God.

Let me begin with a statement uttered by a "faith" preacher whose show I caught on television. The setting was a large auditorium seating about five thousand people. At one point in his sermon, the preacher exclaimed in a loud voice, "God is not angry at you! The devil is angry at you!" The camera panned the crowd capturing expressions of agreement, and nods of approval. This man was preaching to five thousand people, none of whom he knew, but he *knew* that God was not angry with any of them. Either this man has the greatest gift of prophecy on the planet, or his theology states that God is never angry with His people. I can only assume the latter.

But nothing could be further from the truth. It would take a very large book just to list the scriptures where God is angry with His people. Even if most of those scriptures are in the Old Testament, it makes no difference. If anything, it simply highlights God's attitude to His people in any generation, under any covenant, when they backslide, commit spiritual adultery, and do other things that provoke His anger. But there are numerous New Testament examples as well. The most famous is found in Revelation chapter 3.

Here we have Jesus telling the church at Laodicea that they are lukewarm and He wants to vomit them out of His mouth. Most commentators agree that each of the seven letters to the churches in Asia Minor, while written to an existing church, also refers to seven church ages, the last being the Laodicean Age. Again, few would doubt that we are currently living in the Laodicean Age. The Laodiceans had three major failures as indicated by our Lord's instructions to them — sin, selfishness, and lack of sound doctrine. This describes the modern day church, although thankfully, with some exceptions.

But whether it is the actual church in Laodicea or believers alive today, it is still Jesus talking to born-again believers, and He is not pleased. When a person declares that you make them sick, you know that anger and disgust is what they are trying to convey. But after describing the Laodicean condition and expressing His revulsion, listen to our Lord's entreaties:

1) *"Those whom I love, I reprove and discipline; be zealous therefore and repent."* Translation: You make me sick, but because I **love** you so much, I will have to discipline you; so be zealous and repent.
2) *"Behold, I stand at the door and knock; if any one hears my voice and opens the door, I will come in to him, and will dine with him, and he with Me."* Translation: You make me sick, but I **miss** you, and I'd love to just fellowship with you. I'm waiting for an invitation, so please open the door of your life.
3) *"He who overcomes, I will grant to him to sit down with Me on My throne, as I also overcame and sat down with My Father on His throne."*

Translation: You make me sick, but I want you to overcome the sin in your life so I can **bless** you. I want you to share My very throne.

The one-dimensional God we preach just adds to people's confusion. They are quite capable of reading the Bible and can readily observe God's anger. But if we don't discuss this element, then when they experience God's anger for themselves, they will assume that He no longer loves them. Thus the roller-coaster ride continues — He loves me, He loves me not, He loves me, He loves me not. The glory is that, though God can be angry with us, as noted above, He yearns to bless us. Discipline, to be sure, is also a blessing if it saves a soul from death. But God wants to visit us with better blessings — His glorious presence and His throne in the coming kingdom.

The scriptures tell us that God is slow to anger. We are told elsewhere that *"His anger is but for a moment; His favor is for a lifetime."* So it takes a lot to get God angry, and when He is, He doesn't stay angry long. There are reasons for this. When sin requires discipline, He brings it; and like any good parent, He doesn't discipline in anger. And when there is repentance, there is no longer a need for anger. When there is no repentance, then He has made it plain: *"Vengeance is mine; I will repay."* He will repay the wicked, of course, but not just them. God has to bring justice. He defers His righteous judgment against all unrepentant sin till Judgment Day.

God's anger is most apparent when we act in pride and hurt others. God is angry at the Christian husband who abandons his wife and kids for a younger woman because he is full of lust and self-importance. To suppose that He isn't, is to have a very strange view of God. If *my* son did such a thing, I would certainly be angry. Is God less righteous?

Though some of us may never do things that stir God's anger, we all experience His discipline. But we often misconstrue it. As my pastor is fond of saying, "You're rebuking the devil for a situation in your life that is brought about by God." God will use people and circumstance to bring correction and change. But He has no easy job when so many believers see His discipline as abandonment and lack of love, or worse, the work of the enemy.

We don't give God much to work with when we don't tell our critics about His anger. I have often heard atheists on interview programs proclaim their revulsion for a God who claims to be good but does nothing about the evil we see everywhere. They need to know two things. Firstly, God is not standing idly by, for His anger burns against evildoers. Secondly, He has appointed a Day in which He will judge the world. Justice delayed is still justice. But we seldom tell people this.

We express dismay at a fallen world and elaborate on the matter of free will, but, by our silence on God's anger, we act as if there is no consequence, no reckoning, and no Judgment. In our effort to present a God who is only "love", we leave Him without a witness. Scoffers who delight in judging God need to hear about the God who will one day judge them. Telling them in a humble, straightforward fashion is an act of love.

God's Displeasure

The word "displeasure" is another one that is off limits in any discussion of how God relates to His children. I wish I had a nickel for every testimony I've heard from a person who has come out of a legalistic system where they could never please God, no matter how hard they tried. Now they have embraced a God, evidently, who is always pleased with them. But is this true, or is this just another ditch — the ditch of "God is always pleased with me, because that is my theology"?

The scriptures tell us that *"without faith it is impossible to please God."* We are told that *" those who are in the flesh cannot please God."* Do we always act in faith? Or conversely, do we never operate in the flesh? In the gospel of Mark, the disciples forbid the crowds to bring children to Jesus. *"But when Jesus saw this, He was displeased and said to them, 'Permit the children to come to Me...'"*(Mark 10:14).

It is misguided to teach a God who is never displeased with His children. There are a great number of scriptures that tell us to do things that are pleasing to the Lord. These lose their impact in a theology where God is always pleased. Our children need to know both what pleases us as parents, and also what displeases us. This is part of the nurturing process and is totally necessary. So, in taking away from people the knowledge that God can be angry and displeased, we leave Him with only one role — the inconsistent lover. By catering to people's fragile psyches, we deny them the opportunity to work out their salvation with fear and trembling, and to get to know the God of the Bible instead of a wishful caricature.

Lest any of this be misunderstood, let me emphasize one point: Most Christians I know are humble people whose chief desire is to serve God. They may never experience God's anger. I am not preaching a God who is angry at us all the time or even most of the time. This is the extreme that is usually presented the moment we even allow for an angry God. But to ignore the fact that there is much gross sin in the Church, and to preach a God whose response to such sin is benign and benevolent, is naïve and unbiblical.

We are God's children, and generally He is pleased with us. That is His overall attitude. But again, to even suggest that God can be displeased gives rise to the extreme in the minds of many: "I can never please God, poor me." As the saying goes, God *is* easy to please, but He is impossible to satisfy. Till death is swallowed up in life, God will always want more: more praise, more obedience, more faithfulness, more righteousness, etc. It's called sanctification, and it doesn't end till we die or become perfect — the latter being a noble goal, but probably an unachievable state.

All of this is pretty basic, but because we live in an era of extreme-grace, it bears repeating. It is difficult to discuss God's love without talking about His grace; in fact, many see them as inseparable. But they are two very different things, and grace is as misunderstood as love. Consequently, talking about rewards baffles the hyper-grace person. God's judgment, His generous reward plan, and His displeasure with sin can all seem baffling to a person who thinks that grace is the answer to everything.

Grace

A famous author once wrote a book on grace, and rather than define it, he illustrated it with stories. Every pastor knows the power of a story, parable or illustration in bringing clarity to a sermon. But certain things need to be defined very clearly, and grace is one of them, because there are so many misconceptions. If we don't understand grace, we will never understand judgment and reward.

Let me first of all give the common understanding. Grace is unmerited favor. When we were lost, without God and without hope, He took the initiative. He sent His Son to die for us. We deserve hell, but grace did what we could never do. It opened a door for reconciliation. It allows us to be restored to God with no regard to merit on our part. We simply said "yes", which is putting faith in the finished work of the cross.

Now that I'm saved, grace goes out to me daily. I still sin, but when I do, according to Hebrews, I can go to the throne of grace to find help in time of need. There is no condemnation for those who are in Christ Jesus, so the Christian life is not a labor to achieve righteousness. We can rest in what Jesus accomplished, and experience the freedom that grace provides. Paul closed all of his letters, except Romans, with the blessing, "Grace be with you." As Christians, we receive that blessing and revel in the fact that we are under grace, not law. So far, so good.

We saw earlier that if we only understand God as a God of love and have a misconception of the word love, we'll be confused and constantly vexed. Likewise, if we only understand God as a God of grace, and don't know what the word "grace" means, we'll also be confused and vexed. So let us look at what the Bible says further on grace. Call it balance, call it the other side of the coin, but above all, call it truth. We need the truth. It is rare to hear a grace message that tells the truth. Remember, *the truth* is bigger than one or two truths.

It's true, for instance, that Jesus died for the sins of the world. But the truth is much bigger. The truth is that if we don't accept Him as Lord and Savior, we'll go to hell. It's not what books and teachers *tell us* that is often the most important; it is what they don't tell us. There is no intention to deceive, but simply the repetition of truths that have been handed down without exploring truth in its entirety. What follows is what many don't tell us about grace. Let's look first of all at a defining verse in Titus.

The Role of Grace

> *"For the grace of God has appeared, bringing salvation to all men, instructing us to deny ungodliness and worldly desires and to live sensibly, righteously and godly in the present age, looking for the blessed hope and appearing of the glory of our great God and Savior, Christ Jesus; who gave Himself for us, that He might redeem us from every lawless deed and*

69

purify for Himself a people for His own possession, zealous for good deeds." (Titus 2:11-15)

We could easily write a chapter on this verse because it contains such a concise compilation of so many doctrines. Grace is so amazing that when it came, it was announced like a powerful figure who is making an entrance: *"The grace of God has appeared."*

First of all, grace brings salvation to all men. Secondly, it doesn't tell us that sin doesn't matter because we are under grace; it tells us to deny ungodliness and worldly desire. Thirdly, it doesn't tell us to live with lower standards because grace gives us plenty of wiggle room. It tells us to live sensibly, righteously and godly in this present age. Fourthly, grace points us to the age to come. The grace of anticipating our Lord's return encourages us in the battle to deny ungodliness and to live sensibly and righteously. And fifthly, grace equips us to fulfill the great plan of God, *"who gave Himself for us, that He might redeem us from every lawless deed and purify for Himself a people for His own possession, zealous for good deeds."*

So here we see a very different emphasis as to the great work of the cross. Here forgiveness isn't mentioned. The word "redeem" doesn't refer to buying us back from the devil who owned us. The progression is as follows: Jesus dies for us, to redeem us from lawless deeds, to purify for Himself a people He can possess, who are zealous for good deeds.

It is very clear that purification, possession, and passion for good works all hinge on one thing — our redemption from lawless deeds called sin. This is not imputed righteousness, but the actual transformation of our character — imparted righteousness. Let me say it clearly: God loves us, but sin matters.

More on Grace

The writer of Hebrews tells his readers to yield to grace lest a root of bitterness spring up and defile them. Perhaps it is for this reason that a famous teacher defined grace further as "the power to do God's will". When Paul prayed three times for his infirmity to be taken away, the Lord said, *"My grace is sufficient for you."* God's grace was all the enablement Paul needed to live with his affliction. We all understand this concept. If we want to avoid sins like bitterness and bear up under the trials of life, then the Bible makes it plain that something called "grace" is available to help us.

When we speak of difficult people, we often add letters after their name — EGR — Extra Grace Required. We know that we need grace from God to deal with them, and that if we ask Him, He will grant it. We have to want the grace, receive the grace, and let the grace flow through us. God has ordered life in such that a way that without grace and the help of the Holy Spirit, it cannot be navigated. There are just too many snares, pitfalls, hurts, and difficult people. Many Christians do not attend church because they think that church is the problem. But the problem is them. They are unwilling to receive grace and to extend it.

Misunderstandings about the nature and role of grace have abounded throughout Church history. There are two particular heresies that Paul had to deal with in the churches he gave oversight to. I wish I could say that after two thousand years we've finally risen above such faulty thinking, but the evidence proves otherwise.

Two Heresies

The first heresy is explained by Paul in Galatians. He denounces Jewish converts for adding certain practices to grace as additional requirements for salvation. He says it was for freedom that we are set free, and that adding anything to grace brings us back into bondage. I doubt that any denomination, when listing their tenets of faith, would actually deny the sufficiency of grace. But what we call *legalism* is the subtle deception that my good works somehow add to what Christ did on the cross. The flip side is that if I don't do certain things, I am falling short of the grace of God, and my salvation is in jeopardy. People with this mindset have issues with guilt, control, self-righteousness, and judgmentalism.

The other heresy is what we call antinomianism. Paul addresses this in Romans and soundly condemns it. This is the belief that since when sin abounded, grace did much more abound, more sin means more grace. Since Jesus died for my sins, why not make the sacrifice worth the pain by sinning more? Again, no modern Christian would consciously think this way. But on a more subtle level, Christians have the idea that sin isn't that important since we're under grace: God understands my weaknesses and my sins were nailed to the cross, so sin isn't a big deal. People with this mindset are usually selfish, have a man-centered gospel, are soft on sin, and lead worldly lives.

Trophies of Grace

Before we move on to the practical application of grace to our lives, we need to pause for a moment and consider what we call "trophies of grace". While all of us fit under this heading, there are certain people who epitomize the term. Winkie Pratney, an international youth leader, usually introduces his message with the expression that God almost ruined his ministry by not giving him a testimony. He never murdered anyone, was never on drugs, and never spent time in rehab. That's a serious weakness, he says in jest, when you have a ministry to youth.

All jesting aside, we have all seen people whom God has rescued out of the most desperate and broken circumstances to use mightily. Recently our church hosted a couple who found each other during a dark period in their lives. The woman had a history that included abuse, abortion, and mental problems. The man struggled with substance abuse, depression, and chronic unemployment.

Today they exude the grace of God. They have an effective prison ministry and have spoken in hundreds of churches. The lives and testimonies of people like this touch something deep in us. They are a living witness to the power of God's grace. It can reach out and rescue the most hopeless person, but it doesn't end there. God's grace will, if we let it, make us effective ministers to others in need. That completes the cycle. But what if we don't have a sordid background? How does God's grace work in our lives?

Practical Grace

Everything we have is from God. That's grace. When we give it back to God, that's "works". God provides me with employment and the result is income. That income is His grace, and much of it is meant to meet my needs. When God instructs me to give a hundred dollars to someone, I can only do it with His grace. Without grace I would have no job, no hundred dollars, and nothing to give. If, in obedience to God, I give to others what God has given to me by grace, then at the Resurrection of the Righteous He will repay me.

This is similar to a mother giving her young son ten dollars so he can buy Daddy a birthday present. It seems so contrived. What it amounts to is buying the father a gift with his own money. But what is the father's response? Joy! Joy and praise for the son. When the father thanks his son for buying him a gift with his own money, it is no different from God thanking us for giving with generosity what was His all along.

We need frequent reminders of one important fact: Everything we have is His, given to us in grace, and meant to be managed for His purposes. Some people never make this connection and miss out in both time and eternity. They hoard the grace of God as if it would run out, and they think that they are somehow ahead. Quite the opposite.

If I don't give the hundred dollars, I am taking the money and misusing it. This is sin. When Paul talked about people abusing grace in Romans in order to sin, he wasn't just talking about lust and drunkenness. He was talking about selfish living and disobedience.

Abusing grace is on a continuum from not receiving it, to not extending it, to not valuing it. When I choose to live guilt-free, I am receiving grace; when I forgive others, I am extending grace; when I heed our Lord's command: *"Freely you have received, freely give,"* I am valuing grace. I am acknowledging God's grace as the source of everything I possess. And I am using it to live an unselfish life.

A Story of God's Grace

Let me explain grace with an incident from my life. I have a daughter, Debbie, who is now in her late twenties. After she graduated from High School, she took a two-year accounting program at our local college. Our story begins on the Labor Day weekend prior to the commencement of her second year.

At the time I was working for a government office where my main job was to fund students into college courses and pay their tuition. As such, I was keenly aware of enrollment policies and, in particular, tuition deadlines. If a student did not pay their tuition by the deadline, no matter how good their marks, they could not enroll, and they were placed on a waiting list. They could only register if someone ahead of them dropped out.

I had assumed Debbie had paid her tuition. She was an A student and a totally organized person, so I hadn't even discussed it with her. However, on the Friday night of the long weekend she made a curious statement. "One thing bothers me," she said. "What's that?" I asked. She explained that while cleaning her room the day before, she had found the tuition notice. My life passed in front of my eyes. "Deb," I asked with pounding heart, "you paid you're tuition, didn't you?"

Well, as it turned out, she hadn't. There's a term that we use to describe a father who neglects to provide for his own children that which is his stock and trade: the shoemaker's children going barefoot. That's the way I felt. I had helped so many other kids pay their tuition, but I had forgotten my own daughter. And worse, I seemed to recall a time early in the summer when she had asked me if she should pay her tuition and I had answered flippantly, "Naw, you've got plenty of time; the money can just as well gather interest in your account as it can in theirs."

To explain what God did for us in this situation, I have to give you some background of a sports nature. The incident with my daughter occurred at a time when a baseball player named Mark McGuire was trying to break the home-run record Roger Maris had held for 37 years. I'm not a baseball fan, but it was such big news that even I was aware of the media circus surrounding it.

Two angles were being played up by the media. The first angle focused on McGuire. When would he score the tying run? As excitement built to a feverish pitch, his every trip to the plate was awash with anticipation. The second angle focused on the lucky fan who would catch the ball. Who would it be? But of exceedingly more interest, what would he do with it? Would he donate the ball to the hall of fame, keep it, or sell it for a large sum of money?

Now, back to my dilemma. All weekend I tried to get a hold of instructors at the college, but seemingly they had all gone away for the long weekend. The one phrase that kept going over and over in my mind was: "I fumbled the ball. I fumbled the ball." I was convinced that I had blown it, and that was the phrase, a baseball phrase, that I was using to chastise myself.

On Tuesday I was back at work. As I walked down a long hallway in the office, a co-worker shouted, "Hey Mike, you caught the ball!"

"What?" I asked mystified. "What are you talking about?"

He asked me if I'd seen the paper, and I hadn't. Acting mysteriously, he would give no details but encouraged me to read it when I got home. I gave it no more thought as I plunged into the day's activities. But after work my curiosity grew, and the first thing I did upon arriving home was to glance at the paper to see what he meant. When I got to the sports section, I saw a picture of a smiling fan holding a ball with the caption: "Mike Davidson is all smiles...as he catches Mark McGuire's record tying 61st home run."

I was dumfounded. The spelling of his name was identical to mine. Had God actually engineered it so that a man with my identical name caught that landmark ball just to encourage me in a matter as simple as my daughter's courses? Yes, I believe He did. It could not have been a coincidence, not with the phrase I'd been beating myself up with all weekend: "I fumbled the ball, I fumbled the ball." On the other hand, you would have to be an egocentric megalomaniac to believe that out of 330 million names in North America, God specifically chose a fellow with mine to catch the ball just to affirm me.

Or would you? Not if you understood grace. I understand grace.

It was God.

I can see God counting the hours, so to speak, till I got home to read the paper. He couldn't wait to see the look on my face. He knew I'd go through stages of shock, excitement, joy, and consolation. But the last emotion would be the best: wonder and marvel. And God was right. That's what I did. I marveled.

God could have ignored my dilemma or comforted me in some small way. Or He could have simply used it to test my faith. Either way, I'm just another affluent Christian and we all know about the starving masses. Why should He even care about my petty problems?! But He does. He's my Father. And then to drive home the point that He cares, and to leave me weak with wonder, He does exceedingly abundantly above all I could think or ask. And in the end, it didn't even really matter. My daughter ended up getting most of her courses anyway, and was the better for the experience.

But it did matter to God.

He wanted to show me His grace with an extravagance that I would never forget. He knew the challenges that I would face in the future. His plan worked. I have never forgotten that incident and others that were of similar impact. The first time this sort of thing happens our response is that we don't deserve it. But as we learn that "undeserved" is the definition of grace, eventually the "I don't deserve it" response becomes obtuse. It becomes redundant. It's like saying, "I don't deserve what I don't deserve." All we can do is be thankful. All we can do is marvel. I will forever keep that news clipping in my Bible as a testament to God's love and grace.

The Treasure and the Pearl

Let us conclude with two very misunderstood Kingdom Parables. Meditate on the truth of what I'm about to share, and you will never doubt God's love again.

> *"The Kingdom of heaven is like a treasure hidden in the field, which a man found and hid; and from joy over it he goes and sells all that he has and buys that field.*
>
> *Again, the kingdom of heaven is like a merchant seeking fine pearls, and upon finding one pearl of*

great value, he went and sold all he had, and bought it." (Matt. 13:44-46)

We have been taught that Christ is the hidden treasure and the pearl of great price, and that we are to sell all for Him. But this interpretation is contrary to the gospel and breaks down in every particular.

As one person put it: "The 'field' in this Parable is the 'world', the same as in the Parable of the Wheat and Tares, and the sinner is not to purchase the world, but to give it up. Furthermore, the sinner has nothing to sell, nor is Christ for sale, nor is He hidden in a field, nor having found Christ does the sinner hide him again. Salvation is not something that can be bought. It is a free gift. The sinner does not buy Christ; Christ buys him."

No lengthy explanation of how the above details apply to Christ is necessary. What is obvious is that we have mishandled a powerful expression of God's love. We need to ponder the word "joy" in the Parable of the Hidden Treasure. We need to ponder the phrase "sold all that He had" from both parables. In eternity past Jesus saw a treasure that overwhelmed Him. It was the Church hidden in the world. It was us! The joy of what He saw caused Him to sell everything so that He could buy the world and take possession of that treasure.

Think of your favorite gospel song. Mine starts off: "He left the splendor of heaven, knowing His destiny." He who was rich became poor for our sakes. He sold everything He had for the joy of possessing the treasure — us! He suffered and died in poverty that we might inherit all things.

In the Pearl of Great Price, Jesus finds one pearl and sells all He has to possess it. Same story, different focus. Perhaps you have heard someone say, "Even if you were the only one, Jesus would have died just for you." That is what we learn from the Pearl of Great Price. Jesus is not the Pearl of Great Price. You are. I am. He sold everything to buy us.

Where do we get the nerve to tell Him that He doesn't love us? How can we question a love that sells all and does it joyfully? Joyfully! Think of the cross. Spend your life trying to imagine greater love. You can't. It is baffling to witness an unbeliever reject that love and instead choose hell. But it is equally baffling to observe a Christian questioning that love.

It's time to move on. God loves you. God loves me. Let's lay down our lives for Him just as He did for us. And then wonder of wonders, let's read on in the following chapters of this book to discover that dying for us wasn't enough. Even living for us isn't enough. He still wants to repay us for everything we do for Him. It's all through Him and to Him anyway, but He still wants to repay us. It's mind-boggling!

God's love is mind-boggling!

SECTION TWO

The Four Pillars of Judgment

FIVE

The Judgment of Sin

I met Darwin at a party. He was aggressively disputing a
friend, a Christian doctor, over some technical issue of
origins and cosmology. *Who* argues about cosmology? Or
better still, what *is* cosmology? Anyway, something in his
keen mind and combative nature attracted me.

God seldom directs me to visit an unbeliever, but He did
in this instance. He told me to knock on Darwin's door and
give him a copy of the audiotape, <u>Seven Campus Curses,</u>
by the late Dr. Walter Marin. As I anticipated, the first
few moments on the doorstep of his beautiful home were
awkward. With some difficulty, I explained my purpose as
his eyes narrowed with suspicion.

Eventually he invited me in and we had a long talk. The
outcome was more than gratifying, as he devoured the tape
and later ordered everything he could find by Martin. After
a short while Darwin and his wife both gave their hearts to
the Lord, and we became best of friends. We spent many
enjoyable evenings together as couples, playing music and
sharing the Lord.

After a couple of years, my wife and I moved to a larger
city, and soon they did as well. At first we maintained close
contact, but after a few years we began to lose touch with
each other. As we followed their progress, we marveled at
God's ways: I was "mister conservative" and ended up in a
Charismatic Church. He was a radical extravert and ended
up in a Brethren Church. He, along with his wife and eight

children, seemed to savor the reverence and the depth of teaching. Such are God's ways.

A couple of years after we'd last seen them, I got a call from a mutual friend. "Did you hear about Darwin?" he asked.

"No," I replied, concerned at his tone. "What happened?"

I sat there speechless as he told me that Darwin had just been arrested. He had tried to kill his next-door neighbor with three blasts from a shotgun. Miraculously the man was still alive, but the prognosis was not good.

I'll never forget the pain of seeing my friend on the front page of the newspaper, handcuffed, surrounded by police officers, and the picture of despair. I was stunned. How could Darwin — how could any Christian — try to kill his neighbor? And in such a brutal fashion? My mind was reeling.

I learned later that Darwin's neighbor had harassed him for months, openly taunting him and pushing him progressively to the breaking point. On the day of the incident there had been another outrage, and Darwin had snapped. Despite three blasts from a shotgun at short range, the victim lived and Darwin went to trial. His defense was temporary insanity, and people smirked at the use of such a convenient term to describe such a heinous act. But the jury bought it and he was acquitted. However, in the process he lost everything.

Looking Back

As I look back over the years since I received the Lord, I cannot think of a single sin that has not been committed by a professing Christian. Some of these sins I was witness to, others were related to me by friends in the deliverance and counseling ministries. Many of them are too defiling to even mention. Lest the word "professing" bring confusion, let me put it stronger.

I cannot think of a *single* sin that has not been committed by a born again believer whose salvation experience was beyond question.

Most of us have very tidy theology. Good Christians don't commit certain sins. If they do, they probably weren't Christians to begin with. Regardless, once you're born again it's all under the blood. Once this struggle called "life" is over, we meet a loving Father who greets us with open arms. All is forgiven; all is forgotten. At some point rewards are handed out; then we join with others around the throne to enjoy everlasting peace.

How I wish it were that simple.

But the truth is a little more complicated. What you are about to read is what the Word of God has to say on the subject. I'll be the first to admit that it is not very tidy, but it is infinitely more satisfying. And because it is the truth, it has the power to set us free. It has the power to "lead us in the paths of righteousness for His name's sake."

Losing Your Inheritance

We all know that there is a kingdom coming, a detail God saw fit to include even in the Lord's Prayer. The kingdom itself is a mystery to most people, and few have given it much thought. It might surprise many to know, for instance, that there are believers who will have no inheritance in the Kingdom of God. Let me put it stronger: In the age to come, there are many believers, possibly people you know, who, despite their voluminous good works, will receive absolutely nothing. Though born again and apparently industrious, once having passed through the judgment, their entire life will be found to have been in vain.

How can this be?

For now, let us say that there are actions we can take that will disinherit us, and these actions, or sins, are often not what you would expect. We are not talking here about good deeds that will be found to be hay, wood, and stubble in the midst of a virtuous life, but valid works that are disqualified because of a pattern of behavior.

Let us look, then, at what virtually every New Testament believer understood, but which has been sadly lost to all but the most astute modern day Christian. To do this we must give brief consideration to the New Testament context.

The New Testament Context

Life in first century Palestine has at least one parallel to the present day — the countdown to a coming King. At this writing, the Left Behind series, now eleven books and counting, has sold over sixty million copies. That is a staggering figure and shows an interest, not just in literature, but in the Second Coming of our Lord.

But the current interest doesn't evoke the white-hot terror that accompanied the Thief in the Night film of the seventies. And also noticeably absent is the spine-tingling excitement that greeted Hal Lindsay's The Late Great Planet Earth. But happily, despite a myriad of truths the Holy Spirit is anointing in these last days, there yet remains a healthy fixation with the subject of the "Coming One".

That's how it was just prior to our Lord's public ministry. The times were rife with expectation. Certainly the leaders of the four main Jewish sects and most of their followers knew Daniel chapter 2. It is here that we find Daniel's interpretation of Nebuchadnezzar's dream. In that dream the king had seen a great statue with a head of gold, breast and arms of silver, belly and thighs of bronze, legs of iron and feet of iron and clay.

Daniel tells the king that he, Nebuchadnezzar, is the head of gold, and that after him would come three more world kingdoms. That prophecy was given in 600 BC, and every one alive in our Lord's day could look back and see its fulfillment.

As predicted, there had in fact been four world kingdoms — Babylon, Persia, Greece and Rome. In the year 63 BC, Rome, the final kingdom, had conquered Palestine. By the time John the Baptist was preaching the Kingdom of God, nearly a hundred years of Roman rule had elapsed. That created a consternation born of unfulfilled expectation. The Jewish people, slaves in many ways to the Roman Empire, had expected a Savior, referred to in the Hebrew language as Messiah, and in the Greek as the Christ, the anointed One.

And rightfully so!

Daniel had finished his famous prophesy with this statement:

"And in the days of those kings, the God of heaven will set up a kingdom which will never be destroyed, and that kingdom will not be left for another people; it will crush and put an end to all these kingdoms, but will itself endure forever." (Dan. 2:44)

"In the days of those kings" — what could be more clear? The kings had come and gone, leaving the last kingdom to be overthrown by the God of heaven. He would then set up His kingdom which would crush all other kingdoms. Right! So where was it? God's people had waited a hundred years and they were earnestly expecting Messiah, their conquering hero.

The Zealots, one of the main Jewish sects, had even sought to expedite the process. In their fervor, they had instigated numerous revolts that had to be brutally crushed. The Pharisees, on the other hand, were content to work with the Messiah and honor His timing, but were no less frustrated by the apparent delay.

John came preaching the Kingdom of God. Jesus went about preaching the Kingdom of God. Not uncoincidentily, their target audience was expecting the Kingdom of God. That is why, for instance, after the feeding of the five thousand, *"they sought to take Him by force and make Him King."* Jesus, as prophesied, was rejected by the ruling elite. But the common man, having no axe to grind, increasingly recognized in the miracles, particularly the miracles of healing and supply, their prophesied King.

But He projected an enigmatic persona to say the least. He certainly sowed confusion in the minds of those close to Him. Clearly, the disciples had the same expectation as those around them — their Messiah would be a conquering King who would overthrow the Roman rule and set up the Kingdom.

But His words and behavior indicated otherwise.

Rank in the Kingdom

This matter of the Kingdom and its relevance to our judgment has been seriously overlooked. A quick glance at a concordance establishes several things. Firstly, Jesus spent more time talking about the Kingdom of God than any other subject. This is in contrast to the oft-repeated myth that money was His favorite topic. Money was a distant second.

Our Lord's priority, if frequency is any judge, was the Kingdom. And not *just* the Kingdom but, in particular, entry into the kingdom and one's ultimate rank or position there. Try to place yourself in the mindset of the listeners who would hear statements like the following:

"Whoever then annuls one of the least of these commandments, and so teaches others, shall be called least in the kingdom of heaven; but whoever keeps and teaches them, he shall be called great in the kingdom of heaven."

"Not everyone who says 'Lord, Lord,' will enter the kingdom of Heaven, but he who does the will of my Father who is in heaven."

"Do not lay up for yourselves treasures upon earth, where moth and rust destroy, and where thieves break in and steal. But lay up for yourselves treasures in heaven, where neither moth nor rust destroy, and where thieves do not break in and steal."

"Blessed are you when men revile you and persecute you, and say all kinds of evil against you falsely, on account of Me. Rejoice and be glad, for great is your reward in heaven, for so they persecuted the prophets that were before you."

"Whoever then humbles himself as this child, he is the greatest in the kingdom of heaven."

"Jesus said to him, 'If you wish to be complete, go and sell your possessions and give to the poor, and you will have treasure in heaven.'"

"Then the King will say to those on His right, 'Come you who are blessed of My Father, inherit the kingdom prepared for you from the foundation of the world.'"

"Truly I say to you, that the tax-gatherers and harlots will get into the Kingdom of God before you."

"There will be weeping and gnashing of teeth there when you see Abraham and Isaac and Jacob and all the prophets in the kingdom of God, but yourselves being cast out. And they will come from east and west and from north and south and will recline at tables in the kingdom of God. And behold, some are last who will be first and some are first who will be last."

These are but a few of the over 110 references to the Kingdom of God or Heaven found in the gospels.

The Great Expectation

It cannot be said too forcefully that by the time the Book of Acts was written, every believer expected that the Kingdom would be coming immediately. Secondly, they expected it to be preceded by a judgment where rewards were handed out and rank in the Kingdom established.

The last page of the Bible contains a graphic illustration of these two points. Jesus said, *"Behold, I am coming quickly, and My reward is with me to give to every man according to what he has done"* (Rev. 22:12). Jesus isn't just coming, He is coming quickly; and when He does, He has one priority — to administer rewards.

In Acts chapter 1 we are given final details about our Lord's earthly ministry. We are told that, after rising from the dead, He appeared to His disciples *"over a period of forty days, speaking of the things concerning the Kingdom of God"* (Acts 1:3). A few verses later, the disciples asked, *"Lord, is it at this time You are restoring the kingdom to Israel?"* (Acts 1:6).

He had specifically told them the parable of the minas in Luke 19 to clear up this misconception — because *"they supposed that the kingdom of God was going to appear immediately."* But they didn't get the message, no doubt because of the divine prerogative that every generation be led to believe that they are the last. How else to explain *"Behold, I come quickly,"*

In his rebuke to grumblers, James tells them they will be judged, concluding with the threat: *"The Judge is standing at the door!"* (James 5:9). That was a very plausible threat, the more so because James himself truly believed it. Paul in his writings makes frequent reference to the kingdom as if it would appear at any moment, and he doubtless believed it.

One of the reasons Paul wrote the Thessalonian letters was to deal with issues surrounding the second coming.

In the first letter he gives instruction regarding the rapture. In the second, he allays the fears of people who feared that the second coming had already occurred and that they had missed it. He concludes with a rebuke for people who were idle. It seems that an ever-present temptation that existed then, as now, is to regard work and planning as futile when the Lord could return at any moment. Paul's stern rebuttal to this type of thinking was: *"If any man doesn't work, neither should he eat."*

Clarifying the Kingdom

Whenever Jesus spoke of the Kingdom of God, He was referring to one of three things: the spiritual Kingdom, the millennial Kingdom, or the eternal Kingdom. Today we can discern between them, but to the people in Bible times, the Kingdom meant the millennial Kingdom. They were looking for the Kingdom on earth that was promised by the prophets.

The clear teaching of scripture is that there is first the rapture, then the Judgment Seat of Christ, followed by the set-up of the millennial Kingdom, either immediately, or within seven years. It was this event that was uppermost in the minds of every believer. Take the rapture-fever of the seventies, multiply it a hundredfold, and you have the mindset of the people who were the recipients of the epistles.

It should be noted, by way of clarification, that the millennial Kingdom lasts a thousand years. Following this, God creates a new heaven and earth, and time is no more; we enter the eternal kingdom. The scriptures are silent on the role of the saints at this point but most assuredly we will rule and reign with Him forever. Since there is only one believer's judgment, the outcome of that event determines our assignments both in the millennial kingdom, and in the ages to come.

The Significance of the Kingdom

So why is all this important? Because it makes sense of many hitherto confusing passages of scripture, and it gives us tremendous insight into the high cost of sin. Take the following passage in 1Corinthians 5:

> *"I have written you in my letter not to associate with sexually immoral people – **not at all meaning the people of this world** who are immoral, or the greedy and swindlers, or idolaters. In that case you would have to leave this world. But now I am writing you that you must not associate with anyone who calls himself a brother but is sexually immoral or greedy, or an idolater or a slanderer, a drunkard or a swindler. With such a man do not even eat. What business is it of mine to judge those outside the church? Are you not to judge those inside. God will judge those outside. Expel the wicked man from among you."* (1 Cor. 5:9-13 NIV)

Paul doesn't mince words. When he told them not to mix with immoral people, drunkards and swindlers, etc., he wasn't talking about those in the world. He was talking about *Christians*. He explains why: We are not to judge the world, or else we would have to leave it. Judging the world is God's job. Our job is to judge the church.

Paul makes it very plain that the same sins that are in the world are in the church. After naming these sins, he refers to the people who commit them as brothers, and puts them under discipline, which he explains is strictly for Christians and not for the world. He has just told us the earthly penalty for Christians who sin — excommunication. But in the next chapter, he gives us the eternal consequence:

"Do you not know that the wicked will not inherit the kingdom of God? Do not be deceived: Neither the sexually immoral nor idolaters nor adulterers, nor male prostitutes, nor homosexual offenders nor thieves nor the greedy nor drunkards nor slanderers nor swindlers will inherit the kingdom of God." (1Cor.6: 9-10 NIV)

Here we see the same sins listed in chapter 5 along with a few additions. Notice the phrase repeated twice: *"will not inherit the kingdom of God."* The same phrase in Ephesians is translated *"will have no inheritance in the kingdom of God,"* which is a better rendering. Paul does not say these people will not enter the kingdom of God or that they will go to hell. He says they will have no **inheritance**.

Inheritance is the word, and inheritance is the issue.

Before I move on to the significance of this, let me address the verse that follows this passage. Sometimes in scripture we find statements a few verses apart that are contradictory. On the surface, at least, they seem to be saying the exact opposite of each other.

Such Were Some of You

After giving us the list of sinners in 1Corinthians 6 who will be disinherited, Paul says: *"And such were some of you; but you were washed, but you were sanctified, but you were justified in the name of the Lord Jesus Christ, and in the Spirit of our God"* (1Cor. 6:11).

Because Paul says, *"And such **were** some of you,"* we could easily assume that no one in Corinth was presently committing these sins, and therefore would not face the penalty of disinheritance. But in chapter 3 Paul has just castigated the Corinthians for being in different religious camps – some were of Paul, and some were of Apollos. He blasts them with the accusation: *"for ye are yet carnal: for whereas* *there is among you envying, and **strife, and divisions**, are ye not carnal, and walk as men?"(1Cor. 3:3 KJV).*

Strife and division are found in the Galatians 5 "sins of the flesh" list. The words are even identical in the Greek, so there is no question that they are the same sins. This list concludes with the statement: *"those who practice such things shall not inherit the kingdom of God"* (Gal. 5:21).

So the Corinthians were practicing at least two sins that could disinherit them. But that is just the beginning. Paul mentions six more disinheriting sins in chapter 5 that were rampant. He's angry because the people committing these sins weren't being disfellowshiped. Earlier in that chapter, he expresses disgust that a man is living with his father's wife, and he says incredulously, *"You are proud!"*

He pays them the ultimate insult by declaring that even a pagan wouldn't do that.

And then there is the issue which prompted Paul to address "disinheritance" in the first place: Christian lawsuits in public courts. It was Paul's anger at this behavior that caused him to launch the tirade: *"Or do you not know that the unrighteous shall not inherit the kingdom of God?"* He says that those involved in the lawsuits are unrighteous, defrauders, and infers that they won't inherit the kingdom of God.

Given the facts stated above, we must apply some logic. Paul has invested much time and emotion in railing against the carnality of the Corinthians and itemizing the gross sins that they were *currently* committing — sins that would disinherit them. He couldn't possibly, in the next breath then, say just the opposite: that that is the way they *used* to be - *"and such were some of you" (1Cor.6: 11)*. So now that we know what Paul *wasn't* saying in verse 6:11, what in fact *was* he saying?

The city of Corinth was a den of iniquity. Many in the Corinthian church had come from a sinful and sordid background. In acknowledging this, Paul says: *"and such were some of you."* He then describes the work of the cross and the sanctifying work of the Spirit in their lives when they first got saved. He was *exhorting* them and reminding them of how God had found them and changed them. But his earlier comments show that many had slipped back. They **had been** saved and sanctified, but they **were** currently walking in sin and carnality. Therefore they were in danger of losing their inheritance. In Paul's letter to the Ephesians, after threatening disinheritance, he takes exactly the same approach.

The New Testament Mindset

Today the threat of disinheritance means nothing to us because we have not been taught this truth and don't understand it. But a New Testament Christian understood exactly what Paul was saying. They expected the kingdom at any moment, and they understood that they would be assigned positions in the kingdom based on their lives. What Paul has just pronounced is the worst threat they could imagine short of hell — disinheritance.

Honor is very important in eastern cultures, much more so than in western. People are willing to die over issues of honor, and some commit suicide when honor is lost. To tell a person in Paul's day that in the coming Kingdom he or she would lose their inheritance and would be without honor, was the worst thing you could say.

Clarifying Our Theology

Very plainly, we have brushed these scriptures aside or, with no regard for logic, have assumed that the sinners referred to are going to hell. But the same group of people identified in 1Corinthians 5 as Christians are listed again in 1Corinthians 6. Are all immoral Christians really going to hell? If we pause for a moment to consider what we believe, then very quickly our theology will come into line.

So let's ask another question: Do we seriously believe that the pastor who runs away with his secretary has suddenly become an unbeliever, has passed from the Kingdom of Light back into the Kingdom of Darkness, and has had his name erased from the Lambs book of life? No, of course not. We simply think of him as a fallen leader, someone who has sinned, a backslider, but no less a brother in the Lord. He has our prayers and best wishes for his recovery. (The issue of losing our salvation will be discussed in detail later.)

If we consider every sinner in that list, we will come to the same conclusion. Sin separates us from God, but it doesn't send us to hell. "Sin breaks fellowship, not sonship", is how the cliché goes. Granted, some sins strain at our capacity to extend grace, but many of us have dealt with Christians who have committed every one of those sins. We can readily identify with the apostle Paul's analysis — they are indeed believers, but if unrepentant, then they are to be disfellowshipped.

Depending on where you are on the grace scale, this can seem either too harsh or too light a sentence. But it really doesn't matter what you or I think. The apostle Paul, under the inspiration of the Holy Spirit, says that they are to be under severe discipline in this life, but of exceedingly more importance, they will have no inheritance in the life to come.

Greed and Disinheritance

Being greedy, for instance, can disqualify us from any inheritance in the Kingdom of God. It is one of the sins Paul listed. How does this work? Let me give you an example.

Jesus said, *"Be on guard against every form of greed..."* (Luke 12:15). I have periodically gone into David Wilkerson's website where you can download every one of his sermons going back decades. On one such visit I read a sermon where he castigated certain prosperity teachers.

Someone had given Wilkerson a video of a recent prosperity conference. In it, preachers were seen striding arrogantly across the stage, bragging about their jewelry, cars, homes, and other luxury items. Their message was simple: People are poor because they have wrong theology; start believing right, or more exactly, start giving right (especially to them) and you too can be rich.

Wilkerson's anger at these individuals almost burnt my fingers as I scrolled through his message. He declared them to be false prophets. Are they indeed false prophets? I don't know, because the individuals weren't identified, but this I do know: Unless they repent, they are going to be least in the kingdom. Unless they repent, they will have no inheritance in the kingdom of God. They are trapped in the bond of iniquity; they are slaves to their own greed. But even worse, they are teaching others to fall in love with money and are therefore teaching people to sin.

They are not teaching self-denial, the crucified life, a burden for souls, and a life of prayer. They are teaching people to love the world, and the **things** in the world — something that is expressly forbidden. Since I don't know these people, I can only judge the fruit.

It's bad fruit!

Prosperity is a sensitive issue. With so much confusion on the subject of money and so little teaching in most churches, it's important that we not misread what has just been stated. We are talking about greed, not need, nor even abundance. The Bible says the laborer is worthy of his wages. All who serve God are entitled to the fruit of their labor. We will discuss money in the next chapter and hopefully bring clarity to this important topic.

Back to the prosperity teachers. Why have I stressed the issue of these men teaching people to sin? Because that in itself, quite apart from personal greed, can disinherit them. Jesus said:

"Whoever annuls one of the least of these command-ments, and so teaches others, shall be called least in the kingdom of heaven; but whoever keeps and teaches them, he shall be called great in the kingdom of heaven." (Matt. 5:19)

Teaching Others to Sin

At issue here is not just sin, but our *attitude* towards sin and, in particular, the matter of teaching others to sin. So let's look at some applications and get an insight into why this type of trespass brings such severe consequences.

There are female singers who are well known to be Christians, although they are stars in the secular market primarily. It is sad to see them dress like harlots and use sexually suggestive language and gestures in their shows. Their actions not only reveal their own sin, but they also steer young people down a path of immorality. Many Christian actors do the same. They are in danger of being least in the kingdom.

There are ministers who, because of moral weakness, the fear of man, or a liberal mindset, promote ungodly standards. Some divorce their spouses and remarry without missing a beat. Their behavior gives license to others to do the same. Some even teach that homosexuality is a valid expression, and give fuel to people who are tempted in this area. By their teachings, these ministers encourage such people to sin.

Then there is the matter of the tongue. Character assassination through the tongue is a serious sin. When this practice reaches the point where it enflames others and encourages them to do the same, then we have a situation where one's inheritance is at stake.

It is positively appalling to see the number of websites that are devoted solely to the tearing down of well-known Christian ministers. I have visited dozens of them and the ones I saw were clearly hosted by Christians. These people are doing incalculable damage to the Body of Christ by teaching others to revile those anointed by God. We may joke about people who seem to have the ministry of criticism, but it is no laughing matter.

There are many such examples, and there is forgiveness for those who repent. But Jesus makes it very plain: If we are careless about sin, and if we teach and encourage others to sin, we will have tribulation and distress on Judgment Day. And worse, we may lose our inheritance.

The seriousness of this entire matter can be best summed up in the following verse: *"For it is inevitable that stumbling blocks come; but woe to that man through whom the stumbling block comes!" (Matt. 18:7).* It is inevitable that people will be led into sin and get hurt, but woe to the person who does the leading.

In James we have this caution: *"Let not many of you become teachers, my brethren, knowing that as such you shall incur a stricter judgment"*(James 3:1). He then goes on to talk about the difficulty of taming the tongue. The obvious application is that we are all capable of doing damage with our tongue, but the teacher much more so because of his position of authority. As such, teachers have to soberly consider their calling because it comes with an inherent potential for greater harm as well as greater good. The judgment of the fruit of this gift will be severe.

In considering a matter this serious, we must all ask ourselves the question: Is there anything in my behavior or lifestyle that would encourage others to sin? As a parent, do I openly sin and justify it to my children? Or worse, do I try to enforce a double standard? How would I feel if my children chose a sinful lifestyle because of something I modeled? How would God feel? These are hard questions, but for the sake of our souls, they need to be asked.

Happily, the scriptures we are dealing with also present the other side. If we keep His commandments and teach others to do so, we will be great in the kingdom of heaven.

When our words, behavior, and lifestyle encourage others to live godly lives, it is certain that at the end of this life we will have great reward.

Idolatry

Let us continue by considering other scriptural passages that threaten disinheritance, and note the sins that are mentioned. Our second reference is found in Ephesians.

> *"But do not let immorality or any impurity or greed even be named among you, as is proper among saints…. For this you know with certainty, that no immoral or impure person or covetous man, who is an idolater, has an inheritance in the kingdom of Christ and God."* (Eph. 5:3,5)

Here we have a partial listing of the same sins mentioned earlier, with the pronouncement that no one who does these things has *"an inheritance in the kingdom of Christ and God"*. Again, we find no statement that such people won't enter the kingdom, or that, conversely, they are going to hell. We are discussing inheritance, not eternal life. The sin of idolatry turns up on every list we are going to look at, and since it appears to be the common cold of spiritual adultery, it bears looking at.

The reason I call Christian idolatry "the common cold" is because none of us are going to bow down to graven idols, something readily identifiable as hard-core spiritual adultery. Our idolatry is of the less obvious, more pervasive, and presumably less serious type — hence the "common cold" analogy.

We are often told that you can make an idol out of anything, but is this really true? Technically, yes. You and I could be guilty of worshipping our favorite sports team, our new car, the music of Beethoven, or higher education. But there is a vast difference between taking pleasure in something and idolizing it.

There is a common cliché that has the effect of obscuring truth rather than establishing it: "Jesus is either Lord *of* all, or He's not Lord *at* all." It has a curious logic to it, but is it really so? Do we instantly, for all time, make Jesus Lord of every area of our life, or is it a process? Clearly it's a process.

Using the "Kingdom of God" analogy, and speaking in the spiritual sense, we want the Kingdom of God to invade every area of our lives — relationships, finances, sexuality, work, parenting, etc. Then, depending on our vision and calling, we want to take the crown rights of King Jesus into the neighborhood, into the marketplace, and into government. We want the kingdom of God to influence medicine, education, finance, entertainment, etc.

This is a lifetime endeavor and comes under the broad category of sanctification. Will many of our passions trump our commitment to Jesus as we travel this path? Probably. Is this idolatry? If it is, it is not the kind that can disinherit you. Rather, this is the Romans 7 battle with the natural man that wants to serve the world, while the spirit man wants to serve God.

This is an important distinction. It is true that idolatry can disinherit us, but if idolatry is truly as widespread in the church as we've been led to believe, then we are all at peril. But idolatry isn't simply enjoying your new car, spending too much time on the golf course, or insisting on a spotless house.

The truth is that, with rare exceptions, idols in the western world fall into classic categories. The first is fear. Whatever we fear becomes our God. We all occasionally succumb to fear, and some people are even bound by a spirit of fear. But the continual life-long bowing at the altar of fear reduces God from His position of prime authority to a "lesser god" who is incapable of protecting His own people. Fear usually leads to other sins.

Fear in the financial area, for instance, can lead to selfishness, greed, cheating, ingratitude, depression, and a failure to tithe. Fear has to be understood, not as a logical response to a real or perceived threat (unless it is genuine physical harm), but for what it is — sin. Fear is trusting more in Satan's ability to kill, steal and destroy, than in God's ability to provide and protect.

In II Kings we are told that Israel *"feared the Lord and served their own gods"*(II Kings 17:33). That sounds like the ultimate oxymoron! How is this possible? It's possible because fear made them hedge their bets. Just in case God didn't come through, they had to appease the rain god and the sun god to ensure they had a good harvest. That's no different, really, than using your tithe for personal expenses just in case God doesn't come through.

The other common idols are relationships, personal ambition, money, celebrity, and an inordinate addiction to pleasure, especially forbidden pleasure. A minor distinction needs to be drawn here.

Agents of Unfruitfulness

Jesus said there were three things that would cause us to lead unfruitful lives: the cares of this world, the deceitfulness of riches, and the desire for other things. Since these same things have the potential for idolatry, how do we distinguish these agents of unfruitfulness from true idolatry?

Jesus tells us that any attempt to love, follow and serve God, without dealing with worry, money and passion, will be unsuccessful. These things will choke out our spiritual life and make us unfruitful. Jesus is imparting wisdom, not railing against sin.

Idolatry, on the other hand, is loving and serving these things **instead** of the God of heaven. It is most obvious in the area of money and ambition. The greedy man in the

Ephesians 5 passage is called an idolater, so from God's point of view, greed *is* idolatry.

Many people, men in particular, have bowed their knee to the corporate structure. They know God, but don't glorify Him as God. The best of their time, energy, and affections goes to their job, that next promotion, and the bigger paycheck. Wherever God unapologetically occupies second place, there is the possibility of idolatry, and idolatry leads to disinheritance.

Works of the Flesh

Let us move on to our final list of sins that can disinherit us. We find these in the book of Galatians, and they are known as the works of the flesh:

> " Now the deeds of the flesh are evident, which are: immorality, impurity, sensuality, idolatry, sorcery, enmities, strife, jealousy, outbursts of anger, disputes, dissentions, factions, envyings, drunkenness, carousings and things like these, of which I forewarn you just as I have forewarned you that those who practice such things shall not inherit the kingdom of God." (Gal. 5:19-21)

One of the reasons we seldom preach about sin anymore is because we don't know what to say. When we come across a list like the above, we have the inherent belief that such people are going to hell — until we have to deal with one of them. Then, when counseling with a person whose born-again experience is beyond doubt, we reach the inescapable conclusion that regardless of their sin, they are children of God. Someone can say to our face, as one adulterer did to me, "I know what I'm doing is wrong, but I don't care. It feels good!" And we don't know how to respond.

In addition to love and affirmation, such people need at least three warnings. The first warning is that *"God will judge adulterers"* (Heb. 13:4). This is written to Christians, and since God will judge all unconfessed sin, the singling out of this sin tells us how serious it is.

The second warning is that God commands the wicked man to be removed; so henceforth, they can no longer fellowship in the church. That's easy to say, but difficult to enforce in the present age where there are endless places for unrepentant sinners to congregate. That is why the third warning is so important.

Such a person must be told that those who practice these things will have no inheritance in the kingdom of God. Unfortunately, this statement will have little impact on an untaught, carnally-minded Christian. They couldn't care less — now. But they *will* care — then. There will come a day when they would give anything to go back and live their life over again. But it will be too late; all the tears will avail nothing. Without a personal revelation, this will not turn a person from their sin, but we have a duty to speak the truth in love. Love is not always upbeat and ingratiating. Read again Paul's anger in 1 Corinthians 5 at the wickedness described, and remind yourself that warning sinners is an act of love.

Impurity

That is all pretty straight forward when it comes to adultery in the local church, but we are dealing with grave matters that have much broader application. Take the term *impurity*. It is sexual in nature and we could take time to consider its many expressions, but there is no need.

The most common application of this term today is pornography and masturbation, which has reached epidemic proportions amongst church-going men and even pastors. Men, in ignorance, are playing with fire, and it could well cost them their inheritance.

Strife and Jealousy

Then we have the area of strife, envy, jealousy, and enmities. Often a leader of an upstart church in a metropolitan area will suffer attack, especially if the church does well. The attack may well come from the world and the media, but that is a most unlikely source. Usually it comes from other churches. Ministers who feel threatened by the "new kid on the block" will occasionally fuel rumors and, in some cases, even start them.

Most ministers are truly building God's kingdom, not their own, and they rejoice in another's success. Even if they lose members, it matters little, so long as the kingdom prospers. But sadly, there are those who are willing tools in the tearing down of "the competition". Those who practice and encourage such things may find themselves with little or nothing to show for a lifetime of service on Judgment Day.

I remember when there was a shooting in Atlanta in early 2005 that saw four people killed, including a judge. The assailant accosted a Christian woman and kept her hostage in her own apartment for a brief period. During their conversation she read and discussed excerpts from a book she was reading, The Purpose Driven Life. As a result of her later testimony and the capture of the shooter, this book received a lot of press, with the author, Rick Warren, doing many interviews.

The interviews that I saw were universally complimentary to Warren and his achievement — being the author of the best selling non-fiction book in the world. Every interview except one, that is. I wish I could say that the one detractor was an atheist or a humanist, but he wasn't. He was a famous Christian author and pastor.

When asked on TV about The Purpose Driven Life, he dismissed it with a sneer. "Pop Christianity," he said with disgust. Right after his comments, the program host switched over to a panel composed of a theologian and a Christian journalist. When asked to explain the root of this man's evident animosity, with one voice they replied, "jealousy". Pastor Warren has a church of twenty-five thousand people; the other fellow's church has nine thousand. End of story.

I wonder how the Lord feels when the world celebrates one of His sons while a Christian brother becomes the attack dog. If you can imagine the Lord's hurt, then you can understand the reckoning that will one day be necessary. This particular minister is famous for his attacks on Charismatics, so it was not an isolated incident.

Personally, I like the man and have learned more than a few things from his teachings. Were I the judge, I might dismiss his failures. But we have to understand that we are imperfect judges, as much for our ill-placed mercy as for our misplaced anger. We seldom get it right. The fact that we may be a mercy person and prone to overlook a person's sin doesn't make us more righteous than a God who can't. This is where people often miss it. Because of our fallen nature, we will inevitably make less of sin than the righteous, holy God, who alone is Judge.

Factions and Outbursts of Anger

Then we have the area of "outbursts of anger, disputes, dissentions and factions".

I once worked with a fellow by the name of Charlie. Charlie was brilliant and a Christian as well, so it sounds like he had everything covered. But he didn't. Every few weeks Charlie would explode with anger at his supervisor and, doing a very good impression of a preschooler, would stomp off muttering loud threats as people cut a swath in front of him. Rolling their eyes with resignation, his co-workers would give a sigh that said: "Charlie's having another one of his episodes." As a fellow Christian, I found this distressing, but did my best to overlook Charlie's poor witness because he most certainly loved the Lord.

But Charlie's problems didn't end there. He was an elder in a church which believed that every sect, denomination, and independent assembly had erred and compromised Biblical truth. This group had no affiliation with Charismatics, Catholics or even conservative evangelical churches. They participated in no inter-church meetings or campaigns. There is a word for this kind of group. It's called a "faction" or "sect".

Factions don't normally consist of humble people praying that the Lord will bring revelation to the larger body. Instead, they seem to attract carnal people who are blinded by pride and have scorn for the misguided masses. At least, this has been my experience. The scriptures make it clear that those who have this attitude are at risk of losing their inheritance.

Charlie's group planted a satellite church in another section of our city and, not surprisingly, within a few months they were fighting each other. The end result was that the satellite church broke away and ceased fellowship with the original group. It reminds one of the old saying: "Everyone is crazy except me and thee, and sometimes I'm not sure about thee."

Swindlers

And then there are swindlers. I used to work for a large government agency. It was a well-known fact amongst my co-workers that the most despised employers in the city "spouted religious views". Christian views, as it turns out. These people were well known in the Christian community but, in classic blindness, were witnessing out of a corrupt life style. These were people who swindled their employees and lived a double life, thinking nobody would notice. But I have a feeling God did, and although the Church seemed taken in by them, they sure weren't fooling the world.

In the ongoing saga of televangelists who swindle widows, orphans and everyone in between, the man who pretended to be exercising the word of knowledge with a little help from science is back at it. In a television expose which I have seen, this man's wife was overheard feeding him info through a transmitter as she interviewed attendees before the service. He would later use that info to fake the "word of knowledge", elevating his stature as he appealed for funds.

This man still appears regularly on late night television hawking tubes of "miracle water" in between sermons. Examples like this are too good for comedians to pass up. I recently saw a late night talk-show host play a clip of a televangelist appealing for funds. No comment was necessary. The man's quirky, outrageous behavior brought the house down. But I doubt God was laughing. All of this must one day be exposed and recompensed.

Crossing the Line

This is hard reading, to be sure. All of the examples cited above might be construed as simply negative observations on the human condition. It is a well-known fact that we are all sinners. Why dwell on the failures in the Church when there's so much to be positive about? Yes indeed, and we will get to all of that. But for now it is imperative to understand that sin doesn't fall into some black hole or sea of forgetfulness. Sin has consequences, and without repentance the consequences are dire. We need to know this, and it is not bad manners to apply our understanding of these verses to behavior we observe in our own lives or in that of other Christians. Quite the opposite. It is the reality check we need.

We need to connect these glossed-over sins to real people and a real God and to a final judgment.

We could go on and give examples of every sin listed in the three passages in question— 1Corinthians 6, Ephesians 5 and Galatians 5. But one thing becomes very apparent. These sins are rampant in the Body of Christ, even as they were in Paul's day, and a just God cannot simply overlook them. He has chosen the severest of consequences for those who practice them — disinheritance. This begs an obvious question: At what point does a person cross the line? At what point does one of these sins cost you your inheritance?

Very wisely, the Holy Spirit has chosen a somewhat nebulous word to describe the repetitive nature of sin that could cost a person their inheritance. The word is "practice". *"Those who **practice** such things shall not inherit the kingdom of God."* Christians sin all the time. As I said earlier, in thirty-two years I have seen it all. Not only do bad things happen to good people, but good people do bad things.

Sometimes, like my friend who tried to kill his neighbor, the best of us can snap. At other times, like the proverbial adulterous pastor, pride and poor judgment can lead to bad decisions with disastrous results. But happily, that is not where most stories end. We sin, we repent, we go on. In fact, many people who have suffered a moral failure have repented and used that failure as a springboard to greater service. But tragically, such is not always the case. Some are unwilling or unable to repent. We will deal with the "unable" a bit later. But we have to recognize that some people do not forsake their sin. They practice it, and in some cases practice does make perfect.

A case in point is the person in the faction. The longer that he persists in his belief, the stronger it becomes. When your elitist position of being the sole repository of truth depends on witnessing new instances of Christian carnality, the enemy will make sure that you find them. In a church world replete with flaws, Satan has an endless source of ammunition.

People involved in the sins of the flesh are usually not deceived. They know that what they are doing is wrong. That is why God never defines "practice". If we knew how many slips we were allowed, human nature dictates that some would try to stay just under the line. Does "practice" mean once a day, once a week, or once a month, and for what duration of time?

Two Principles

There are two general principles that will guide us in this matter. First of all, *"God resists the proud but gives grace to the humble"* (James 4:6). Frequency of sin is not as big an issue as attitude. Someone sincerely trying to break free from a sinful lifestyle will receive more mercy in that day than someone who toys with sin.

Secondly, *"If we confess our sins He is faithful and just to forgive us our sins"* (I Jn. 1:9). No reasonable person would choose sin over eternal inheritance, but it can take a lifetime to get the victory. When the victory comes, God offers forgiveness and, with it, repayment for any service rendered in His name.

But saying you are sorry is not the same as repentance. Judas was sorry, but that fact was of little consolation to him. Being sorry must lead to repentance — a change of heart, a change of mind, and ultimately a change of lifestyle.

The Issue of Confession

Let me take you to a conversation you may have overheard at some time. In it a young believer in the Lord is witnessing to an unsaved person. The conversation goes something like this:

New Believer: The Lord Jesus died for your sins. Just accept Him into your heart and you'll be saved. You don't have to wait till you die; you can have assurance right now that you're going to heaven.

Unbeliever: Yeah right. Once I'm "saved" I can just commit any sin I want and I'm still going to heaven. Is that what you're saying?

At this point our zealous young witness will sputter: "But, but… if you're saved, you won't want to sin."

Hmm…you won't want to sin? The problem, of course, is that you *do* want to sin. If you didn't want to sin, you wouldn't, and then there'd be no need for most of the New Testament epistles which deal in large part with sinning saints. However, we do agree that it's the old man who wants to sin, and not the new man made in the likeness of Christ Jesus. But I'm not sure our unbelieving friend would appreciate these subtle distinctions. So what should our young witness have said? Something like this:

"Your point is well taken. Getting saved doesn't produce overnight obedience in every area of life. That's a process, and for most of us, progress is slow. Yet we are all accountable for our actions and will reap what we sow. Plus, whether saved or unsaved, we all face judgment and thus we are told to fear God. So I don't want to mislead you by saying that sin doesn't matter or that it doesn't have consequences. But I *can* promise you that if you put your trust in Jesus, you won't go to hell."

I think an unbeliever could probably accept this answer because, you see, even the unbeliever has a conscience. Even he knows that regardless of your relationship to God, there's no free ride. You can't sin with impunity just because you're "saved".

Unfortunately, with so little teaching on sin and consequences, it's not only young believers who fall into the above trap. We are all a bit fuzzy on the journey from the cross to the throne. Theologically, most of us understand the atonement, but in our zeal to give God His due, we forget to do our part. We feel that as long as we don't intentionally sin, then everything is fine.

The road to hell is paved with good intentions, but so, as it turns out, is the road to heaven. On Judgment Day we'll need something besides good intentions. What is it then that we'll need? For openers, we'll need forgiveness and confession.

Two Key Scriptures

God has given us two scriptures to spare us a lot of
resentment and also a lot of pain. The first one has to do with
our relationship with unbelievers and is found in the book of
Romans.

> *"Never take your own revenge, beloved, but
> leave room for the wrath of God, for it is written,
> **Vengeance is mine, I will repay, says the Lord.**
> But if your enemy is hungry, feed him, and if he
> is thirsty, give him a drink; for in so doing you will
> heap burning coals upon his head.
> Do not be overcome by evil, but overcome evil
> with good."* (Rom. 12:19-21)

Since we have been made in God's likeness, we have
a sense of justice. That's why He doesn't say, "Don't take
your own revenge because that wouldn't be right." No, He
doesn't appeal to our conscience. Instead, He satisfies our
need for justice. He tells us that vengeance is His and He *will*
repay. This sets us free from bitterness. We can trust God to
bring justice. With this as a backdrop, we are now free to
obey the following command: *"If your enemy is hungry, feed
him."* If we were bitter, we wouldn't be able to do this. But
the realization of what is going to happen to our enemy if he
doesn't repent sets us free from that temptation.

Furthermore, God, knowing that much of our conflict is
within the Body, has given us a scripture for the believers
we have strife with as well. Have you been hurt, betrayed or
rebuffed by a fellow believer? Do you sometimes feel like
that unbeliever in the dialogue above? It just doesn't seem
fair! Just because the person is a Christian, he shouldn't be
able to get away with such hurtful behavior. Exactly. You
can rest assured that he won't.

The Bible says: *"If we confess our sins, He is faithful and righteous to forgive us our sins and to cleanse us from all unrighteousness" (1 John 1:9).* What is the reverse of this scripture? If we don't confess our sins, He won't forgive us our sins; He won't cleanse us. That sounds like heresy only because we don't understand what it means. For the believer, not being forgiven doesn't mean he is going to hell. It means that he will meet every unconfessed sin on Judgment Day.

The Scriptures are plain that there are sins that are forgiven in this age and those that are forgiven in the age to come. The age to come begins with the believers' judgment. Sins that aren't forgiven now will be forgiven at the judgment. This distinction is made clear in the following scripture:

> *"Therefore I say to you, any sin and blasphemy shall be forgiven men, but blasphemy against the Spirit shall not be forgiven. And whoever shall speak a word against the Son of Man it shall be forgiven him; but whoever shall speak against the Holy Spirit, it shall not be forgiven him, either in this age, **or in the age to come**."*(Matt. 12:31,32)

We are naïve if we think that everything is under the blood, whether we confess it or not.

This also solves the mystery of Matthew 6:15: *"But if you do not forgive men, then your Father will not forgive your transgressions."* If this scripture means that every believer who doesn't forgive is going to hell, then a high percentage of Christians will be in hell because many of us struggle in this area. It's not that we don't *want* to forgive the offender necessarily. It just means that, time and again, events prove that we haven't, in fact, done so. All it takes is the right trigger and "whoosh", back come the old feelings of resentment.

No, this verse doesn't mean we are going to hell, but it does mean that if we refuse to forgive, we'll face a lot of chastisement on Judgment Day. Imagine, if you will, meeting every sin you have committed since your new birth at the judgment, simply because you refused to forgive. I can think of nothing more sobering.

After giving us the general principle in I John, why does Jesus single out this one sin as an illustration? Because for a believer, not forgiving a little when he has been forgiven much is, in a sense, the worst sin. That sin will bring him tremendous grief on Judgment Day.

God has given us a verse that sums up our responsibility with respect to the matter of sin.

> *"But if we would judge ourselves we would not be judged. But when we are judged we are **chastened** of the Lord, that we should not be condemned with the world." (1Cor. 11:31,32)*

The Self-Judgment Imperative

If we judge ourselves in this world, we will not be judged in the next. If we don't, we can expect chastening. Is it possible that there are many Christians for whom daily self-judging is foreign? I believe so. I believe many people justify much of their sinful behavior or, worse, are largely indifferent because "it's all under the blood".

I was present recently when a guest speaker with a prophetic mantle was encouraging us in the area of God's love. He repeatedly exclaimed in a loud voice that God had forgiven us before we were even born — and not just the sins of the past, but all our future sins as well. He had good intentions, but his exhortation just added to the confusion. It is very unwise to **ever** teach forgiveness without confession. The Bible doesn't, and neither should we.

Let me ask you a question. Can you remember every conversation you had on Tuesday three months ago? Of course you can't, but God can. He's got it all written down.

Why would He do that, you ask? We don't have to wonder. He told us.

"And I say to you, that every careless word that men shall speak, they shall render account for it in the Day of Judgment." (Matt. 12:36)

You and I are going to face the words of a lifetime. If we do a daily accounting, then this won't be so onerous. But if we continually sin with our mouth, a thing James said was inevitable, then, without daily repentance, we're racking up quite a debt.

And these are just our words. The judgment applies as well to thoughts, actions and motivations. If we let things slide in any area of life, we can get behind very quickly. If we let self-judgment slide, we'll end up in a very uncomfortable position. We'll be accountable for a mountain of things we can't even remember.

"God loves me; He would never make me feel uncomfortable," we reason. If that were true, then why would He tell us to judge ourselves in this world? Why would we go through the discomfort of daily judgment here, if standing before Him there, all is forgotten? Time and space mean nothing to God. He judges us in this lifetime. It certainly won't be less severe when we meet Him face to face.

Everyone who has gone through the fire of God and felt his disciplining hand knows how relentless He can be, and how seemingly indifferent to our pain. Will that suddenly change at the great accounting? Everyone who has seen His wrath against His own people in the Old Testament knows that He will readily inflict pain as chastisement for sin. Will a different God appear at the Judgment?

The apostle Paul put it this way:

*"For we must all appear before the judgment seat of Christ, that each one may be recompensed for his deeds in the body, according to what he has done, whether good **or bad**. Therefore knowing the fear of the Lord we persuade men...."(2 Cor.5:10,11)*

So Paul says that it's not just the good that we are going to be judged for, but the bad as well. Then he concludes with a warning: *" Knowing the fear of the Lord, we persuade men."* He persuades men about holiness in the fear of the Lord. Today the term "fear of the Lord" is greatly misunderstood. Because there is a dearth of teaching on this subject, it's primary role as a deterrent to sin has been blunted. Later in this section, I will share some insight on this important truth.

The Good with the Bad
Suppose you were the wisest man that ever lived. Your wisdom was known in all the earth and throughout all the ages. It was captured in books which men read as signposts for living. But you didn't take your own advice and had some difficult times in the latter part of your life. You even became cynical. Now death is approaching, and you want to leave one last nugget that encapsulates the one truth you want people to remember. What do you think you would write?

Happily we have the record of such a man. It was Solomon. In the last two verses of Ecclesiastes, the man who has seen it all, done it all, leaves us with these words:

"The conclusion, when all has been heard, is: fear God and keep His commandments, because this applies to every person.
*Because God will bring every act to judgment, everything which is hidden, **whether it is good or evil**."(Ecc. 12:13,14)*

Notice the key words which we've encountered before. Every person will be judged; every act will be judged; both the good and the evil will be judged; everything that is hidden will be judged. Solomon saw judgment day coming and, though he had penned hundreds of proverbs and wise sayings, he had one final and overriding piece of wisdom for us — fear God and keep His commandments.

This is a bit of a stretch, but now imagine you're God Himself. You've come to earth and completed the work for which you were sent. You've inspired Biblical writers to leave a wealth of teaching as to how people should live after you're gone. But on the last page of this massive book you want to reiterate one critical point. What would it be? Again, we don't have to guess, because Jesus is that God, and this is what He said: *"Behold, I am coming quickly, and my reward is with Me, to render to every man according to what he has done" (Rev. 22:12).*

Again we have much the same elements. Every man will be judged, everything he has done will be judged. The word "reward" doesn't just speak of recompense for good things, but for bad things as well. It's the same Greek word used of Judas in this verse: *" Now this man acquired a field with the reward of his wickedness"*(Acts 1:18).

Do we see a pattern here? Solomon, Paul, Jesus. The Old Testament, the New Testament, and the Living Testament. All three agree as one. They all say the same thing. They all describe a day when everyone who has ever lived will be judged for the things they have done in the flesh, good or bad, and this fact should produce one response above all — fear of the Lord.

This can be confusing if we have a one-dimensional view of God. God is our Father, our Savior, our Advocate, and many other things. But He is also our Judge, and we must never forget this.

Our Father as Judge

To assist us in our understanding of God's different roles, it may help us to consider a famous illustration. Suppose a court judge leaves for work in the morning. On his way out he hugs his teenage son and they exchange pleasantries. You can tell they have a good relationship. But his son has a drinking problem that has long been hidden. On that particular day he drives while intoxicated and is pulled over and arrested. The boy has a hearing the same day and is brought into court.

Imagine his surprise to discover the identity of the man behind the bench dressed in somber judicial robes — his father. Without doubt his father still loves him, but for the moment his role has changed. During the proceedings he is acting in the capacity of judge, not father. As judge, his duty is to see that justice is done. And further, that it be done without partiality. But when the proceedings are concluded, regardless of the outcome, outside the courthouse father and son embrace once again.

Every illustration is imperfect, but that, in a sense, is what it will be like. So there will be pain on Judgment Day. There will be the pain of loss — loss of reward. There will also be the pain of realizing that you failed God. There will be the pain of exposure — everything that is hidden will be made public. There will be the pain of regret — there's nothing you can do to change how you lived; it's too late. And finally there will be the pain of chastisement.

The scripture doesn't say for nothing that He will wipe away every tear from our eyes. There will be tears of joy and there will be tears of sadness, all in direct proportion to how we have lived.

Preparing for Heaven

Let me add one more thought as we leave the matter of sin and confession. The sanctification process is progressive and lifelong. It may happen that early in our Christian life or during protracted stages, we are guilty of repetitive sins in the area of anger, lust, abusive speech, greed, gossip, etc. These sins may happen so frequently, or our heart may be so hard, or our repentance so shallow, that there could be a sizeable amount of unconfessed sin awaiting us upon death.

I believe that when we come to true repentance in an area and gain total victory, we can ask God to wash away all related sins, even though we may not remember every instance. I believe this is something He longs to do. Where there is true repentance and victory over defilement, He wants to offer a clean slate. This can happen in several ways, and God confirmed this to me through Billy Graham.

Mr. Graham was on Larry King Live on June 16, 2005. They were discussing his medical problems and his ultimate passing. Larry asked him, "If you were to die this very night, would this be a good night?" Mr. Graham answered in the affirmative, talking briefly about his salvation experience and the glories of heaven. Then, more to the point, he discussed his experience in the Mayo Clinic in 2001 while being treated for hydrocephalus.

One night he felt himself slipping away and thought his time had come, so he asked the Lord to "receive him". I'll let him tell what happened next in a direct, verbatim transcript of the broadcast.

"All of a sudden, all of my sins came before me, everything I'd ever done wrong that I'd **forgotten** about years ago came into my mind. And I prayed 'Lord, forgive me! May the blood of Jesus Christ cleanse me from all of my sins.' And I had the greatest peace come over me, and that peace has not left me since. I'm very certain that the Lord was ready to receive me at that time, not because of my good works or because of all the things I'd tried to do, **but because the Lord had forgiven me.**"

Notice the word "forgotten" and the phrase "Lord forgive me". These weren't just sins that he'd confessed and forgotten about, but sins that hadn't *been* confessed. If they *had* been confessed, he would not have needed to ask for forgiveness. Also notice the result — peace — and Mr. Graham's explanation of why he is now ready to go at any time: not because of his good works, but because "the Lord had forgiven me".

This is so important. As Christians, we have to realize that there is a preparation that is necessary for all of us, as we one day leave this world and stand before God. Even if you are the greatest evangelist who has ever lived, you need that preparation. Your good works are only one side of the equation; your unconfessed sin is the other side. If we are to take Billy Graham's words at face value, the unconfessed sin seemed to be more important than the good works in terms of that preparation.

We must remember two things. First, any one of us could die suddenly, and thus it is important always to "be ready to meet our Maker". To many of us, this has only meant salvation, but in fact it means much more. Specifically, in the matter we are discussing, it means dealing with unconfessed sin.

Secondly, when we have a terminal illness, it *is* important that we heal any broken relationships. But for many of us, this is as far as our thinking goes. God wants to deal with much more than this. He wants to totally forgive our past, and if we ask for the gift of total repentance, He will make it available to us.

The Fear of the Lord

One of the reasons preparation for heaven has not been taught is because we have sown confusion on the subject of the fear of the Lord. First of all, we have seldom taught on the subject, and, secondly, with the current overemphasis on cheap grace, we have been unclear as to what this fear really is. Ask anyone what the fear of the Lord is, and they will quote a proverb such as *"The fear of Lord is the beginning of wisdom,"* or they will say that it simply means "reverential awe". Neither of these answers is very helpful, and the last one is actually misleading.

Any one of us can define "fear" without hesitation. It means exceedingly afraid, fright, alarm, terror. But as soon as we talk about the fear of the Lord, immediately all the rules of language go out the window, and fear ceases to be fear, but morphs into reverential awe. I understand why. Surely we aren't supposed to actually *fear* the One who loves us so much that He submitted to brutality and torture to redeem us? But indeed we are, as the scripture plainly states, and the reasons will become evident as we progress.

Earlier we quoted Paul's statement that each one of us will one day stand before the judgment seat of Christ. He follows with: *"Therefore knowing the **fear** of the Lord, we persuade men...."* We have already seen some of the things that he persuades men about — practicing sin for instance. But what does the word for "fear" in this verse really mean?

The Greek word translated "fear" in this verse is *phobos*. *Phobos*, according to Strongs, means exceedingly afraid, fright, alarm, and terror. This should come as no surprise, because that is the same definition any literate person would ascribe to the word "fear". That is the dictionary definition. *Phobos* **never** means reverential awe. The same word, for instance, is used in describing the response to the death of Ananias and Sapphira: *"And great fear came upon the whole church, and upon all who heard of these things"* (Acts 5:11).

In 1Peter 1:17 we are told the following: *"And if you address as Father the One who impartially judges according to each man's work, conduct yourselves in fear during your stay on earth."* The word for fear in this verse is again *phobos*. Notice the context in which it is found. We are told to conduct ourselves in fear during our lives because of the coming *judgment.*

One day our Father will judge our works with total impartiality, and a legitimate and scriptural response to this fact is fear. The whole idea of a Christian living in fear is so abhorrent that we stumble over this statement. But why should we? We have been taught from day one that we are to fear nothing and no one **except** God. But again, we have always explained away real fear by calling it something else — primarily "reverential awe".

One reason for the lack of holiness today is because we have taken away the connection between fear and holiness. God is not reluctant to use one as a motive for the other. *"Having therefore these promises, dearly beloved, let us cleans ourselves from all filthiness of the flesh and spirit, perfecting holiness in the fear of God"* (2 Cor. 7:1). Holiness isn't perfected in isolation. It is perfected in the fear of God. The word for "fear" in this verse is again *phobos.*

But surely the fear of the Lord sometimes means reverential awe? Yes, it does. Another Greek word for fear is *phobeo,* which means frighten, be alarmed, be in awe of, reverence. It occurs 97 times in the New Testament. In only a couple of cases can it be construed to mean reverential awe. The bottom line is that in scripture, fear usually means fear, and the fear of the Lord means the fear of the Lord. This is not bad news; it is good news.

By not teaching people about sin, judgment, and the fear of the Lord, we have taken away one of the greatest incentives for holy living. In our misguided desire to defend God's reputation as merciful and loving, and to free people from guilt and pain, we have left them very vulnerable. The fear of the Lord is a protection that all of us need in our lives. But let us go further and explain the conundrum of living in fear while simultaneously being a peaceful person, something we would all agree is essential.

Working Out Our Salvation

"Therefore my friends, as you have always obeyed
- not only in my presence, but now much more in my
absence — continue to work out your salvation with
fear and trembling, for it is God who works in you
both to will and do according to His good pleasure."
(Phil. 2:12,13)

. In the above verse we are told to work out our salvation with "fear and trembling". The Greek word for "fear" is *phobos* and we already know that it means genuine fear. The Greek word for "trembling" is *tromos,* which means "quaking fear", a bit like *phobos* on steroids.

At first glance, this verse appears a bit baffling. Why are we to work out with fear and trembling, something that God offers freely — our salvation? In the second part of the verse, He gives us the answer: *"**For** it is God who works in you both to will and do according to His good pleasure."*

Now we're really puzzled. That is one of our favorite feel-good scriptures. Why should that cause us fear and trembling? Because God is working for **His** good pleasure — not ours. Like any good parent, His chief pleasure, in a general sense, is to see His children succeed. Again, we might ask, why should this cause us trepidation?

Because God cares much more about our success than we do. Some parents can totally identify. It is not uncommon for a son or daughter to be content with only a pass mark, but what the parent demands is excellence. That is what God wants as well, and the fact that He will be relentless in pursuing it should give us pause. According to Hebrews 12, as our Father and disciplinarian, He will do whatever is necessary to achieve that aim.

There are really two threats and one promise in the passage under consideration. The two threats are discipline in this life and loss in the next. The promise is that God is working for His good pleasure, not ours.

God's Pleasure

So what is God's good pleasure, in real terms and in the ultimate sense? Certainly our holiness, obedience, worship, and any number of things bring God pleasure. But God is not short-term oriented like we are. He always has the ultimate in view. To discover it we must go back to the gospels. We find the same word translated "pleasure" in another famous verse: *"Fear not little flock; for it is your Father's good pleasure to give you the kingdom"* (Luke 12:32).

Though there are mysteries yet to be revealed, in one sense God's ultimate pleasure is to give the kingdom to the saints. It is impossible to comprehend the pleasure that this will bring Him. In Daniel 7 we find a description of this future event:

> *"But the court will sit, and his (Satan's) power will be taken away and completely destroyed forever. Then the sovereignty, power and greatness of the kingdoms under the whole heaven will be handed over to the saints, the people of the Most High. His kingdom will be an everlasting kingdom, and all rulers will worship and obey Him."* (Dan. 7: 26,27)

But before that event can take place, there must first be the Judgment Seat of Christ. It is there that each person's life is assessed, and their inheritance in the Kingdom allotted. This brings us back to a verse we have considered earlier: *"And if you address as Father the One who impartially judges according to each man's work, conduct yourselves in fear during the time of your stay upon earth."* We are to conduct ourselves with fear, and work out our salvation with fear and trembling, knowing that one day we shall stand before God and be assigned our eternal position based on our deeds.

The Fear of the Lord Illustrated

This raises an important question: How can I have love, joy and peace — things I am commanded to have — when I am living in fear and trembling? To put it simply, God's pleasure is that you and I live our lives in a mental state that will allow us to inherit all things. God describes this mental state as "fear and trembling", and it is not inconsistent with love, joy and peace. In fact, it produces love, joy and peace. Here is how, in three simple examples:

1) Out of fear of the Lord, I watch everything I say. Jesus Himself said, *"And I say to you, that every careless word that men shall speak, they shall render account for it in the Day of Judgment"* (Matt. 12:36). In doing so, I experience peace. Why? Because I no longer say the first thing that comes to mind, which could be angry, sarcastic or demeaning. I fear God. By having my speech seasoned with salt, I have peace with God and peace with men. Conclusion: the fear of God produces peace.

2) The scriptures tell us to *"bring every thought captive to Christ Jesus."* I know He will one day judge the thoughts and intents of my heart. In order to defeat thoughts that would be judgmental, bitter or negative, I have to replace them with praise and thanksgiving. When I do this, it brings joy. Conclusion: the fear of the Lord produces joy.

3) I am told that *"pure and undefiled religion is to care for widows and orphans in their distress and to keep oneself unstained by the world."* I know that on this basis, my brand of religion will one day be judged by God. Out of the fear of the Lord, I avoid the contami-

nation of the world, and spend part of my time giving to the less fortunate. As I do this, God teaches me how to love, just as He has many others. Conclusion: the fear of God produces love.

These three examples cover the three main areas of thought, word and deed. We must work out our salvation in all three areas. God will not do it for us. In the area of deeds, there is much to consider, but none more important than the sins of the flesh.

The Bigger Picture

We are commanded to *abstain from fleshly lusts which wage war against our souls* and to *flee youthful lusts*. Avoid them! Treat them like a plague and show them the fear they deserve. God will help us, but it is something WE must do. When we gain victory in this area, we experience a freedom and peace we didn't know existed. *The Kingdom of God is righteousness, peace and joy in the Holy Spirit.* Before it can be peace and joy, it must first be righteousness.

A huge area with respect to our words and our hearts is the issue of jealousy, strife, factions and divisions. We should fear any action on our part that would tear down legitimate ministries or bring division to the Body of Christ. We are told that people who practice these things *will have no inheritance in the Kingdom of God.*

But it's not just obvious sin that is at issue. Jesus said no one could be His disciple who does not give up (not give away) all his possessions. John states forcefully that we are not to love the world nor the **things** in the world. It's a sobering fact, but we must relate to our possessions and the world's goods with fear and trembling. Though insignificant in themselves, they have the power to disqualify us from discipleship and to steal our inheritance. A lack of concern in this area should signal that something is wrong.

But it's more than just things; it's EVERYthing. Jesus said if we don't deny self and pick up our cross, we can't follow Him, though outwardly it might appear that we are. Thus we must fear selfish living because it is the rank opposite of self-denial. Every time life begins to crowd out God, alarm bells should go off. If this doesn't happen, then it is God's job to intervene in our lives and get us back on track. But it is our job to respond; He won't do it for us.

My dictionary records over ninety hyphenated self-words: self-defense, self-interest, self-pity, self-preservation, self-reliance, etc. Until we understand that every one of them is an enemy of the cross, and thus an enemy of Christ-like character, we will never fully understand the need to work out our salvation with fear and trembling.

Let us look at one more Kingdom statement. In this example we don't find the word *fear*, but instead *reverential awe*:

> *"Therefore, since we receive a kingdom which cannot be shaken, let us be thankful, and so worship God acceptably with reverence and awe; for our God is a consuming fire."* (Heb.12: 28, 29)

Here we have the introduction of other elements that complete our response to the Kingdom promise.

For Our Protection

To summarize, the Bible gives two attitudes we are supposed to have concerning the good news of the Kingdom:
1) Fear and trembling less we be disinherited;
2) Thankfulness, worship, and reverential awe for such a great gift.

But even in the case of #2, the writer finishes off with *"for our God is a consuming fire"*. Even in the midst of our thankfulness, worship, and reverential awe, the writer wants to remind us that God is Judge. It seems that this fact, above all others, is something that needs to be stressed. Worship can bring us to God, but in so many cases, it takes fear to keep us there. *"The fear of the Lord is a fountain of life."*

We don't worship God strictly, or even primarily, because He gives us a Kingdom. But it's vital that we understand the import and gravity of what we do receive, so that we don't squander it. Obviously we are meant to meditate on the Kingdom, for how can we be thankful for it, if we never think about it? And this appears to be one of our problems.

As we have discussed earlier on, the context of the New Testament is that people expected the Kingdom. They expected it immediately, and they knew it would be preceded by a judgment that would assign them inheritance in the kingdom. They lived in light of this fact and many of the instructions to Christians in the epistles have this under-standing as a backdrop. We have lost that knowledge and, as a result, many of the scriptures that are intended to warn us and waken us have lost their meaning. We are playing, so to speak, with only half a deck, and the results are devastating.

A Christianity Today poll found that 37% of pastors struggle with pornography (Dec. 2001). A Promise Keeper's poll found that 50% of men had viewed pornography in the previous week. Promise Keepers has been around for decades and it operates on the buddy system — brother caring for brother. That poll suggests that this approach, while neces-sary, has limited value. The support of the Body is critical, but it is no substitute for the fear of the Lord.

Christian men are in much greater jeopardy today than they were twenty years ago, despite all the men's ministries. Care can never accomplish the work of fear, but must work together with it to bring results. As an aside, Today's Christian Woman (Fall 2003) found that one out of every six women struggles with an addiction to pornography. That is not supposed to happen because women by design are not visually stimulated. But it *is* happening. These women need support and counseling, but they also need the same warning as men.

We need to be promise-keepers. We *need* to keep our promises to God. But if we don't, we need to know that He will still keep His promises to us. One of those promises is that *"each one of us shall give account of himself to God."* We need the holy fear this verse produces.

An oft-quoted passage is: *"Where there is no vision, the people are unrestrained" (Prov. 29:18)*. While it may have several meanings, it has one overriding application: When people don't understand their future, they lose control. Our future is the kingdom. We need to remind ourselves of that fact.

For most of us, eternity is just a few years away, and it's doubtful that the Kingdom age will be delayed much longer. God is looking for people to worship in His presence night and day. He is looking for people who will rule and reign with Him forever. He wants to reward faithful service on this earth with crowns and thrones. It is His good pleasure to give us the Kingdom. But for the honest seeker, the real prize is God Himself. And that is ultimately what He offers — intimacy there for faithfulness here.

Preaching on Sin

I saw the pastor of the biggest church in America on Larry King the other night. Nice fellow. He was born positive, preaches a positive message, and according to his wife, lives what he preaches. He judges no one and never preaches on sin because, as he put it, "People know they are sinners; they don't need to be told."

Oddly, this fact never restrained the epistle writers, who, as we have seen, spent copious amounts of time addressing sin and sinning saints. These letters make up a large part of the Bible, and it is my understanding that it is the Bible we are to preach.

I have no problem with a person having a life message and preaching that message. But it is imperative that a senior pastor share the pulpit with others who can balance out his message, to ensure that the whole counsel of God is taught. If we don't do this, then we will fail in our responsibility to rightly divide the word of truth.

It *is* true, as our enemies often state, that you can use the Bible to prove just about anything. If your only goal is to teach a benevolent God who is indifferent to sin, it's easy to do, but people deserve better.

Preaching the Negative

Many pastors, such as the one above, are on record as saying something like the following: "There's enough negative in the world; just turn on the TV and all you get is bad news. People don't need more negative in their lives; they come to church to hear the good news and be lifted up." There are two things wrong with this well-meaning statement.

First, by the implied definition given to the term "negative", much of the scriptures must be considered negative. We need to say it again: Anything that gives us temporary consolation is not good news if there is sin in our lives. Anything that convicts, confronts, and moves us higher in God is positive, even if it disquiets us. Sin isn't just lust and rage. It is worry, vanity, self-indulgence, ungratefulness, neglecting the poor, etc.

The second problem with that statement is that, once you make it your church policy to only peach the "positive", you have just quenched the Holy Spirit. You have told Him in no uncertain terms exactly what He is allowed to say in **your** church services. I would be suspicious of a church that always brought a hard word, but even more suspicious of one that *never* did.

The devil is sly. If I stood before a church, Bible open, and used a pair of scissors to cut out every reference to sin, the people would be appalled. If I then proceeded to remove every Godly rebuke and every instance of God's anger and judgment, they would be outraged. I would be left with a book about half the size of the Bible, and I would be branded a heretic.

No one would do that, nor would they have to. There is another way to get rid of those troublesome verses and still keep the crowds. All I have to do is say that God has given me a positive message and then only preach half the Bible — the "good" half. People will bless me, I will have a huge following, and I may even grow rich. But woe is me, even if my intentions are the best.

Because there is no difference between the two approaches. None.

The net effect is the same: deception.

The Role of God's Word

We must never confuse the Word *of* God with the word *from* God. We are told in 1Corinthians 14 that prophesy — the word from God — is for edification, exhortation and consolation. Not so the Word of God. The verse that describes the Bible's role is an interesting one — not at all what you'd think, were you to randomly sample the Sunday sermons of a thousand preachers. We are told in 2Timothy 3:16,17 that the Word of God has four functions.

"All Scripture is inspired by God and profitable for teaching, for reproof, for correction, for training in righteousness; that the man of God may be perfect, equipped for every good work."

The Greek word here for *teaching* is most often translated *doctrine* in the King James. Of the 21 times this word occurs, about a third have a negative connotation – *"will not endure sound doctrine"; "teaching for doctrines, the commands of men"; "every wind of doctrine"; "doctrines of devils"*, etc. This should alert us to a common danger: the human propensity to make the scriptures say what we *want* them to say.

A preacher's job is to make the scriptures say what they *do* say, nothing more and nothing less, as unpopular as that may be. We are to preach the Word in season and out of season. Interesting word — "season". Like clothing that is out of vogue in a certain season, certain truths seem to suffer the same fate.

The Greek word for "reproof" means conviction. The proper teaching of the Word should bring conviction. Thirty years ago, a wise older Christian told me why he had recently changed churches. He had this to say: "I never felt convicted during the preaching or at any time during the service. If you never feel convicted and challenged to go further in Christ, something is wrong with the message." I agree. That brings us to the word "correction".

The Greek word for correction means to "straighten up". That phrase has the same connotation today that it did then. It is not uncommon to correct a person with the exhortation to "shape up!" or "straighten up and fly right!" in the hippy lingo of the sixties. Conviction makes us aware of sin; correction tells us what to do about it. Both are works of the Holy Spirit, but most often God will use the minister of the gospel as His agent or messenger. The tool the minister uses is the Word of God. We need preaching that both convicts and corrects.

Finally, there is "training in righteousness". Here it is possible to teach character qualities and godly behaviors by strictly accentuating the positive. In most cases, though, this is a one-string fiddle that limits the notes the musician has at his disposal. The other three strings of doctrine, conviction and correction give the Holy Spirit more to play with.

Fear, for example, is a sin that is rampant in the Body of Christ. It needs to be addressed. Approaching the subject of fear through teaching on faith and the power of God has its place, to be sure. But we need to be aware of the consequences of yielding to fear in our lives. We need to know the impact it will have on our children, on our health, on our relationship to God, and ultimately, on our eternal destiny.

There are a hundred such examples of topics that need to be taught in a thorough manner with no regard for ruffled feathers because the word "sin" is employed. Messages that are upbeat, feel-good, and humorous have their place, but as a steady diet, they don't contain enough nutrient to build God's army.

The Goal of God's Word

So the Scriptures have four functions, but to what overall purpose? There are two purposes, we are told, and they are set out in the concluding words of this verse: Firstly, that the man of God may be perfect; secondly, that he may be equipped for every good work.

The Greek word for perfect means "complete", and it is the only occurrence of this particular Greek word in the New Testament. To put it simply, the role of the scriptures is to bring perfection or completion to a person's life. It is separate from all the other influences such as parent, pastor, spouse, etc. To emphasize the unique place of the scriptures, God chose a unique word to describe the result of its work in our lives: *artios,* meaning "complete". But it takes the complete scriptures to produce the complete man. Anything less will fail.

The second goal of the scriptures is that we might be equipped for every good work. The proper teaching of the scriptures won't focus on our *needs,* our *affirmation,* our *pros-*

perity, etc., but our *equipping.* That is the test of the message. Are we better equipped through what we have heard? Was there something that was communicated through teaching, convicting, correcting, or training that has elevated us to a new level of works? Or was it just words? Do we simply feel better about ourselves — the self-absorbed passion of far too many Christians? Are we better equipped to produce what God wants, as opposed to what we want?

The two should be the same, and ultimately will be for those that are trained by the Word. But without the teaching of an able minister and the conviction of the Holy Spirit, we can easily be pursuing selfish goals that are at odds with God's purposes, both for His kingdom and our place in it.

Notice, as well, the word "every". Is the preached word equipping us for *every* good work? Are we so complete in Christ that we are capable of visiting the sick, throwing a banquet for the needy, and taking in strangers? Are we equipped to say "no" to the wiles of the devil when he tries to seduce us into loving the world? Saying "no" to worldly compromise *is* a good work. We need to be told that. In fact, the two areas just mentioned — caring for the poor and keeping oneself unstained by the world — comprise what James called pure and undefiled religion.

"Pure and undefiled religion" summarizes the good works of a complete Christian.

Actually, the book of James is an interesting one. I recently did a study on it. The book contains 106 verses. The first 18 are upbeat and encouraging. The rest of the book is basically a harangue, a diatribe, a rant — choose your word. I can't imagine a modern day apostle, any apostle, writing such a letter nowadays to a church, any church. And yet the Holy Spirit wrote that letter to His church, and I found it very helpful.

Choosing a Church

This is all very interesting, but what do these observations on the Word of God have to do with The Judgment of Sin? In the next couple of verses Paul tells us:

> *"I charge thee therefore before God, and the Lord Jesus Christ, **who shall judge the quick and the dead at his appearing and his kingdom;***
>
> *Preach the word; be instant in season, out of season; reprove, rebuke, exhort with all long-suffering and doctrine.*
>
> *For the time will come when they will not endure sound doctrine; but after their own lusts shall they heap to themselves teachers, having itching ears;*
>
> *And they shall turn away their ears from the truth and shall be turned unto fables." (2Tim. 4:1-4 KJV)*

It's because of the Judgment that Paul elaborates on the purpose and importance of scripture. It's because of the Judgment that he commands Timothy to preach the Word of God. It's because of the Judgment that Paul tells him to stand his ground and issues this strange command: *"reprove, rebuke, exhort with all long-suffering and doctrine."* Reprove and rebuke are synonyms, and exhort, in this case, means *beseech*. No fancy footwork; Paul comes right to the point. Timothy is to rebuke and beseech people for one important purpose: that they might obey sound doctrine. And, oh yes, it will require one thing above all else — long-suffering. Why long-suffering? Because it will be hard.

The reason it will be hard is because *"they will not endure sound doctrine"*. The Greek word for *endure* is translated "suffer" in almost every other instance. Following sound doctrine, by its very nature, brings one inevitable consequence — suffering. It demands one character quality above all others — endurance. Why is that? Because sound doctrine doesn't present an unreal world of myths and fables. It's not about projecting my carnal passions for money and success onto the gospel narrative. It's about embracing the true gospel with its righteous demands. It's about the cross and self-denial. It's about loving people to death — my death. Till I die to self, I can't truly love. There's suffering involved.

And so it matters!

It matters where you go to church. It matters whether or not you are hearing sound doctrine. It matters because of the Judgment. What you hear will guide your life and determine your actions and your destiny. But Paul isn't just talking to you and me; he's also warning Timothy. Timothy, and by extension every preacher, is charged with teaching sound doctrine because of the Judgment. To do otherwise is to *invite* judgment.

There is no polite way of saying that America is riddled with people who won't endure sound doctrine. They don't want to suffer. There is no polite way of saying that America is riddled with preachers who do not preach sound doctrine. If my church and pastor teach a lifestyle that is opposite to that of Christ Jesus, then I am being taught a myth and a fable.

The Power of Correction

We have forgotten the power of correction. When a book is written with convicting authority, it is considered heavy, overly serious, legalistic and unloving. However, the God of the Bible never frets about the negative fallout from a stern reprimand, but rather about the reverse — false comfort. *"And they have healed the wound of My people slightly saying, 'Peace, peace', when there is no peace"(Jer. 6:14).*

It does not surprise me to hear that the largest church in America is pastored by a man who never preaches sin, but only preaches a positive message. It is only human to want to hear of a God who only wants to bless. That is, after all, who God is. But there are people He cannot bless, and those He must "bless" with the rod. To never hear of this God, and to never find Him in the scriptures, is a fool's paradise.

The books of Proverbs and Ecclesiastes have several recurring themes, one of them being that "*It is better to listen to the rebuke of wise man than to the song of fools*" (Ecc. 7:5). An honest seeker will go to great lengths to hear the truth about himself, because he loves the truth and knows it can set him free. It may disturb and unsettle him briefly to see his character exposed, but repentance brings righteousness. Righteousness has eternal value that will reap benefits, eons after the pain of correction has been forgotten.

The song of fools, unfortunately, is what we hear most often in a fool's paradise.

"*Faithful are the wounds of a friend...*" is one of the great standards by which relationships are measured. There are few relationships more important than the one that exists between a church leader and his flock. All leaders will one day give an account for the souls they watch over. They need to consider very carefully what they preach. If there is an absence of "faithful wounds", there is seldom the corresponding friendship, but instead a people-pleasing accommodation.

Judge Not Lest Ye Be Judged

Before we bring some concluding thoughts on sin, there is one other matter we must deal with. We have seen in our Lord's discussion of the believers' judgment, that He singled out unforgiveness. But there is a second sin that also draws special attention: judgmentalism.

"*But you, why do you judge your brother? Or you again, why do you regard your brother with contempt? For we shall all stand before the judgment seat of God.*

For it is written,
'As I live, says the Lord, every knee shall bow to
Me,
And every tongue shall give praise to God.'
So then each one of us shall give account of
himself to God.
Therefore let us not judge one another any more."
(Rom. 14:10-13)

Why does God single out the sin of judging a brother? The reason is because, like unforgiveness, judgmentalism is in a category by itself.

By way of clarification, let us revisit the issue of unforgiveness in a very famous parable Jesus gave, the parable of the unforgiving debtor. This parable is preceded by a question from Peter: " *'Lord, how often shall my brother sin against me and I forgive him? Up to seven times?' Jesus said to him, 'I do not say to you, up to seven times, but up to seventy times seven.' " (Matt. 18:21,22)*.

What follows is the familiar parable where a slave begged for mercy from his master because he couldn't pay a huge debt. The master had pity on him and forgave him the debt outright. The slave then went out and found a fellow slave who owed him a pittance. Despite cries for mercy, the forgiven slave choked him and threw him into debtor's prison.

When the master heard about this, he was enraged and ordered that his own slave be handed over to the tormentors until he paid every cent of his debt. Then we have these sobering words from the Lord Jesus Christ: "*So shall My heavenly Father also do to you, if each of you does not forgive his brother from your heart.*"

In the most forceful parable and in the strongest language, Jesus tells us that for a Christian to not forgive a small debt when he has been forgiven a huge debt is unconscionable and will bring retribution. Jesus makes no concession to the truly horrible abuses that have been perpetrated against some of us, except to say: *"Vengeance is mine; I will repay."*

Forgiveness has nothing to do with the magnitude of the act, for in comparison to our own debt, it is insignificant. Our feelings of self-righteousness and self-pity often obscure this fact, and so in our minds we often feel justified in holding unforgiveness. It is for this reason, the fact that we are always easy on ourselves, that Jesus must be firm to the point of seeming harsh.

The sin of judgmentalism is similar. God will not judge us, in the sense of eternal damnation, for the multiplied thousands of sins we have each committed. Therefore it is a terrible thing when we judge and condemn a fellow Christian for a personal failing.

James says if we judge one another, we judge the law and put ourselves above the law. That is the sin, then: putting ourselves in the place of God who alone is Judge. James concludes with: *"There is only one Lawgiver and Judge, the One who is able to save and to destroy; who are you then to judge your neighbor?" (James 4:12).*

Both the sin of unforgiveness and the sin of judgmentalism speak of ingratitude and self-deception, but also of something far worse — playing God. When these sins are committed with self-righteousness and great energy, they provoke God in a unique way. It is plain, then, that people who are judgmental and unforgiving will get a particularly rough ride on Judgment Day.

As an aside, the second reason God gives us such strong warnings is that few of us will escape these particular sins. For many people lust, greed, and anger will never be a problem. But who of us has not been guilty of judgmentalism? Who of us has not been deeply wounded by a parent, friend, spouse, boss, or even a spiritual overseer, with the resultant struggle to forgive? The answer is, virtually no one. These are truly universal sins.

The Mechanics of Judgment

The mechanism by which judgments operate is misunderstood and, along with it, the sin of judgmentalism. The sin of judgmentalism occurs when we delight in someone else's failure, or when we attack those who fail in an unloving fashion. You and I are built to observe behavior and come to conclusions. The more astute and prophetic we are, the more we tend to do this. It is not wrong to conclude that a person is failing in some area of their life when, in fact, they are. To try to suppress this knowledge under the guise of not judging is a kind of misguided denial bordering on neurosis.

Instead, it is what we do with this knowledge that determines what kind of a person we are. If we pray for the individual and truly seek their welfare, we are godly. However, if we despise their failure and feel righteous by comparison, God will judge us in the same way that we have judged them.

It is important to remember that sin is against God. In describing his acts of adultery and murder, David said: *"Against Thee, Thee only, I have sinned, and done what is evil in Thy sight" (Ps. 51:4).* Our judgments and unforgiveness may hurt people, but our sins are against God. In this connection He gives us solemn warnings: *"Judge not lest ye be judged,"* and *"If you do not forgive men, then your heavenly Father will not forgive your transgressions."*

Are we beginning to see why Paul said, *"It is a terrifying thing to fall into the hands of the living God"(Heb. 10:30,31)?* That statement is prefaced by Paul's declaration that *"The Lord will judge His people,"* so this is written *to* Christians *about* Christians. Many of us have not treated sin or judgment with the respect they deserve. We have tuned out verses like the above and will some day face the consequences of this complacency. It is because God loves us that

He gives us these warnings. If we repent of sinful attitudes and practices, His forgiveness is instantaneous.

It would be unfair to spend so much time on the consequences of sin without also talking a little about sin itself, and the matter of victory *over* sin. Until we understand sin, we will never comprehend the critical role it plays in the interaction between God and man, Christians included. There are many fine books on this subject, so I will limit my comments.

Understanding Sin

Let me start with a simple observation on sin. There is a fine line between the two extremes of taking sin too lightly on the one hand, and constantly engaging in self-flagellation on the other. It's a road with a ditch on either side. On the one side is shipwreck, and on the other is self-condemnation and paralysis.

I had a Christian friend who struggled with a sin issue. A number of years ago he committed suicide. Why, you might ask, would a Christian commit suicide? Because he was overcome by sin and, in a final act of self-hatred, he took his life. We can never underestimate the destructive power of sin. As someone said: "Sin will take you places you never intended to stray; it'll keep you longer than you intended to stay; and it'll cost you more than you intended to pay."

Jesus said, *"If your eye causes you to sin, pluck it out."* We often remark on our Lord's use of hyperbole, since this was surely just an illustration He was using. Perhaps, but if it *was* just an illustration, His use of what we would call "gross language" had one overriding purpose — to warn us in the strongest possible language against sin.

To the man who was bed-ridden for thirty-eight years and couldn't make it into the healing waters of the pool Bethesda, He had one message after healing him: *"Do not sin any more so that nothing worse may befall you" (John 5:14).* The man

141

has been bed-ridden for thirty-eight years and Jesus warns him about something worse? And the warning against sin is, in itself, perplexing. How big a sinner can you be when you've been in bed for thirty-eight years?

Surely Jesus should have focused on the man's temple attendance, his relationships, and other things that were on hold for decades. Surely the wisest Man who ever lived could have given more practical advice. Actually, His advice was very practical — sin again, and you're dead meat. That's how we would say it today. It's certainly no more offensive than telling a person to gouge out his eye.

Would it be fair, then, to say that Jesus was "hung up on sin"? I think so. We call it a hang-up because we haven't seen hell. Probably five minutes in that place would change our attitude pretty quickly. Have you ever had a non-believer mock you as a guilt-ridden, sin-obsessed freak? I have, several times. They find Jesus frightfully boring. How unen-lightened He was, how provincial, how pedestrian — always obsessing over sin. But God will have the last word. In a future age, they will rue the day they trifled with sin.

The epistle writers are no less severe in their attitude toward sin. In Paul's letter to the Romans, he makes the definitive commentary on the subject in this terse comment. *"There will be tribulation and distress upon every soul of man that does evil"(Rom 2:9)*. And he later adds — *"without partiality"*. We find then, what appears to be a "zero toler-ance" policy towards sin both in the teachings of Jesus and in the epistles.

The Far-Reaching Effect of Sin

Why *is* this when, if we confess our sins, He is faithful to forgive us our sins? There are several reasons, but let us note two: the law of sowing and reaping, and the exceeding sinfulness of sin. Sin leaves its mark on everything it touches. You don't have to explain that to a teen who was molested as a child. All the repentance in the world on the part of the perpetrator can't erase the mark that's been left on such a person. And for the perpetrator, there is a harvest of unrighteousness that God will not cancel, no matter how much repentance is involved.

It is impossible, therefore, to minimize the effect of sin both in our lives and on those around us. I once heard a well-known prophet commenting on the effect of sin. He said it effects individuals and families, it affects cities and nations, and it affects even the earth and the cosmos.

Cops for Christ have done some excellent work correlating earthquake activity with significant moral lapses. There were significant earthquakes surrounding Supreme Court decisions on abortion and others favoring homosexuals. But it even extends to the cosmos where there is increased travail in the heavens — sunspot activity, etc, as a result of sin.

The Other Side of the Coin

On the other side of the issue are the people that are easily deterred from serving Christ because of sin. They live under the constant condemnation of repeated failure, often in the moral sphere. But life is short and ministry time is limited. Sometimes it takes a lot of faith to believe that we are indeed forgiven and still qualified to serve Him. The thought of standing before Him someday, empty-handed because we didn't try, is too abhorrent.

Imagine not serving God because we let the enemy beat us up over the things He died for. Imagine seeing our hidden pride exposed, the pride of not feeling worthy to serve Him, that somehow our sin was too big for His perfect work on the cross. We would suffer great loss.

We have the example of King David, who sinned greatly and yet was greatly loved and greatly used of God. We have the seventy-times-seven forgiveness mandate in the gospels. We have the injunction to draw near to the throne of grace for help in time of need. God knows that the last thing we feel like doing after we've sinned is facing Him, and yet that is precisely the time we need to come to Him. And it is there that He waits for us, always forgiving.

But there is something better than forgiveness: not needing it; not sinning in the first place. The work that God does in our souls after the new birth is called sanctification, and its goal is imparted righteousness. This goal is certainly attainable, but the presence of one element is paramount — purpose.

The Importance of Purpose

There are many motivations for avoiding sin, and they would include such things as a desire for personal peace, a desire to avoid pain, a desire to please God, and a desire to grow up in God. These reasons have appeal, but without a greater purpose many will still lack the motivation to be relentless with the flesh. Purpose comes before desire, for we seldom desire things for which we don't see much purpose. And if we don't desire them, we are not going to exercise the discipline necessary to secure them.

There are two main purposes that God has given us. These purposes have God at their center, but in His wisdom He has given us an incentive plan that rivals that of any multilevel marketing firm.

Temporal Purposes

What are these two purposes? The first one is temporal and has two components. Let us begin by looking at a familiar passage: *" In My Father's house are many dwelling places; if it were not so, I would have told you; for I go to prepare a place for you" (Jn. 14:2).*

This scripture has two applications, and we'll start with the lesser-known one. The phrase "dwelling places" in the NAS Bible is a more accurate rendering than the King James

144

word "mansions". In this verse, Jesus declares that He is going to prepare a place for believers in the Father's house, the House of God. This is the church that our Lord told Peter in Matthew 16 He was going to build. The "place" referred to is the position He has for each of us in this structure.

To many of us, our calling seems of little importance. But Jesus put a high priority on giving specific gifts and callings to each believer which would, in turn, allow them to function in a unique way. This becomes clearer as we look at another passage. These same two Greek words rendered "house" and "prepare" in John 14 appear in another passage and are translated exactly the same:

> *"Now in a large house there are not only gold and silver vessels, but also vessels of wood and of earthenware, and some to honor and some to dishonor.*
> *Therefore, if a man cleanses himself from these things, he will be a vessel for honor, sanctified, useful to the Master, prepared for every good work."(2 Tim. 2:20-22)*

Here we see the same picture, except now from the believer's point of view. Here it is the believer who has to prepare himself if he wants to enter the place of service already crafted for him by the Lord. He does this by cleansing himself from sin. If he is successful, he will be sanctified, able to do good works, and, most important of all, be useful to the Master. Here, then, is the first component or enticement: *being greatly used of God.* You don't have to be perfect to be greatly used of God, but you do have to be sanctified.

The second component is honor. Sanctification causes us to become a vessel of honor in the House of God, as typified by the gold and silver vessels. It should be stressed that this has nothing to do with our level of gifting. It relates to the honor that comes from assuming our place in the Body after going through the cleansing and sanctifying process.

This honor takes two forms. First, God honors people that love Him and are co-laborers together with Him. He plainly says: *"Those who honor Me I will honor, and those who despise Me will be lightly esteemed" (1 Sam. 2:30).* This honor takes numerous forms, but every servant experiences this and it is a great blessing. We struggle with this because we confuse God's love, which is universal, with His honor, which is not. We want God to treat us all the same, but He plainly doesn't, despite the fact that He loves us all the same.

Secondly, there is an honor that comes from the church. Obviously, high profile ministers receive the greatest honor, and this is scriptural according to I Timothy 5:17. But it by no means ends with them. Though some people serve behind the scenes, their works are nevertheless seen and appreciated by many, in particular their leaders. Leaders view these people as part of the team, joint workers in the Lord's vineyard, and they esteem them for their faithfulness.

This covers the chief temporal purpose for submitting to the sanctification process: being placed in service for the God we love and becoming a vessel of honor. But there is a second purpose that is eternal in nature.

Eternal Purpose

Returning to the scripture in John 14, we note its primary interpretation. Jesus, since His ascension, has been very busy. One of His main activities is intercession and another is preparing "mansions" for the faithful. This is figurative language for inheritance. Most believers have an inheritance in the eternal kingdom that will be distributed at the time of the judgment.

In speaking of the coming judgment, Paul says of God: *"...Who will render to every man according to his deeds; to those who by perseverance in doing good, seek for glory and honor and immortality, eternal life" (Rom. 2:6,7).*

What Paul says is that God will give eternal life to those who persevere in doing good. But in the middle of the verse he explains their motivation for doing good as those who *"seek for glory and honor and immortality"*. This is just a small part of what faithful people will receive in heaven. But let's be very plain. For those who do good, there *is* glory, honor and immortality in the eternal kingdom.

Immortality is not the same as eternal life. We refer to someone as being immortal because he or she is remembered for achieving something great. This is but one of the many distinctions in heaven, and it is contingent on cleansing oneself and doing good.

In Summary

For those who have lived diligent lives and are vessels of honor, the judgment experience will be glorious. But for those who are vessels of dishonor, it will be painful. If we don't teach about the judgment, we remove one of the greatest incentives God gave for living a holy and productive life. I realize that the absence of teaching on the subject of the believers' judgment has not been intentional. Most pastors simply have no knowledge or revelation on the topic. But it does put people at risk.

I have heard many sermons on growth and maturity. Often a pastor will address a personal fault, such as anger. He will discuss the human tendency to justify our faults with excuses like: "That's just the way I am; accept it. I'm from such-and-such an ethnic group, and that's how we are." These people are then encouraged to drop the excuses, admit their failings, and allow God to change them. This is good advice. But we never take it to the next level, the level of accountability, and that is why it is seldom effective.

People are left with the impression that change is simply a personal choice. If we choose not to change, there are no consequences, because consequences are never mentioned. Occasionally we hear mention of the affect that our faults will have on personal relationships, but that is as far as it goes.

Most of us have heard the quip: "Insanity is doing the same thing in the same way, and expecting a different result." That can't be insanity because that is the norm. Insanity is supposed to be outside the norm. Preaching the same old message while expecting a different result *isn't* insanity, but it is counter productive. It is self-deceptive. It is business as usual. It is boring.

I don't recommend that a young pastor preach his first sermon on pornography with the exhortation: *"If your eye causes you to sin, gouge it out!"* But we must recognize that he would be well within the bounds of scripture to do so. Yes, Jesus was probably using hyperbole when He issued that statement. But we need occasional reminders of just how radical He truly was, and how timid and genteel we are by comparison. Jesus taught consequences.

God wants us to get radical about sin. He wants us to teach consequences!

A Final Word — Losing Our Salvation

There are certain non-essential doctrines where it is best not to be dogmatic. Eternal Security is one of them. Those who accept the five points of Calvin, culminating in the perseverance of the saints, will never accept what I am about to share. That is fine, but I have to share my conviction.

I have taught that the same sins that are in the world, are in the Church. I have taught that those who practice certain sins are in danger of losing their inheritance in the Kingdom of God. I have taught that only God knows when a person has crossed the line and is disinherited. This, as I have clearly shown, is what the Word of God teaches.

The reason I have to address the subject of losing one's salvation is, firstly, because the Bible does. Secondarily, if I don't teach this, then by default I'm teaching that the worst that can happen to a believer is that they can lose their inheritance. As bad as that is, words aren't adequate to describe how preferable disinheritance is to eternal damnation.

So let me present briefly what I believe the Bible teaches on this subject. We will use as our major text Matthew chapter 7:

> *"Not everyone who says to Me, 'Lord, Lord,' will enter the kingdom of heaven; but he who does the will of My Father who is in heaven.*
>
> *Many will say to Me on that day, 'Lord, Lord, did we not prophesy in Your name, and in Your name cast out demons, and in Your name perform many miracles?'*
>
> *And then I will declare to them, 'I never knew you; depart from Me, you who work lawlessness.'"*
> *(Matt. 7: 21-23)*

This would probably get most people's vote for the scariest passage in the Bible. I have certainly had more questions about this verse than any other. Notice, first of all, that these individuals had cast out demons. This tells me they were believers and defuses the argument that this passage doesn't deal with Christians. How does this make them Christians? For the answer we need to look to a verse in Acts:

> *"But also some of the Jewish exorcists, who went from place to place, attempted to name over those who had the evil spirits the name of the Lord Jesus, saying, 'I adjure you by Jesus whom Paul preaches.'*
>
> *And seven sons of one Sceva, a Jewish chief priest, were doing this.*

And the evil spirit answered and said to them, 'I recognize Jesus, and I know about Paul, but who are you?'

And the man, in whom was the evil spirit, leaped on them and subdued both of them and overpowered them, so that they fled out of that house naked and wounded." (Acts 19:13-16)

So here we see some Jewish boys getting their clocks cleaned because they made a fatal mistake — trying to cast out demons without a saving knowledge of Jesus Christ. This scripture underlines the fact that only a believer can cast out a demon in the name of Jesus.

So if the people in question were believers and did mighty works, why were they rejected by God at what, we presume, is the final judgment? The answer is found in two phrases our Lord utters: *"I never knew you"* and *"you who work lawlessness"*. These issues are almost inseparable, so we will deal with them together. In Hebrews we have this instruction: *"But encourage one another day after day, as long as it is still called 'Today', lest any one of you be hardened by the deceitfulness of sin" (Heb. 3:13).*

There is a progression in the heart of a backslider: lawlessness, hardness, and estrangement. When a person sins, the Holy Spirit convicts them, and if they repent, their conscience remains sensitive. But sin is deceitful, and if we're not careful, it has the capacity to harden our hearts. What does it mean to "harden our hearts"? It means that if we persist in a certain sin, we'll no longer consider it a sin.

This is a very dangerous position to be in for two reasons. First, you can't repent of something that you don't believe is a sin. Secondly, if you don't think you are sinning, then you'll assume your relationship with God is intact. Here we have a recipe for disaster.

Let us look first at issue of being unable to repent. Again we turn to Hebrews:

"For in the case of those who have once been enlight-ened and have tasted of the heavenly gift and have been made partakers of the Holy Spirit, and have tasted the good word of God and the powers of the age to come, and then have fallen away, it is impos-sible to renew them again to repentance, since they again crucify to themselves the Son of God, and put Him to open shame." (Heb. 6:4-6)

There is much that could be said concerning these verses. However, we will confine ourselves to the issue of falling away where there is no possibility of being renewed to repentance. God, of course, will never reject anyone who repents. So what is described in this verse is not the unwillingness of God, but the desperate place of the sinner. The sinner cannot repent because he does not believe he is sinning. Let me give you an example.

Though the subject of this example is a man who has been exposed and deliberately marked, I will not name him because I do not believe it is my place to do so. This man was in the prophetic ministry for decades and had garnered worldwide esteem for his gifting and godliness. However, he had never married, and it was later discovered that he had been having sexual relationships with men for many years. When he was exposed, he initially submitted to discipline, but then bolted, denying any wrongdoing.

Rick Joyner, one of the men administering the discipline, said the man claimed that since he only had sexual relation-ships with one man at a time, he was not, in fact, a homo-sexual, but was working to overcome homophobia. Rick said the reasoning was laughable, but strangely, the man himself appeared to believe it. And that is the problem. He probably did and does. That is the deceitfulness of sin.

But there is a second problem. When you talk to people such as the man in question, they invariably say they have a good relationship with God. It is frustrating and slightly mind-boggling to be told by someone who is in an adulterous or perverse relationship, that they have never felt as close to God as they currently do. But that is all part of the deception and, therefore, accounts for their surprise at our Lord's words to them in Matthew 7.

As well, because the gifts and callings of God are without repentance, these people may still enjoy a thriving ministry. These people in Matthew 7 weren't struggling Christians who battled the flesh, but seemingly victorious believers who were shocked by the Lord's response to them. They genuinely expected commendation, not the rebuke, "I never knew you!"

It is indeed true, as some have noted, that the Greek word for "know" in this text was also used in the following verse with reference to sexual intercourse: *"And Joseph...did not **know** her until she gave birth to a Son" (Matt. 1:25).* So it is plain that our Lord was saying He didn't know these people intimately. There are many believers who lack intimacy with God, but Matthew 7 is of a different order, arising as it does from gross sin and a hard, unrepentant heart.

So we have the completed circle. Sin leads to hardening, and hardening reaches the point where the person no longer recognizes it as sin. Sin, as the scripture says, comes between a man and his God. But the hardened sinner has grieved the Holy Spirit to the point where he is unaware of the breach. Quite the opposite, he thinks things are fine.

But from the Lord's point of view, the intimacy is gone, the relationship is dead, the connection is broken, and the final pronouncement can be made: *"I never knew you; depart from me, you who practice lawlessness."*

A Final Sobering Note

It is disconcerting that the Lord used the term "many" when describing the group that would receive this horrific sentence. As in the issue of disinheritance, it is not easy to judge when a person has crossed the line and has been excluded from repentance. We must pray for all who go astray, but we must keep our distance from those who lead unruly lives while claiming closeness to God. This is doubly true of those who are highly gifted. Without repentance, they will continue the downward spiral, becoming false prophets and ravenous wolves.

We will witness many tragedies on Judgment Day, but none greater than seeing once great men of God whose names have been stricken from the Lamb's Book of Life.

A Final Edifying Note

To say that there *will* be tragedies on Judgment Day is far different from saying that there have to be. And that is the bigger tragedy: it is all so unnecessary. God has made provision for every test, trial and temptation we will face in life. But in the end we must choose.

Sin is like a gated compound with a sign reading "Trespassers Will Be Prosecuted." We would like an asterix that says "Except for Christians", but it isn't there. Instead, inside the compound there is another sign which says: "It is not too late to turn around." Turning around is what we call repentance. That sign appears repeatedly in the compound just as it does in Scripture. God offers us daily repentance. He wants us to walk in the light as He is in the light so that the blood of Jesus can keep on cleansing us.

I want to leave this earth clean, don't you? But there is someone who wants it even more than we do: God. I have a feeling that as He watches our lives, He frequently muses, "Please don't make Me bring this up on Judgment Day." We can make God's day just by coming to Him with a contrite heart. Most of us have heard the simple question with the surprise ending that goes something like this: "Want to find God's will for your life? Check it out!"

"For this is the will of God, your sanctification" (I Thes. 4:3).

We know that it was sin that brought Jesus to earth. We also know that it was love that brought Him to earth. We know that there are numerous reasons why a God of love can't just ignore sin, even in the lives of the redeemed. We have looked at some of them. God has ordained that the Christian life be a time of sanctification where we take on the likeness of Christ. To do this we must forsake sin. Jesus said if we loved Him we would keep His commandments. So we can't discuss love without discussing sin. The one is but a reflection of the other.

What do you want to see reflected on that Day?

SIX

The Judgment of Stewardship

The society had languished for years while the board, of which I was a member, tried to find a mission. First it was youth, then offenders, then unwed mothers, then nothing. First we bought *this* property, then *that* one, always trying to mesh the location with the half-formed vision. Finally we settled on the idea of a seniors' home and purchased a building that would meet the need. I say "we", but really it was the brainchild of our director. This man labored to put all the pieces into place.

I thought running a Christian school was difficult, and it is. But providing care for people in the final stage of their life can be equally challenging. You have medical problems; you have staff and volunteer problems; you have problems with the building. There are the grounds to keep, the frequent renovations to oversee, the residents' families to deal with, and the constant pressure to keep the rooms rented. It is never-ending, and much of it fell on the shoulders of our director.

And that was the part I didn't get.

This was a man in his seventies who had been a pastor for fifty years. He had "retired" several years ago, but was busier than ever. He held a leadership position in a denomination, gave apostolic oversight to about ten churches, and had an international ministry. I knew he had the energy of ten men, but I couldn't understand his interest in this affair. He just didn't need the headaches. Sure, it was a work of compassion, but hardly one that would change lives. We all know that old people rarely get saved.

But one *did*.

Then another, and another. Families were touched, volunteers were impacted, the Health Department gave us accolades, and the community gave us their support. It would take more space than I have to report all the good that was accomplished. But it came largely because of the stewardship of this one man.

I don't know if he is a workaholic, but I do know that he chose people over leisure and labor over ease. His plate was already full, so he could have easily justified his non-involvement. But he never wavered, tackling everything from dispute resolution to carpentry.

You see, this man has a gift of leadership, and he knows it. Where there is ability, there is responsibility. As a faithful steward, he was always looking for ways to use that ability, no matter the cost. That is what good stewards do. As I observe men like this, I am challenged. I am challenged by the question: What has God put into my life for which I will one day give an account?

This is the question we must all address.

Introduction to Stewardship

When a person is newly saved, he is usually in a bubble. In western culture there is seldom a price to pay. In fact, quite the opposite. For most converts, the new life is all about receiving. Like any parent with a new baby, God usually showers a new believer with His manifest glory and ministers to him in a variety of ways. Who can forget the excitement of praying for a parking spot, only to see one miraculously open up! It's not up there with raising the dead, but to a babe in Christ, it is a heady experience.

But soon the believer's life will need the balance of both giving and receiving. In due course he will hear about tithing and will face what appears, at first, to be a daunting challenge — that of giving a tenth of his income. Like most of us, he is probably in debt, so a ten per cent tithe seems unfathomable. But by starting small, getting out of debt, and getting used to the novel idea of giving money away, many Christians progress to a full tithe. But, unfortunately, many do not.

The Barna polls reveal that only a small percentage of born-again believers actually give a tenth of their income to a church or to missions. This, in itself, speaks volumes about our lack of understanding on the subject of stewardship. If we don't think God owns ten percent of our income, how will we ever handle the concept of God owning everything? We won't; we can't. So as we become cognizant of the full implications of stewardship, we will see that, at least in this area, few Christians are prepared to meet their Maker.

Indeed, without a Judgment, what would be the point of even probing this? If we are simply born-again, autonomous people who have the option of giving part of our lives and substance to God without repercussions, then end of discussion. But such is not the case. Whether we know it or not, we own nothing, are stewards of everything, and will one day give an account to God.

Definition of Steward

In the Greek, the word for steward means "manager or overseer, one in charge of the household". Paul takes this word and applies it in a spiritual sense to himself in 1Corinthians 4:

> "*Let a man regard us in this manner, as servants of Christ, and stewards of the mysteries of God. **Now it is required that those who are stewards be found faithful.** I care very little if I am judged by you or by any human court...It is the Lord who judges me.*

Therefore judge nothing before the appointed time; wait till the Lord comes." (1 Cor. 4: 1-5)

The main thing demanded of a steward, according to that verse, is that he be faithful.

While it is patently obvious that God owns everything and that we are temporal managers, it helps to have a proof verse. If God owns us, then by extension, everything we have is His. He establishes that claim in 1 Corinthians 6: *"You are not your own, you are bought with a price...."* We belong to God.

Paul opened the letter to the Romans with this phrase: *"Paul, a bond-slave of Jesus Christ...."* That wasn't just a mushy sentiment written in momentary fervor. It was a fact. He was owned, body, soul, and spirit, by his Master Christ Jesus. So are you; so am I. We're not our own; we belong to Christ; we're bought with a price. If we don't even own the thoughts in our head, why then would we presume to own the car in the driveway or the boat at the lake? I refer, of course, to the command to *"bring every thought captive to Christ Jesus"*. He owns them.

We know that a steward is required to be faithful and will one day be judged by God, but what does it mean to be faithful? And faithful to what? Before we can make sense of this, we have a huge mental hurdle to overcome. The foundation of democracy and freedom is property rights. That is why forbidding the private ownership of anything from a gun to a piece of land is a step down the road to slavery. Private property rights are a good thing, but for a believer the words "private" and "rights" can be problematic.

From the moment we are old enough to understand phrases like "possession is nine-tenths of the law", we have a very clear understanding that what we own is ours. Additionally, we have the full power of the state to enforce our claim. A person can go to jail for removing our car ten feet from our driveway. All our programming tells us we are owners. Once saved, we truly need an attitude adjustment. Only the most resolute will be able to delete the ownership program and install a new one — the "God's Manager" program. Why is this so hard? Because the exchange has never taken place.

The Exchange

John is a typical middle class heathen. He's affluent, but in debt; successful, yet unfulfilled; educated, but confused. And above all, he's discouraged by the barrenness of life without God. He cries out from the depths of his despair and is wonderfully saved. He finds a Bible and discovers the crown rights of King Jesus to everything he is and owns. He has a conversation with God. Thus begins the exchange.

God: You call Me Lord and so I am. My claim upon your life and possessions is absolute. Give an account of yourself. What do you have?

John: A house.

God: I'll take that. What else?

John: A car and a boat.

God: OK, I'll take those. What else? Do you have a wife, kids and a job?

John: Yes.

God: All right, I'll take those.

After the inventory is complete and God has everything, including John's bank account and the change in his pocket, John thinks to himself, "Well, I've lost everything, but I've found eternal life. Here I'll be sleeping in the street, but there I'll see thrones of glory. All and all, a pretty good deal."

Then God interjects, "You know, John, I really don't need another empty house. I already own the cattle on a thousand hills and My heavenly vaults are full. Tell you what, I'll lend you the house, but now let's be very clear. I am the owner and you are simply the manager. If it were your house, you'd be tempted to use it for *your* purposes and your pleasures, and it might become a curse to you. But I'll let you sleep in my house if you will use it for the kingdom."

John replies with excited disbelief, "Really, God? You'd let me sleep in your house?!"

"Yes," God replies, "but now I want you to be attentive to the needs of others. I want you to show hospitality to strangers and perhaps even minister to a homeless person."

"Wow," exclaims John. "That's the least I can do!"

As the conversation continues, John is given back the stewardship of all his former possessions, but with explicit directions from the Lord as to how to use them.

So there you have the exchange, and it fosters a heart that says: "That's the least I can do." The problem, of course, is that in most of our lives the exchange hasn't really happened. We hear sermons on stewardship versus ownership, but it's all just words, and we jealously guard our possessions against all intruders, including God. A scratch on "our car" is enough to incite rage at the perpetrator.

What is the basis for this attitude? Very simply: "I earned it, so therefore I own it. I was the one that held the job that earned the wage that bought the house. Therefore it's my house. Right?" Well, not exactly. You see, Paul covered all that in his letter to the Corinthians when he said: *"And what do you have that you did not receive? But if you did receive it, why do you boast as if you had not received it?"* (I Cor. 4:7).

But, we could still protest, I surely *did* earn it.

In today's vernacular Paul would say something like the following: "What part of 'given' don't you understand? Was it your good planning that caused you to be born in America instead of a ghetto in Bombay? Was it your foresight that gave you a keen mind and a good job, instead of a life on welfare? Was it your cleverness that caused you to hear the gospel instead of dying with the shirtless masses, never even hearing the word of truth?"

No, everything you have, you have from God, and the proof is that He can take it from you at any time. Sobering thought. You don't have to be an evil person to make the gospel of no effect in your life. You just have to say, "What's mine, is mine," and everything unfolds from there.

It is important to see that all the blessings we experience are from God and have little to do with us, though our forefathers undoubtedly paid a price for our freedom and prosperity. But even the prosperity was not of our choosing, and this is where many stumble. It's hard to believe that most of the factors that led to our current situation had nothing to do with our choices. We made choices within an eternal destiny that was mapped out. But the fact that those choices happened in prosperous 21st century America, and not in Europe during the Dark Ages, had nothing to do with us. Let me clarify this.

Stewardship and Destiny

Stewardship is usually thought of in terms of money. This, of course, is only a small portion of what we manage, but let me use money to give an explanation of stewardship. With regards to money, there are three dominant views:

1) Poverty Theology: All Christians should essentially take a vow of poverty like Catholic priests. (This conveys a misunderstanding of God, His heart, and His purposes for our lives.)

2) Prosperity Theology: Every believer could be rich if they just had enough faith. (This demeans the faith of many

courageous believers who have lived in times of great social injustice, under the most oppressive conditions.)

3) Stewardship Theology (The correct view): God decides for each person, in which country and at what time in history he will be born; which social class, race and family he will belong to; what his personality, giftings, intelligence, and physical abilities will be; who he will marry (or not); and his probable education and work.

These factors constitute "Part A" of our stewardship quotient, and they are sovereignly chosen by God. They put a boundary around the limits of our financial prosperity. That is why Paul was emphatic that we should be content with what we have, and not strive to be rich or envy the rich. Riches, in large part, are a gift.

But Paul also said, *"He who sows sparingly will reap sparingly."* He also talked about having *an abundance for every good work.* Jesus said, *"Ask and it shall be given unto you."* He also said, *"Give and it shall be given unto you."* These and many other commands and principles suggest there is a second part to the equation, Part B.

Part B consists of the following:
1) Substance: Everyone has something, even if it's only a little. Using it wisely will bring increase.
2) Faith: The more we exercise our faith, the more faith God gives us; and faith moves mountains, even financial ones.
3) The ability to ask: It's called prayer and is very powerful. Jesus Himself said we are to ask for "daily bread".
4) The ability to give: God makes many promises regarding sowing and reaping.
5) Wisdom: If we ask, He will give us wisdom abundantly, and this is part of the power to make wealth.
6) Energy: There are many promises for the diligent and the hard-working, and this also is part of the power to make wealth,

7) Gifts and skills: Properly employing our gifts and skills, as well, is part of the power to make wealth.

8 Time: We all have twenty-four hours a day. How we manage our time impacts greatly on our productivity and our subsequent blessing.

Part A and Part B make up our stewardship quotient. This is what we have to work with during our brief stay on earth. This is what we are accountable for on Judgment Day. The determining issue is "increase". We must be reminded that *"the race is not to the swift"*. Many people are born with little, and their beggarly circumstances might suggest great disadvantage. But in the exercise of their faith, wisdom, generosity, and hard work, they are overcomers. The sum of their life's work may greatly exceed those born rich, in terms of fruitfulness and faithfulness. Fruitfulness and faithfulness are the key issues, not riches.

Our chief concern should not be: "Will we be able to pay the bills?" But rather, "Will we be a good steward of all that we've been given?" If we are good stewards, for sure the bills will be paid, and we will have an abundance.

Within the Scriptures are principles we can use to maximize our stewardship. There is no formula for getting rich; there is only a formula for managing well what God has given us. If we manage well, we will be rich — in heaven, in the eternal Kingdom. If we don't understand this, then we don't understand the theology of stewardship, and therefore can't understand the principles of prosperity.

Settling Accounts

In the Bible, the judging of our stewardship is referred to as the "settling of accounts" or "giving account". The same word or combination of Greek words is used in three instances. First, we find it in the Matthew 18 Parable of the

Unforgiving Steward: *"Therefore the Kingdom is likened unto a certain King which would **take account** of his servants."*

Secondly, we have a passage in Romans 14:10-12 that says:

> *"But you, why do you judge your brother? Or you again, why do you regard your brother with contempt? For we shall all stand before the judgment seat of God. For it is written, 'As I live,' says the Lord, ' every knee shall bow to me, and every tongue shall give praise to God.' So then each of us shall **give account** of himself to God."*

Thirdly, we find the same phrase in the Parable of the Talents, a passage we will give greater attention to: *"Now after a long time the master of those slaves came and **settled accounts** with them."* In the Parable of the Minas in Luke 19, we have the same concept but different wording. But these two parables together teach us much about our final accounting and the judgment of our stewardship. So let us look at the Parable of the Talents in greater detail.

> *"For it is like a man about to go on a journey, who called his own slaves and entrusted his possessions to them.*
>
> *And to the one he gave five talents, to another two, and to another one, each according to his own ability; and he went on his journey.*
>
> *Immediately the one who had received the five talents went and traded with them, and gained five more talents.*
>
> *In the same manner the one who had received the two talents gained two more. But he who received the one talent went away and dug in the ground, and hid his master's money.*

Now after a long time the master of those slaves came and settled accounts with them.

And the one who had received the five talents came up and brought five more talents saying, ' Master, you entrusted five talents with me; see, I have gained five more talents.'

His master said to him, 'Well done, good and faithful slave; you were faithful with a few things, I will put you in charge of many things, enter into the joy of your Master.'

The one also who had received the two talents came up and said, 'Master, you entrusted to me two talents; see, I have gained two more talents.'

His master said to him, 'Well done, good and faithful slave; you were faithful with a few things, I will put you in charge of many things; enter into the joy of your master.'

And the one also who had received the one talent came up and said, 'Master, I knew you to be a hard man, reaping where you did not sow, and gathering where you scattered no seed.

And I was afraid, and went away and hid your talent in the ground; see, you have what is yours.'

But his master answered and said to him, 'You wicked, lazy slave, you knew that I reap where I did not sow, and gather where I scattered no seed.

Then you ought to have put my money in the bank, and on my arrival I would have received my money back with interest.

Therefore take away the talent from him, and give it to the one who has the ten talents.

For to everyone who has shall more be given, and he shall have an abundance; but from the one who does not have even what he does have shall be taken away.

> *And cast out the worthless slave into the outer*
> *darkness; in that place there shall be weeping and*
> *gnashing of teeth.'" (Matt. 25: 14 – 30)*

A talent was a monetary unit in circulation at the time of the gospels. While our talents or giftings make up part of our stewardship, this parable is not dealing with "talents" in that sense. This parable actually deals with money. But money is simply the vehicle our Lord uses to graphically illustrate the connection between stewardship and judgment. Good stewards receive commendation; bad ones receive rebuke.

During our judgment, we will all be examined on how we stewarded everything that was given to us. The issues are not just increase, but increase for the master. Concerning our talents, for instance, two things are important: that our talents be developed, and that the goal of developing them be an increase in the Kingdom of God.

Our stewardship includes our time, talent, treasure, energy, relationships, and health, as well as our various roles (son or daughter, father or mother, grandma or grampa, brother or sister, employee or boss, church member or leader, etc.). The role of the church member or leader is one I want to enlarge upon. It will help us illustrate, in a graphic way, one of the primary truths this parable seeks to convey, and how it is reflected in what we observe in the Body of Christ. In doing so, I draw on some comments made by Derek Prince.

The Message of the Parable of the Talents

Returning to the parable of the talents, we observe that God gave each a certain number of talents according to their "ability". Who is the man with the five talents? He is like one of the five-fold. He is gifted of God. He knows that he can make a difference and expends his life trying to do so. He may be a pastor, an evangelist or an itinerant minister. Or he could be an apostle to the workplace and his primary ministry could be outside the church. If he is faithful to his calling, he will one day receive the "Well done!" commendation.

Who is the man with two talents? He is like the one who has lesser but still obvious ability. God may gift him to be a worship leader, a Sunday school teacher, a cell group leader, or a twelve-step facilitator. Like the man in our first example, he knows he can make a difference and is rarely reticent in trying. If he is faithful to his calling, he as well, will hear the much-coveted commendation.

Burying Your Talent

Then we have the one-talent people. They lack the obvious ability and giftings of the other two groups and make up the majority of the people in the Kingdom of God. They have just as strong a call on their lives as the others, but they have a tendency to say, "I can't teach, I can't preach, I can't sing, I'm not a leader. Therefore God doesn't expect anything from me." Of course not all "one-talent" people think this way, but many do. So they bury their talent. They just sit and become an observer. If this pattern of behavior is consistent across all areas of their stewardship, then the outcome will be fearful.

Outer darkness is their destination, not the lake of fire. Weeping and the gnashing of teeth will be their experience, not the torment of the damned. These people will be saved, yet as through fire. Once the judgment is over, they will enjoy heaven as much as anyone. But they will enjoy it from the perimeter called "outer darkness", because by contrast to the glory of the throne room, it will be dark. Campbell Morgan speaks of it as "the darkness that is outside the Kingdom of responsibility".

What is their crime? Murder, incest, blasphemy? No. Their crime is neglecting to invest their lives, despising what the King had given them, and, in effect, calling it worthless. That is a great sin. Perhaps the King's response seems out of proportion to the severity of the crime — to us at least, who view things differently. But the Master called the one-talent person a *"wicked and lazy slave"* in verse 26. God esteems sound and wise investment. Waste your life, and you will pay a price.

However, I must emphasize that neglecting your ministry to the Body doesn't equate to wasting your life. Such a person could be a good steward in other areas, be rich in good works, and be of sterling character. This will be discussed later in a separate treatment of both our good works and our character. But for the sake of clarity, we must use this simple, if extreme example, to give some insight into the issue of "burying your talent".

Why, in the parable, does God have the one-talent person burying his gifting? Why not the five-talent person? Because that is what we observe in life. Rarely do we find one of the five-talent people plagued with indifference. The gifted person comes under a host of temptations, including pride, greed, and lust. But rarely is he tempted with laziness, which is the curse of the one-talent underachiever who thinks God expects nothing of him.

Being Honest About God

Many people may find this analysis of the one-talent person a bit shocking. But the Parable of the Talents is written for believers, to instruct them on the coming judgment and the consequences of good and bad stewardship. To have the one-talent steward suddenly morph into being an unbeliever just because we don't like the outcome, is disingenuous and exegesis at its worst. Or to assume that the one-talent person has lost his soul, is to preach salvation based on works, which is clearly heretical.

It is important to understand that the God of the Bible is our Judge. He deliberately portrays Himself as angry with the one-talent slave. We don't need to be an apologist for

God. Our finite minds cannot grasp his infinite attributes, but we must not ignore the many representations of Himself that He provides. If we do, we end up making up a God after our own carnal desires.

I personally prefer the God of John 17 over the God of Matthew 25, but it is, after all, the same God. He has no qualms about revealing certain aspects of His nature. He wants us to see His fury. He wants us to know that He is a consuming fire. He wants us to live in the fear of the Lord. In an immature reaction to the "hellfire and brimstone preaching" of a century ago, we have ceded to the unbeliever many of the scriptures that are directed at the believer.

Regardless of the one-talent slave's excuse that he was afraid, the Master never mentions this. The real issue was that the slave was lazy. I have seen believers who are industrious in every area of their life but one — the spiritual. Towards God and the work of God, they are lazy. I believe this is one of the reasons behind the charge of wickedness. To take all God has given you, including the precious gift of salvation, and use it strictly for your own pleasure while ignoring Him, is wicked.

But I believe there is another reason behind the charge of "wickedness", and we find our clue in the slave's view of his Master as "hard". I have known Christians who have a distorted view of God. Serving and giving must come out of a grateful heart and a belief that God is good. The wicked slave had a different view of God and a different heart attitude. He took no joy in trying to bring profit to the Master. Instead he exhibited the very trait that he accused God of: hardness of heart.

In conclusion we note the commendations given to the first two stewards: they are exactly the same. Even though the first gained five talents and the second gained two, the percentage increase for both was the same. So ultimately the issue of how much we have been given is not important since we have no say in that. What is important is how we manage what we have for maximum increase. It is this that will garner our Master's highest commendation.

With this as a background, let us now look at certain areas of stewardship in greater detail.

The Stewardship of Money

Money, in great amounts, has God-like properties. On the one hand, it offers some of the same benefits as a relationship with God — security, identity, and affirmation. And on the other hand, those that possess it can exert influence that is God-like in nature: power, authority and control. The security issue is probably the chief pitfall for most Christians, and the one most often addressed by our Lord. For this reason it deserves special attention.

Following God

To follow God, you have to go against many of the most entrenched human traits. Jesus didn't mince words in His description of the challenges inherent in doing so. *"The foxes have holes, and the birds of the air have nests; but the Son of Man has nowhere to lay His head."* But the issue is bigger than discomfort, as He tried to caution His listeners. He said some things that are hard for us to hear. We tend to read them through the lens of our own culture, thus softening their demands.

Take this statement from Luke's gospel: *"So therefore, no one of you can be My disciple who does not give up all his own possessions" (Luke 14:33)*. When we read this passage, we interpret it as Jesus saying that if we don't give up our possessions, He **won't let us be** His disciple. Whereas, what He actually means is **"we won't be able to be"**.

This is confirmed by the two illustrations He has given us in the preceding verses. Let us look at the parable of the man building a tower:

> *"For which one of you, when he wants to build a tower, does not first sit down and calculate the cost, to see if he has enough to complete it? Otherwise, when he has laid a foundation, and is not able to finish, all who observe it begin to ridicule him, saying, 'This man began to build and was not able to finish.'"* (Luke 14:28-30)

Notice that building the tower was the builder's choice. No one forbade him to build because he didn't have the resources; but if he didn't have the resources he **wouldn't be able** to finish what he had started. That gives us an insight into the problems inherent in trying to follow Jesus. If certain things aren't dealt with, we won't be able to do it, and we'll look foolish. What is the application?

In our Lord's day it was pretty straightforward. Jesus was an itinerant preacher. If someone wanted to follow Him, he couldn't continue to run a business, keep a house, feed animals, etc. If he were one of the twelve or seventy, he understood that following Jesus required, in effect, giving up his possessions.

Let's say that one of the seventy had bade farewell to his family and, with great fanfare, had signed on with Jesus. Weeks later he found himself in a distant city. What if news reached him that a business affair back home required his immediate attention? What if he wasn't able to pay the price and press on with his mission? He would return discouraged, and undoubtedly suffer the ridicule of being someone who started but couldn't finish.

Today this matter of discipleship is somewhat different. As discussed earlier on the subject of the exchange, you don't have to give everything away to have no possessions. You just have to give them to God. This then frees you to be a steward who is able to follow Jesus. It's the "obsession with possession" that makes discipleship impossible.

Mammon

So let us look at the subject of money. The book <u>Wealth, Riches and Money</u> by Craig Hill and Earl Pitts brings clarity to a confusing subject. For openers, when Jesus said in Matthew 6:24 that you can't serve God and Mammon, He wasn't talking about money. In some translations the word money is used in place of Mammon. But Mammon is the correct word. Mammon is a spirit much like Dagon and Molech, and he is the devil's Minister of Finance. In the heathen world of multiple gods, each has a role, whether it's the rain god, fertility god or the money god. And they all have to be appeased because they all have malevolent power.

Jesus wasn't declaring that it would be *wrong* to serve both Mammon and God, but that it would be impossible. We must choose. Mammon tries to entice people to serve him through various persuasions, the chief of which is the idea that money has inordinate power. When a person sees money as his source and allows money to govern his life choices, he has unknowingly given the spirit of Mammon power to rule his life.

Money is to be our slave, not our master, and it is to be pressed into service to do the work of God. In Luke 16, Jesus refers to money as *"a little thing"*. In the parable of the talents, Jesus, commenting on the steward's management, declares that *"you have been faithful in a little thing."* The spirit of Mammon wants to create the opposite impression: that money is huge. He attempts to use the fear of its lack as a driving passion in our lives.

"Why all this talk of Mammon?" one might ask. "Doesn't money belong to God?" No, it doesn't, as Jesus Himself made plain in the gospels. When challenged on the issue of paying taxes, Jesus requested a coin and asked whose likeness was on it. When they said to Him, "Caesar's," He responded, *"Then render to Caesar the things that are Caesar's and to God the things that are God's."* In Jesus' own words we have confirmation that money belongs to the state, the world system.

Money is different than wealth. Wealth is gold, silver, lands, servants, cattle, etc., and it belongs to God. He tells us that *"the silver is Mine, and the gold is Mine"* (*Hag. 2:8*), and that He owns *"the cattle on a thousand hills"* (*Ps. 50:10*). But when gold is melted down, formed into coins and stamped with the image of a man, it changes systems. It goes from being wealth in the kingdom of God, to money in the kingdom of this world. And as money, it is now subject to the spirit of Mammon.

Grace and God's Provision

A further perversion, as pointed out by the authors, is the modern day approach to financial need in a person's life. In many books and conferences, people are taught that the answer to all their financial needs is to sow money into the kingdom. This violates two principles. First, it reverses the master/slave relationship. It sees money as the goal and God as the agent. But God will not be our slave to get us money. We are to use money as our slave to do the work of God. We cannot give our way out of debt because the whole concept of "using" God is demeaning and challenges His care. Which brings us to our second principle.

God has made the meeting of our needs a matter of grace, not works. In Matthew 6, Jesus refutes the lie that through sowing and reaping He will meet human need. He does this by giving the illustration of the sparrow and the lily. He provides for them without their sowing and reaping, toiling or spinning. In other words, their provision is in no way dependent upon their works. It is likewise with us.

Sowing and reaping have a place, but not in the meeting of our needs. There are many ways that God can meet our needs, but the most common is through employment. It is imperative to realize that regardless of who signs our check, God is our source. If we truly believe this, then we will not be panic-stricken when there is a change in our provision. We may lose our job, but never our Source.

We achieve stability in the financial area in several ways. First, we trust that God will meet our needs based on grace, not works. Second, we see Him as our source and He, not our employer, becomes our trust. Third, we give tithes and offerings. This is very important. The world system operates on the principle of buying and selling, while God's kingdom operates on the principle of giving and receiving.

As the authors point out, whenever we take that which is meant for buying and selling, namely money, and freely give it, we profane the sacred properties ascribed to money by Mammon. In profaning money, we prove that it is not our source, our idol, or our god. As we do this, the spirit of Mammon loses its grip on our lives.

Money is a problem in the west. Jesus said, *"If you are not faithful in the use of unrighteous mammon, who will give you the true riches?"* Much of the weakness of the church today is a result of poor money management. According to Barna, only 6% of born-again Christians tithe a tenth of their income. Fifteen percent of Christians purchase lottery tickets versus just 12% of atheists. Though the average Christian may earn $3 million over his lifetime, fully one half of that will go to interest payments. All of this speaks of waste, wrong priorities, a lack of faith, and, in many cases, outright greed.

God wants to funnel much money into the harvest through Christians, but unfortunately many Christians can't be trusted. Any large financial blessing would in most cases be diverted away from the kingdom and into personal consumption. We are responsible as stewards for every penny that passes through our hands. What may appear to be a blessing, could come back to haunt us if we spend it carelessly, without inquiring of the Lord.

Furthermore, by blessing Christians indiscriminately with money, God would be violating one of His own principles. We find this principle at the end of the parable of the talents in Matthew 25. Concerning the man who buried his talent, which was a currency of that day, the scripture says the following:

> *"Therefore take away the talent from him, and give it to the one who has the ten talents. For to everyone who has shall more be given, and he shall have an abundance; but from the one who does not have, even what he does have shall be taken away."*
> (Matt.25:28, 29)

What is the principle? Good stewards get more money; bad stewards get less. The amount of finances we have right now is probably the amount we can be trusted with.

However, there are exceptions. The management of money is a burden that God doesn't often place on those who have certain callings. The term "financial freedom", with all that it implies, isn't scriptural. Any money beyond what is required to meet our basic needs, brings responsibility. The term "prosperity" is often used to describe these "excess funds". But because these funds have to be managed for the Kingdom, they can actually inhibit us from pursuing the pure call of God on our lives. The reason wealthy people usually work such long hours is because it takes time to wisely manage money.

The Illusion of Financial Freedom

We need more perspective on the whole concept of "financial freedom". I knew a fellow once who lived a wild lifestyle that included heroin addiction. He got wonderfully saved and turned his life around. His church at one point invited Dick Mills to lead a series of meetings. Dick has the unique prophetic gift of ministering to gatherings by giving encouragements from the scriptures. Remarkably, he can give a set of related verses along with references, to hundreds of individuals – all without a Bible in his hands. He received that gift through the laying on of hands, and it's a marvelous thing to witness.

This fellow, Brian, received a prophecy that he would be a pastor some day. Fast-forward about five years. Dick Mills is back at the same church, and who should be leading worship but Brian, the one who received the prophecy. He was now a worship pastor at that church. It brought tears to my eyes as Dick and Brian rejoiced at God's goodness.

Unfortunately, that's not the end of the story. Some Christian fellows came to Brian and told him that they had an exclusive franchise on a product that could make him a wealthy man. There was a snag, however. In order to be successful, he couldn't just work at it part time. Not to worry, Brian was told. A couple of years of hard work would yield such positive results that he would be financially independent for the rest of his life.

Brian fell for the oldest of all deceptions. He reasoned that if he was financially independent, he could serve God a lot better. He wouldn't be limited by the constraints of a job, even a pastoral job, but would be free to go wherever God called Him. He fantasized about a life free from financial limitations and obligations, and how life without these pressures would allow him less distraction and more commitment to God.

Ah yes, life without financial constraints. We would all be able to serve God so much better. It has a curious logic about it, does it not? I've run into several young men that have come under the same deception. Some think they can serve money just for a season and then revert back to their undivided pursuit of God. But money changes people, and so does time away from God, trying to get it. This is a recipe for disaster, and whatever its initial appeal, it soon awakens a torrent of greed that begins to take over our life.

Paul put it well when he said:

> *"But those who want to get rich fall into temptation and a snare and many foolish and harmful desires which plunge men into ruin and destruction.*
> *For the love of money is a root of all sorts of evil, and some by longing for it have wandered away from the faith, and pierced themselves with many a pang."* (1Tim.6:9,10)

Yes, "many a pang" is what people experience who pursue money, however noble their initial purpose. Brian left the ministry and poured himself into this "can't miss opportunity", but within a short time things went badly, and he quickly abandoned it. He then opened a series of businesses, all of which floundered. Not long after, I heard from a friend that he was backslidden and back on drugs. Sad, very sad.

Money is not the currency of the kingdom — faith is. It's faith we should want more of, not money, for it's faith that will enable us to serve God better. And the thing that develops faith, as well as endurance, diligence, longsuffering and a dozen other qualities, is none other than good old-fashioned work. It's going to a mundane job and giving it our best that pleases God. It's taking our leftover time and energy, and offering it as a sacrifice to our family and others that blesses Him and produces growth in our lives. Money has benefits, but it can insulate us from many of God's dealings, and therefore stymie our growth.

Investing from a Kingdom Perspective

We live in an age of investment, and investing is a good thing. The problem is that the secular definition of investing is the opposite of the Biblical definition. Jesus said in Matthew 16:24: *"If anyone wishes to come after Me, let him deny himself, pick up his cross and follow Me."* But He didn't stop there. In case we missed the point, He continues: *"For whoever wishes to save his life shall lose it; but whoever loses his life for My sake shall find it."* This is pure discipleship.

What is our life? Five things: time, energy, money, gift-ings, and influence. The word "save" in the Greek means, in this case, to selfishly expend for the benefit of self. If you "save" or use your talents for personal ambition and gain, you will lose them. From an eternal standpoint, you'll waste them, and on Judgment Day you'll have nothing, and you'll be exposed as a selfish fool. The same applies to the other four. If you seek to save your money, you will lose it. If you lose it — that is, give it away for the sake of the kingdom — you'll save it. Our proof text is in Matthew 6.

> *"Do not lay up for yourself treasures on earth, where moth and rust destroy, and thieves break in and steal. But lay up for yourselves treasures in heaven where neither moth nor rust destroys, and where thieves do not break in or steal; for where your treasure is, there will your heart be also." (Matt. 6:19-21)*

It couldn't be clearer. Yet people have never before felt such pressure to put money into monetary vehicles that store up treasure on earth. Couples in their early twenties are investing for retirement. But isn't that a good thing, you ask? Hasn't every fifty-year-old bemoaned the fact that if he'd put aside $50 a month for 30 years, he'd now be rich? That depends.

If a young couple takes money out of consumption to put into savings, it can be a godly thing. But if that money comes out of their tithes and offerings, or if their bank account becomes their trust instead of God, then it's vanity; it will be found one day to be hay, wood, and stubble. These are the issues at the core of investing. It's never just simply a question of investing money; it's where the money came from, and for what purpose it was set aside. These questions involve the larger issues of trusting God, managing His money, and expanding His kingdom. This is not rocket science. And yet it's the easiest thing to stumble over.

As well, there's more to investing than simply giving. We must give where the Master can get the best return. There's one evangelistic ministry, for instance, that can win a soul for about $1.00 US. In other words, when they divide their expenses by their decision cards, it's a ratio of one-to-one. From an eternal perspective, where can you get a better return on your money than that?

Why would a person store up treasure for a retirement that is iffy at best, when right now there is a world harvest taking place? We have to change our thinking. There is an unhealthy preoccupation with retirement at this time, and it has no witness in scripture. We are managing funds for the Lord of the Harvest and His instructions are clear. Sow, don't save. Store up in heaven, don't squander on earth. Work while it is yet light, for the time is coming when no man can work. *"When no man can work!"* — that's a reference to the end of the age, but also to your death and mine.

What would you rather have, a cushy old age, or ten thousand souls waiting for you in heaven?

That's a choice we may have to make.

The Stewardship Focus

Because we are emphasizing stewardship, our focus in this section is somewhat different from that of traditional teachings on money and finance. Of course God wants to bless us and see us prosper in our finances, but that is such a given that it hardly bears mention. Virtually every Christian seminar on finances focuses on debt reduction, prosperity and giving. But stewardship assumes a greater degree of maturity. It assumes that there is little debt. It assumes that we are enjoying God's blessing but have moved beyond simply prospering. It assumes that we are givers. It takes things to the next level: the level of the disciple.

At the discipleship level, money is not a gargantuan thing that we wrestle with all our lives. It is simply one of the many aspects of our stewardship, and like the others, it requires faith, diligence and obedience. Marriage counselors tell us that when sex is working, it's ten percent of a marriage; but when it's not, it becomes ninety percent. Money is like that. When it is managed well and "working", it is a small part of our lives — "a little thing", to quote our Lord. But when it is not, it can rule our lives. And as an aside, money issues, not sex, are the main reason for marital failures.

The Shrewd Use of Money

We have a preoccupation with money, but Jesus wouldn't even keep it on His person. He left it in the care of a thief. Perhaps that should tell us something. Legend has it that Jesus talked more about money than any other subject. That is incorrect, although He talked about money often, because the love of money is the root of all evil. It has always been the main competition God has had for the hearts of men.

These facts alone should alert us to the importance of handling money in the most circumspect fashion. Jesus was hard on people who were careless with money. He had an ill-disguised regard for shrewdness, even if it came from people of dubious character. Jesus gives a most unusual example of shrewdness in the following parable. The apparent purpose, beyond simple instruction, is to humble us.

"There was a certain rich man who had a steward, and this steward was reported to him as squandering his possessions.

"And he called him and said to him, 'What is this I hear about you? Give an account of your steward- ship, for you can no longer be a steward.'

"And the steward said to himself, 'What shall I do, since my master is taking the stewardship away from me? I am not strong enough to dig; I am ashamed to beg.

'I know what I shall do, so that when I am removed from the stewardship. They will receive me into their homes.'

"And he summoned each one of his master's debtors and he began saying to the first, 'How much do you owe my master?'

"And he said, 'A hundred measures of oil.' And he said to him, 'Take your bill and sit down quickly and write fifty.'

"Then he said to another, 'And how much do you owe?' And he said, 'A hundred measures of wheat.' He said to him, 'Take your bill, and write eighty.'

"And his master praised the unrighteousness steward because he had acted shrewdly; for the sons of this age are more shrewd in relation to their own kind than the sons of light.

"And I say to you, make friends for yourselves by means of the mammon of unrighteousness; that when it fails they may receive you into the eternal dwell- ings." (Luke 16:1-9)

What we have here is a man who knows a transition is coming in his life. He's going to be out of work. In order to make the transition a good one, he defrauds his boss. He cuts a deal with the man's customers and reduces the debt they owe. If he does them favors, he knows that when he is unemployed and has to move on, they'll give him a grand reception. He's therefore using money from the old life to ensure blessing in the new one.

The guy is a villain, but look at the Lord's response. He praised him for his shrewdness because he had acted more shrewdly than the sons of light. Then He makes this cryptic statement: *"And I say, make friends for yourself by means of the mammon of unrighteousness; that when it fails they may receive you into eternal dwellings."*

What is the message and the chastisement in this passage? Jesus is saying that this guy had more smarts than the average Christian. At least *he* was able to use money, even if it wasn't his own, to win himself friends and favor. The inference is that Christians waste their money. Jesus then exhorts us to invest our money in the kingdom, so that on the other side, in eternity, souls will be there to welcome us.

Notice, in reference to money, He uses the phrase "when it fails". He is declaring here the truth of the old adage — "You can't take it with you." At a certain point money will fail; it won't be of any use to you because you'll be dead. So now is the time to use it, not on vain pursuits, but to make sure you're welcomed into eternal dwellings. In other words, use it to spread the gospel.

But there is one undercurrent to this story. It is the Lord's grudging admiration for the steward whom he calls "shrewd". God loves it when people can distinguish between the sacred and the profane, the worthless and the valuable. He has more respect for someone who wants something that has value and goes about getting it in the wrong way, than he does for the person who has no sense of value. That is why He loved Jacob but hated Esau.

Because the proper use of money is so connected with fruitfulness, the Lord repeatedly linked both subjects. Take the long passage from Matthew 6:19-34. How you "do" this passage will have a large impact on the type of life you live, and whether it is fruitful or not. Jesus begins by telling us to lay up treasure in heaven, not on earth. He then declares that we can't serve both God and Mammon. And finally we are told not to worry about food and clothing. He concludes with the statement: *"Seek first His kingdom and His righteousness, and all these things shall be added to you" (Matt. 6:33)*.

So here He establishes three main principles: investing eternally versus investing temporally, serving God versus serving money, and making God your center and supply versus trying to meet your own needs and suffering the resultant anxiety. Much of the substance of life is wrapped up in these teachings.

In Summary

Let me summarize with a few comments. You cannot divorce the stewardship of money from who you are as a person. The more you serve God, make the kingdom your priority, and grow in the knowledge of Him, the easier time you'll have managing money. If you submit to God, grow in character, and get a vision for the eternal, you'll not be hampered by greed and waste. But as soon as you begin to backslide and leave your first love, the struggle with money begins. If God doesn't fill the God-shaped vacuum in your life, the next best thing is usually money. That's why financial responsibility is one of the clearest signs of spirituality.

We are all a "work in progress". Amongst my relationships are people at every place on the financial-management continuum. Plus, our styles vary greatly. I'm reminded of an apostle who keeps a ledger in his briefcase where he records every purchase he makes, down to the breath mints in his pocket. In his own words: "When I have to one day give an account, I won't have to scramble for receipts. It's all in here."

I know others who never let the left hand know what the right hand is doing, and yet live abundant, generous lives.

They appear to be as faithful in their stewardship as the afore-mentioned apostle. Whatever system you use, I recommend you analyze what you are currently doing and ask yourself the ultimate question: "Am I a good steward? Will I be able to stand in the Day of Judgment?"

The Stewardship of Work and Ministry

Work

The Bible declares that we're all in full-time ministry, but this is more of a mind-set than a job description. Full-time paid ministry is the calling of the very few. For the rest, our calling is the marketplace where we see an increasing emphasis on evangelism. Though our jobs may indeed be our mission field, the fact is we are paid to do something, and that something will take up the greater part of eight hours a day.

The scriptures tell us to do our work quietly and to be prepared to give to every man an answer, a reason for the hope that lies within us. We are also told to do our work heartily as unto the Lord and not unto man, for it's from the Lord that we will receive the reward. So though our work gives us oppor-tunities for the gospel, it is first of all something we are to do faithfully and diligently **unto the Lord**, and this will one day bring us great reward. So we should never see boring work as the enemy of productive activity, but as an essential and dominant part of what we daily offer to God.

Still, all of this can seem like a good idea gone awry. After all, the world *is* in fact dying in sin while we "waste" precious time making a living. But it's in sharing our common humanity with the lost, including the need to work, that we relate to them and teach them something about righ-teousness. That is how God has ordered life. There's nothing wrong with standing on a street corner handing out tracts;

it's just not a high percentage proposition. Bringing God's glory into the workplace is.

We must also remember that, historically, work was six days a week and ten to twelve hours a day. I still recall when my father, who was in the military, was given Saturday afternoon off. Reducing the workweek to five and a half days was huge progress and is a very recent occurrence. Though the fantasy of the thirty-hour workweek has run headfirst into the train wreck called "outsourcing", we must thank God for the great advances in working conditions that most of us enjoy.

We must also remember that, historically, you could be anything you wanted to be, as long as you wanted to be a soldier, merchant, farmer, tradesman, tax collector, laborer, priest or doctor. That was pretty much it. I spent many years as a career counselor, guiding people into a seemingly endless variety of sometimes mundane, but often exciting, careers. But this is purely a function of the modern labor market. It is not our God-given right to have an exciting career.

As well, the concept of a "job" is a recent thing, and dates from the Industrial Revolution. The idea of having an employer who gives you a set wage, employs you year round, and gives you security and benefits, is relatively new. Many countries have yet to experience the Industrial Revolution, and work in these places hasn't changed much from what we observe in the New Testament. We should be grateful to have jobs, since most generations simply had piecework wherever they could find it.

I say all of that to put a context around work, which is part of the package that came with the fall. It is only recently that the idea of developing your talents has had any real relevance. Historically, the average person couldn't read, had no access to education, and was born poor. Work was a practical necessity that put bread on the table. The power to gain wealth, as outlined by Solomon and others, certainly allowed for upward mobility, but only for the most wise and industrious, and usually over several generations.

We need to be grateful for progress and for our place in history. But in all of our discussion of careers, talents, vision, and God-given dreams, we have to make sure that work has its proper place in our lives. First of all, it functions as a way to bless God and support our families. Secondarily, it provides us with satisfaction and fulfillment. These two purposes don't need to compete, but they too often do.

No doubt the twenty-first century didn't catch God by surprise. He is able to program into each person's DNA a desire and talent that is needed in the marketplace. Doing that for which you have gifting and passion is honoring to God and will, no doubt, result in greater success. But we should never lose sight of the fact that work is first of all unto God and not essentially for the building of a career that can dominate our lives to the exclusion of God, ministry and family.

Our work constitutes a large part of our lives, even for a homemaker. How we steward our work will have a large impact on our eternal reward. The instructions to slaves in the Pauline letters should help us twig to the fact that it's not our position (slave or free) or our work (small or great) that determines our reward, but our attitude — faithfulness, diligence, gratefulness, etc.

If we treat work as a drudgery that we tolerate with a surly, ungrateful attitude, we will waste a great deal of our lives. To infer that this would not impact our judgment and thereby our eternal state would, of course, be ludicrous. On the other hand, to treat work as an idol that captivates our hearts and consumes our passions is an affront to a jealous God. For such a mishandling of our talents, we would likewise pay a great price.

Ministry

So let us turn now to ministry. We all have a ministry to both the church and the world but, as already stated, usually these take place outside of our commitments to family and work. However, they nevertheless must take place if we are to fulfill the call on our lives.

This section is on stewarding our gifts, as opposed to identifying them. However, it is obvious that it will be difficult to steward what we do not understand or acknowledge. One of the hardest jobs any church leader will encounter is that of helping people find a place of service. What church leader hasn't struggled with the following passage?

"We are to grow up in all aspects into Him, who is the head, even Christ, from whom the whole body, **fitted and held together by which that which every joint supplies, according to the proper working of each individual part,** *causes the growth of the body for the building up of itself in love." (Eph. 4: 15,16)*

We would all marvel at a church that operated like the well-oiled machine that we see pictured here. But the reality is very different, and it is obvious that the Body, and each church member, is a work in progress. So to make some sense out of stewarding our ministry, we must deal with what we do know, not the mystery of what we don't know. We must deal with what we currently have, not that which is yet to come.

Called, Chosen and Faithful

Let us revisit a few thoughts to gain further insight. First, God has vessels of honor in every church. These are people who have submitted to the sanctification process and are now able to assume their position in the Body. They were called of God, and after going through sanctification, they are then chosen of God. But there is a third phase — faithful. We find these three phases in Revelation 17:14: " *And those who are with Him are the called and chosen and faithful.*" The word faithful refers to another step beyond being called and chosen. It speaks of stewardship. It speaks of managing faithfully that which you've been called and chosen to do.

Called to What?

We have already said that one-talent people make up the majority of church members, so one thing must be stressed: the ministry of service or "helps" is probably where most people are called to function. As one person said, ninety percent of Christianity is just showing up. Whether it is prayer, worship, work bees, visitation or ushering, the work of God depends on the hard work and commitment of foot soldiers.

We have already seen that greatness lies in serving. The beauty of ministry is that anyone can be great because anyone can be a servant. This truth is second only to the profundity of the gospel itself: anyone can be saved because anyone can say "yes" to God. Unfortunately, because high profile ministry is perceived as having more value and status than humble service, one-talent people often miss opportunities for greatness.

The Ministry of Helps

One insight concerning the ministry of helps will assist us greatly in seeing things from God's perspective. We find a very interesting passage in 1 Corinthians 12:

And God has appointed in the church, first apostles, second prophets, third teachers, then miracles, then gifts of healings, helps, administrations, various kinds of tongues. All are not apostles are they? All are not prophets, are they? All are not teachers, are they? All are not workers of miracles, are they? All do not have gifts of healings, do they? All do not speak with tongues, do they? All do not interpret, do they? (1Cor. 12: 28 –30)

Paul gives a list of ministries and ministry gifts in verse 28, and then he gives the "all are not" list in verse 29. Guess which two he leaves out of the "all are not" list? Helps and administrations. That means we are *all* called to do these two things, but it means much more than that.

This passage is the only place where these two Greek words for *helps* and *administrations* occur in the New Testament. Secondly, they both mean the same thing. In English we would call these words synonyms. Thirdly, they are both defined as *"helps, governments"*.

This may sound confusing, because though the words are synonyms, the definitions seem contradictory. How can the word *helps* be synonymous with the word *government*? Let's look at government. The role of government is to bring order out of chaos. It is easy for us to be critical of our government, but if it was abolished tonight, tomorrow there would be anarchy and chaos.

The role of *helps* is the same — to bring order out of chaos. When you set up chairs for the service, you are bringing order out of chaos. When you help an infirm person from the car to the wheelchair, you are bringing order out of chaos. You are in essence bringing government to bear on a situation. But here is the main point.

The word *helps* is listed right along with all the other "power" ministries in 1 Corinthians 12. And this is where the confusion occurs. Let me set the scene. It's a Sunday night miracle service and someone has to set up chairs. You volunteer to help set up chairs so that the healing evangelist can minister, right? Wrong! The scripture takes a very different view.

What actually occurs is this: You minister by helping set up the chairs so that the healing evangelist can minister the message of healing. Both jobs are equally important and both are ministry. If you set up the chairs with the same faithfulness and diligence that the preacher sets up his message, you'll also receive the same reward. **There is no difference!!**

But there are many ways to set up chairs, just as there are many ways to minister healing. If the healing minister operates in pride, or if he does not keep his life free from the love of money, he may lose some or all of his reward. If the minister of helps does a poor job of setting up chairs because "it's only chairs", he may lose some or all of his reward. It is one thing to have a ministry; it is quite another to steward it wisely for the Master.

As previously stated, it is not wrong for the teaching elder to receive a double blessing, because that is what the scripture commands. It *is* wrong, however, to have a priesthood and a laity. It is wrong to treat pastors as the only "ministers" in the church when the Bible teaches that we are all ministers. All ministry is important. Someone who has the ministry of helps must steward that responsibility with no less diligence than an evangelist would his next crusade.

One last point bears repeating: The temptation of the high profile minister is to do things to be seen of men. Of this person, Jesus said, *"You already have your reward."* The prominent minister, then, runs the risk of receiving his reward now, instead of in heaven. The minister of helps has the opposite challenge. He will get little reward on earth even if he is hard-working and faithful. His leaders will appreciate him, but there is no glamour in what he does. Most of his reward comes in heaven. But because he is seldom taught this, he may be tempted to despise his calling. Should that be the case, a loss of reward would be the result.

Serving Through Gifting Versus the Gift of Serving

Many people have a keen desire to follow in the footsteps of Mother Theresa. They just want to serve the poor. That is a high calling, but unless it is *your* calling, you probably wouldn't last long in such a situation. First, you wouldn't have the grace, but secondly, you wouldn't be in God's will. We must all do our part to help the poor, but we are responsible to minister out of God's call on our life.

Our gifts are subject to the Gift-giver and cannot be cast aside, however much we may want to follow another path. We are all most effective when we are doing what we've been called and equipped to do. That is how the Body is supposed to operate as pictured in the Ephesians passage.

We must all be *willing* to do the most menial task, but it is a bad use of resources to have your pastor cleaning toilets. In this connection, I remember a story told by a famous teacher. He was about to host a camp for supporters of his ministry when the water pipe to the bathrooms started leaking — eight feet down. That's where he was when a guest speaker yelled down to him, "Could you please tell me where I can find the camp director?"

"That's me," came the voice from the pit.

"No, no, I mean so-and-so, the head of such-and-such world-wide ministry," repeated the visitor.

"That's me," came the voice from the pit.

Someone had to stop the leak, and, as this leader later explained, he was the only one around. So we must all be willing to offer the gift of service any time it is required, but as well we must be willing to serve *through* our gifting.

I asked a young man the other day what he thought his ministry was. He answered me using the language of the Romans 12 "motivational gifts" (Rom. 12: 6-8). He said his ministry was service, and I agree. But he also has natural abilities. He is an electronics engineer and he served me for about a week by debugging my computer and re-installing software. He served me through his ability. In most cases, this type of serving is the wisest stewardship of our time.

The Gifts of the Spirit

We should also note briefly the gifts of the Spirit outlined in 1 Corinthian 12. We cannot take time to teach on this except to say that just before the gifts are listed, we find this statement *"But to each one is given the manifestation of the Spirit for the common good"* (1 Cor.12:7). These gifts are under the administration of the Holy Spirit, but they are for the good of everyone.

This means that when I'm prompted by the Holy Spirit to exercise one of the gifts but fail to do so, I am denying others the benefit of that gift. That is bad stewardship. If I refuse to prophesy out of fear, for instance, I am not being a good steward. We seldom think of it this way.

Good leaders encourage their people to "step out in faith" and exercise the gifts. Good leaders exhort their people to take risks because failure is a necessary part of their development. That is correct, and God has the same attitude. But unfortunately, stewardship and accountability are usually left out of the equation.

Without a teaching on stewardship, a teaching on the gifts of the Spirit may not be very effective. If I'm not taught that I'm accountable to God, then why should I risk failure? If I'm not taught that stewarding a Corinthians 12 gift is the same as stewarding the gift of music or evangelism, then why should I struggle to develop that gift?

The Parameters of Gifting

According to Romans 12, *"…since we have gifts that differ according to the **grace** given us, let each exercise them accordingly; if prophecy, according to the proportion of his **faith…**"* (Rom. 12:6).

From this verse we can make two observations about gifts. The first is that, regardless of which gift we might discuss, some people are more gifted than others. That's called *grace*, and God gives gifts to whomever He chooses and in whatever dimension He chooses.

If grace is the tent, then faith is the tent pegs. God has put a boundary around each person's gift. It is our responsibility to find that boundary because gifts don't manifest initially in their full-blown state. Instead, they grow as we exercise them and increase in faith. Wherever there is growth, there are growing pains. We pay a price to grow in our gifts. But when we do, the Master notices. He notices how we steward our gifts and will one day reward us accordingly.

Ministry Pressures

In the exercise of any gift, we will be challenged by fear, laziness, selfishness, fatigue, and a host of other struggles. Temptations of every kind abound for active ministers: temptations to stop short of what God has called them to, as well as temptations to go beyond. There can be wrong motives, jealousies, manipulations, operating in fear, etc. There are many ways to fall short.

Greed, lust, and power are three temptations prominent ministers have to contend with. But jealousy and power-struggles can show up in the strangest places. I know a street ministry— the last place you would expect to find prideful ambition — where there are turf wars, power struggles and petty jealousies. To serve out of a pure heart and a love for the Lord is a difficult thing, even in the most humble of ministries.

The worship ministry, which I know something about, is strewn with land mines. Of course, the intent of a worship leader is to see God lifted up, but in the process he receives a lot of attention which can blur his focus. As well, there is often a tension between the pastor and worship leader as

The Invitation

they compete for time when they should be deferring to one another. Artistic people are sensitive and often melancholic, and these attributes can provide challenges in a ministry that is front and center. To steward this ministry with no concern for personal ambition, impervious to other people's opinions, is no small thing.

In any ministry there are temptations to turn back or give up. Twenty-five years ago God called me to be a worship leader in a large Pentecostal Church, and He gave me ten different confirmations. That should have been my first clue that there were going to be bumps in the road. Worship style was a contentious issue in many churches at that time, and this church was no exception.

It's a long story, but in the end the church split over that very issue. I took a lot of flack, but I knew I was in God's will. However, the pressure to quit didn't just come from "the other side". Friends who were careless with their tongues had no idea how they undermined my resolve. One told me point blank, "Get out!" But I couldn't; I knew I had a call. (As an aside, twenty years later there was a reconciliation service and both churches that came out of that split buried their differences.)

My story, I'm sure, has been repeated in the lives of ten thousand ministers. If I had quit at any point, my destiny would have been forever changed. I don't want to diminish what an omnipotent God can do with second best, but we must always strive to achieve our calling in God. Everything flows from there. I have seen so many turn back. But I have seen many others despise the shame, take the flack, and go on with God.

How many people that are now in heaven, race finished, in perpetual peace, away from the battle, have one recurrent thought: "Thank God I didn't turn back. Thank God, despite every demon in hell, and the pressure of well-meaning and not-so-well-meaning people, I did God's will." Joy floods over them as they see their inheritance and the pride in their Father's eyes.

The movement from life into eternity has many analogous expressions within life itself. We tell kids in high school that the peer pressure to do drugs, to engage in imitative behavior, and to fixate on acceptance, largely ends when you graduate. It's just a phase, and if you can survive it, then at nineteen you see it for what it was. When it's over, you look back at friends who were destroyed through drugs, sex, crime, and other high-risk behaviors, and say "thank God". Thank God I made right choices, knowing that in the end it would work out. Ministry is like that.

When we read books like <u>The Church Unleashed</u>, we think of the big picture. We think about the impact on the world if the sleeping giant is ever roused, if the troops are ever mobilized, and if every soldier takes his place in the army. We dream of a church like the one Paul writes about in Corinthians: a body where everyone knows their place and labors faithfully, causing the entire body to function properly.

But right now we are not talking about the big picture. That is, after all, God's problem. Our problem is what to do with what we've been given. If we do nothing, because we undervalue God's investment in us, then we will one day lose what He intended to be our investment in Him.

Us Versus Our Ministry

God does not view us primarily as ministers, nor does He relate to us primarily through our giftings. Neither does He ascribe worth to us on the basis of our giftings, since He Himself is the One who determined what those would be. We are God's children, and we have value from just *being* that should not be confused with anything that would involve *doing*. But in the present context we are dealing with stewardship and inheritance, not personal worth. We are dealing with God as Judge and Gift-giver, not as Father.

This is where so many people misunderstand important concepts like stewardship and inheritance. All they have ever heard is that God is our Father and Savior, and that one day we will all die and go to heaven in a seamless transition. It is true that since the resurrection has not yet occurred, no believer has yet been judged. But Judgment Day will eventually come, and when it does, the focus will be on what we have been *doing*.

But to keep things in balance, let us address the issue of *us* versus our ministry. It is hard for us to truly appreciate the depth of the statement that "God is more interested in winning all of us, than in winning all of the world *through* us." In a man-centered gospel, God is fretting over the lost; and since we are His chief agents, He's totally preoccupied with our performance. God, however, is far more interested in us than in our performance.

Derek Prince has always been one of my heroes. His teachings have been a source of great insight over the years. At sixty he was contemplating retirement, as he had already been a university professor, pastor, missionary, author, father to twelve daughters, and a number of other things. But he asked the Lord, "Is there more?" He reflects later on this with embarrassment, because with God there is always more.

And there certainly was. Derek accomplished more in the next ten years than he had in the previous forty. He almost single-handedly introduced the deliverance ministry to America. He started a radio program that even today reaches over one-third of the world, and launched other initiatives that affect millions.

At about age 70, he and his wife decided to take a sabbatical. It was a critical point in their ministry, so they decided to take six months to wait before God. Their plan was to relax, pray, and spend time with the Lord every day. A few days into the sabbatical, Derek's wife, Ruth, had an emergency. Her sister had been diagnosed with a terminal medical condition, so Ruth was called away to be at her bedside for a protracted period. Then Derek developed heart problems and had to be admitted to the hospital. What followed was a long period of weakness and treatments. It was just one thing after another.

Finally God began to speak to him. Not about his ministry, but about a personal fault: the impatience that he had never surrendered to God. Here was a man who was the head of one of the most effective ministries on earth. He takes a sabbatical to hear from God, and everything falls apart. Then when God finally does speak, it has nothing to do with the ministry. No, it's all about him, about personal issues like impatience and other "minor concerns". That's God.

Our ministry is never as important to Him as we are. Every sin is a hindrance to our union with Him and the complete surrender He is looking for. But secondly, as we saw earlier in the case of Billy Graham, revealing our sin to us is God's mercy. He knows far better than we do what will prepare our hearts for heaven. The sin of impatience in the life of a spiritual giant seems inconsequential to us. But the fact that God brought Derek's life to a halt to address it, shows us how important character truly is.

Purpose

We live in remarkable days. The Purpose Driven Life at this writing has sold 35 million copies, making it the best selling non-fiction book in American history. Because this book has been anointed seemingly above its peers, we can deduce from the title what God perceives to be the greatest need among Christians: purpose. This book, if you will, has found the heartbeat of much of the Christian world. It tells me that people need purpose, want purpose, and are willing to read and invest in trying to find that purpose.

A book can't change a person's life, but a book can give insight and revelation. Knowledge, in that sense, is power. But only by engaging the will and applying what one has read, can real change take place. Knowledge brings accountability. We are responsible for what we know. We have high literacy levels, the deposit of centuries of truth, and an ever-current word that God is releasing in the earth. In the parable of Luke 13, the person who knew His master's will but didn't do it, received more stripes than the one who didn't know His master's will.

What you and I have been called to do is written in heaven. There is nothing haphazard about the lives we have been given. We have free will within a narrow choice of options. If we are wise men, then what has already been written in heaven will be written on earth. We should be able to write down our calling, take inventory of our giftings, and be able to gauge our progress towards our destiny in Christ.

The Stewardship of Time

Math can either be fun or painful. It can be painful to take a simple calculator and see how most of us will spend our lives. Those of us who make it to the age of seventy will likely spend twenty-three years in bed, sixteen years at work or school, three years eating, three years watching TV, a thousand hours commuting and fifteen hundred hours waiting in line-ups.

Bad, huh? But it could be worse. There are poor African countries that are extremely defoliated because of all the trees that were torn down centuries ago. To find fuel for the evening meal is no small matter. Someone has to find and gather the necessary branches and sticks. For the unlucky person, this involves scouring the countryside from dawn till dusk for a one-day supply. And the next day? Well, the next day it starts all over again.

Life under communism, with its chronic shortages, was hard. It was hard doing without, but sometimes even harder to do "with" because of the insufferable patience required. One person in the family was designated as the "waiter". Dispel any thoughts of restaurant work. This waiting was in line-ups for everything from food and medicine to gasoline and cooking oil. Imagine spending the better part of your life in a line-up. That is the way it is in "modern-day" Zimbabwe and many other poverty-stricken countries ruled by tin-pot dictators.

These facts, and they *are* facts, make it obvious that we are in a contest of sorts. We live in a world where much of the external control of our time is taken from us — as much as ninety percent. Yet we have a mandate that is breathtaking, both in its scope and in its importance. How do we reconcile the two? Is it just resolve and good time management that are required?

These will obviously help, particularly resolve. I think of the circuit riders in early America who logged hundreds of thousands of miles on horseback, bringing the gospel to native peoples. I look at some of the commentaries and concordances in my library, and ponder the incessant labor that must have gone into just one of those volumes. I think of Bill Bright who, in the last two years of his life while being treated for a terminal illness, finished eighty projects, including a full-length book. Clearly, identifying your calling, subduing the flesh, and being extremely focused, are requirements to leading a productive life.

The Importance of the Internal

But as important as those things are, and despite the fact that we are all ministers, few of us will ever be in full-time ministry and generate the staggering statistics of a circuit rider. Our discipline needs to be of another kind. In the passage above, I mentioned that about ninety percent of the external control of our time has been taken from us. Happily, that still leaves the internal, and it is no small thing to say that herein lies the key for many of us. In Ephesians we have an interesting passage:

> *"Therefore be careful how you walk, not as unwise men, but as wise, making the most of your time, because the days are evil... be filled with the Spirit, speaking to one another in psalms and hymns and spiritual songs, singing and making melody with your heart to the Lord."* (Eph. 5: 15,16,18,19)

In this letter the Ephesians are told to make the most of their time because the days are evil, just as they are in the twenty-first century. But Paul's instruction to them is not to quit their jobs, restrict their sleep to three hours, and hit the gospel road. Rather, he connects "making the most of their time" to worship.

This is a bit dumfounding to the person who sees value only in what is tangibly accomplished and can be readily seen with the eye. Secondarily, ministry unto the Lord seems a poor investment when there are so many people that need ministry. Surely the Lord is the all-sufficient One, and our time is better spent with people. Encouraging people is indeed part of our mandate as the above verse suggests, but this is not to be our main focus.

Our focus is to be the infilling of the Holy Spirit. We are to sing in our hearts to the Lord. We are to rejoice always, pray without ceasing, and in all things give thanks. We are to abide in the Word, and meditate on it day and night. This brings us into union with God and the outcome is powerful: if we abide in Him and His words abide in us, we can ask what we will, and it will be done. So "without lifting a finger", we can change the external world. But there is more.

If we look after the *in*ternal, we can dwell in the *e*ternal. What is the eternal like? In the eternal, celestial courts of God, praise and thanksgiving go up before the throne night and day. That is how God wants us to live our lives, and He calls it making the most of our time. There really isn't time for worry, lust, or negative thinking when we are obeying the command to always do the following: pray, rejoice, sing, worship, give thanks, meditate, and abide in Christ. According to Psalm 1, our spirit can do this even while we are sleeping.

It is important to realize that these are commands. But how is it possible to do all of this and still function in a job, marriage, etc.? It is entirely possible, due to the fact that we are spirit beings who can abide in Christ while simultaneously performing a task and carrying on a conversation. This is the true secret to a productive life, but it certainly requires discipline. We think of the self-life as "me doing what I want to do". But, in fact, the self-life begins with "me thinking what I want to think", and it progresses from there.

If we abide in Christ, our prayers will be answered; that's what Jesus said. That is fruit. It is a rare person that won't find time for good works, but we often ignore the greater works while lamenting our inability to become more involved. Worshipping, thanking, praying, and rejoicing is as involved as it gets. No one who does these things will lose their reward. No one who does these things will be unproductive.

Character Is Fruit

But these inner disciplines don't stop there. In Peter's second epistle we are told to grow in certain character qualities: "*...applying all diligence, in your faith supply moral excellence, and in your moral excellence, knowledge, and in your knowledge, self-control, and in your self-control.... For if these qualities are yours and are increasing, they render* *you neither useless nor unfruitful in the true knowledge of our Lord Jesus Christ "* (II Pet. 1:8).

The construction of this verse is in the negative, so let us put it in the positive. If we have these qualities, we will do more than acknowledge a relationship to Christ; we will be useful and fruitful. We have said it before, but we need to say it again: character is fruit. Who we are is eternal fruit, not just what we do. Who we are, to a great extent, comes from choices we make. These choices come out of how we think. How we think is determined by our obedience to engage in the inner disciplines we have just discussed.

So making the most of our time involves spiritual disciplines that exalt God, touch the unseen world through prayer, and forge character in us that is everlasting in nature. This is fruit. And the nice thing about this kind of fruit is that it almost always passes the test of pure motives. None of this is seen of men. By contrast, some of the most visible and vibrant good works in history may not survive the fire of judgment because they were done to be seen of men.

We saw earlier that just our attitude towards our work can result in great reward. If, while we are faithfully carrying out our duties, we simultaneously engage in praise and prayer, we will have a fruitful life. How easy it is to miss these two points and thereby squander a good portion of our lives. As the scripture says, we perish for lack of knowledge. Unfortunately, what perishes is not just the temporal, but also the eternal.

If we don't understand and act on these things, we may one day be surprised. We may end up with an unfruitful life, not because of some terrible sin, but because of a mere oversight— we forgot to engage our spirits. To put it in the vernacular: "We had to be there anyway, so we might as well have gotten something done." Translation: Something has to fill our days, so it may as well be gracious and God-honoring; something has to fill our minds, so it may as well be elevating and praiseworthy.

The concept of time is inextricably linked with that of priorities. If you work in any but the most routine job, you must prioritize your assignments because "there is never enough time". The same is true of our personal lives. As husbands we have to prioritize the "honey do" list that magically appears every Saturday morning. But in a more global sense, we also have to consider the "big five" and how we allocate time to them. The big five are: God, family, job, ministry, and everything else.

Priorities

Following God does require thinking outside the box. Often in a discussion of managing their time, people will describe their priorities in this manner: God first, then family, then job, then ministry, then everything else. It sounds right, and it is definitely progress over what the previous generation would have said, but is it correct?

I remember seeing the daughter of World Vision founder, Bob Pierce, in an interview once. Musing on the problems they had had in their family life, she laid no blame. She said her father was simply a reflection of his generation, and that they were taught that ministry came before family. Sad, but true.

But although we have made progress, the priorities listed by most people in our day aren't God's either, because He has only one — Himself. "*Seek first the kingdom of God and His righteousness,*" we are told. The Greek word for "first" is that which has no antecedent. We are to seek the Kingdom first, second, and third, etc. No nice neat little boxes; life in God doesn't come that way. If we are to love the Lord with **all** our heart, soul, mind and strength, there really isn't much left over for other "priorities".

So what is the answer? The answer is that we are to put God first and He will direct us as to the management of our time. For instance, there are times when people with itinerant ministries have to leave their families for prolonged periods. They shouldn't feel guilty about this, as if they are putting ministry before family. The best benefit that can come to their family is if they themselves are obedient to God. If the evangelist, for instance, is obedient to God, God will not only look after his family while he is away, but a special blessing will accrue to them. For one thing, they will share in the eternal reward.

It can work the other way around as well. A pastor with an international ministry once took leave from his work for six months to look after his errant brother. Would God actually ask a person to do this? Yes, He would and does, but many aren't listening because of the mistaken priority issue.

There are even times when God may ask us to put our job first, and if we are in His will, He will look after the other areas. All of this involves walking in the Spirit. It is far easier to have a formula, because it lessens the burden to hear His voice. But if our first priority was hearing His voice and heeding it, the other priorities would fall into place. Plus we'd be spared much needless pain and wasted effort.

Conclusion

In conclusion, there are many poems, songs, and other art forms dedicated to the subject of time. The shortness of life has intrigued men throughout history. "I will only pass this way once" is a phrase that touches something deep in us, as does the conclusion: " If there is any good that I can do this day, let me therefore do it."

In <u>Don't Waste Your Sorrows,</u> the author exhorts us to extract value from the things that come wrapped in suffering. But even more so, to redeem the time. This is very reminiscent of a story from the <u>Book of Virtues.</u> A person was given a device that would allow him to pull a string whenever difficulties arose. The string represented time, and he could avoid the worst parts of life simply by pulling on the string.

This he did, but later lamented how much shorter his life had been, and how some of the difficult moments were also the most poignant. By foregoing the one, he had also lost the other. Life in the end was easy, but correspondingly shallow. By trying to have only good times, time, the most precious commodity of all, had been squandered.

The shortness of life is a great enigma. "Time flies" is the most enduring cliché. There is never enough, and most of us feel cheated no matter at what age we go to the grave. Part of the reason is that we are meant to live forever, and will surely do so. But the other reason is that we can never accomplish even a small part of what we want with the time we are given. This presents all of us with choices, sometimes hard choices.

If you are someone who truly engages life, you must accept the inevitable frustration that this will create. But in the end, the wise man makes a resolute decision: I have all eternity ahead of me, so let me expend my brief temporal life in the pursuit of that for which I was created. Let me serve God with all my heart and despise the trappings of this world. Let me go to my grave and stand before God, having made the most of my time.

But there is more to stewardship than the wise use of our time. There is also the need to reach our *appointed* time. This is a separate subject and must be dealt with as such. Let us look, then, at the whole matter of longevity and the role we play in it.

The Stewardship of the Body

The Cost of Premature Death

How long do you want to live? We've all been asked that question on occasion. Most people respond without hesitation, and I have found the figure to be fairly predictable if somewhat optimistic. The Bible is probably our best guide as to the length of a realistic lifespan. And, not surprisingly, it agrees with the actuarial tables of the insurance industry. We are told in Psalm 90 that the days of man are seventy, or, if due to strength, eighty.

Right now the average lifespan in the US is seventy-seven: seventy-three for men and eighty-one for women. So living to eighty, which is what most people want and expect, is both scriptural and attainable. However, the phrase "due to strength" suggests that the last ten years are conditional. We will look at those conditions and at the whole issue of premature death.

I read the obituaries every day, and it is not readily apparent that the average life span is 77. If I didn't know this, I would put it much lower — about ten years lower. So many seem to die in their fifties and sixties. As well, perhaps now that I am sixty, my definition of old has changed, and it seems all the more tragic when people die "before their time". Why is this happening? And equally important, does it even matter, since for a Christian death is graduation?

First of all, yes, it does matter. The body is the receptacle for the eternal spirit, so we need it to do the work of the Lord. When it dies, all ability to "store up treasure" dies with it, and so the timing of the body's death is important to our eternal state. When discussing death with an unbeliever one usually encounters fatalism. Most believers, on the other hand, have a sense of optimistic destiny. I understand the unbeliever's fatalism, but when I note the diet of many Christians, I wonder at their optimism.

In Psalm 139 we find this telling statement: "*And in Thy book they were all written, the days that were ordained for me, when yet there was not one of them.*" The word "ordained" speaks of the length of life God has set for each of us. In Ephesians 2:10 we have the other key element: "*For we are His workmanship, created in Christ Jesus for good works, which God prepared beforehand that we should walk in them.*"

Two things we can know for sure about life and death. First, God has ordained a life span for each individual; and secondly, He has determined the works that are to be accomplish during that span. But just because God has ordained a life span, it doesn't necessarily follow that we will reach it. However, it does follow that if we don't reach it, we can't possibly accomplish all the works He has for us.

In a previous chapter I mentioned the experience of Brian Bailey, a well-known Bible teacher. He had the experience of dying at a rather young age. I have heard him recount the details of what happened as his spirit left his body. He was drawn upwards towards the Lord but had an encounter that left him shaken. He was a faithful pastor at the time, so he should have rejoiced as he neared the gates of heaven. But instead he felt a sense of dread. He knew he was dying before his time. With a sense of anguish, he exclaims on a tape recording of his experience: "Whatever you do, don't die before the time. For the agony of seeing what you were meant to accomplish, and to see that you fell short, is worse than any pain on earth."

He talked of the Elijah experience, and how people, in acute depression, ask to be taken home before their time. This, he admonished, is a huge mistake. There are some who have reached a place in God where He may indeed grant that request. But the outcome will be eternal loss. Brian urged his listeners with great intensity to cry out for the strength and mercy to finish the race, knowing the severity of falling short.

Further to the matter of premature death, Brian quoted Psalm 90 to illustrate that our manner of life can influence our lifespan. If we eat well and look after our body, we may extend our life by at least a decade. Later Brian questioned God as to why he had had that experience and he was told, "so that you might warn my people." The end of the story was that Brian was resuscitated and is still alive at this writing. As a Bible teacher he has many messages, but one of the strongest is a warning to God's people against disrespecting the body and going home early.

All of this suggests something that we must be cognizant of with respect to physical life. It can be stolen from us in any number of ways, and the eternal consequences are serious. Our health has to be managed or stewarded just like our money or anything else we've been given. But before we look more closely at our health, let us look at some other causes of premature death.

Causes of Premature Death

We are all in a battle, and the bullets are real. We must never forget that. There was an apostle in Central America who had a significant ministry in a very spiritually oppressive area. He was tragically killed in a freak accident in midlife. After his death it was discovered that he had evaded taxes and mishandled funds. We can never know for sure, but his associates speculate that, through breaking the law, he had left a chink in his armor that the enemy was able to penetrate and exploit. The result was premature death.

Another major apostle from Australia was living in an adulterous relationship. Despite entreaties from friends, associates, and prominent ministers, he persisted in this lifestyle. A short time later, he developed an aggressive form of brain cancer and died quickly, apparently without repentance. Those who witnessed the event had no doubt that his moral failure led to his premature death. We can only guess at the number of those who have suffered a similar fate. People with great spiritual authority have to be doubly careful to walk in integrity, or the results can be disastrous.

We are fond of saying that there are no accidents in the Kingdom of God. If that is indeed true, then there is much human error that leads to devastating consequences. To say that God *allows* something is very different from saying that He intends it. Close to where I live, a van carrying a group of Christian athletes was involved in a terrible accident on their way to a tournament. A pastor and several students were killed and others were left with crippling injuries. There is little doubt, from the details that emerged, that proper precautions weren't taken, and that driver error was the most likely cause. Stories like this impress upon us not only the need for prayers of protection, but also the need for wisdom.

Generational curses are another thing that can lead to an early death. God's people perish for lack of knowledge. With proper teaching, those curses can be broken and lives can be spared. There are many ministries now that are active in the area of deliverance, and there are many success stories of people set free from generational curses.

The list goes on. A search of the Bible will uncover causes of premature death almost too numerous to mention — everything from pride and rebellion, to eating the Lord's Supper in an unworthy manner. In summary, a premature death is tragic and has eternal consequences that most of us are unaware of. To finish the number of days God has given to us is, in fact, quite an achievement. Like every aspect of our walk, success in this area will require diligence, wisdom, godliness and prayer.

Fearfully and Wonderfully Made

We must remember that the body has honor. There have been heresies, especially in the early church, that dismissed the body as unimportant. Heretics made such a separation between the spirit and the body that sins of the flesh were regarded as acceptable and inconsequential. Only the eternal spirit mattered.

However, because we are fearfully and wonderfully made, the body deserves the respect and treatment due God's highest creation. We are told to *"present our bodies as a living sacrifice, holy and acceptable unto the Lord" (Rom. 12:1)*. We read further in the writings of Paul that *"the body is for the Lord, and the Lord is for the body"(1Cor. 6:13)*. And lest we not give the matter its due gravity, we are given the stern warning: *"The body is the temple of the Holy Spirit, if any one defiles the temple, him will God destroy" (1Cor. 3:17)*.

We are told of the gravity of sexual sin with the caution that *"every other sin that a man commits is outside his body, but the immoral man sins against his own bo*dy *"*(1Cor. 6:18). So clearly, the body has a sacred quality about it. And for final proof, we need only consider this statement in 1 Corinthians: *"You are not your own, you are bought with a price, therefore* **glorify God in your body."**

It seems that heresy and hedonism go hand in hand in almost every era, and ours is no exception. We live in a youth culture, or a "cult of the body". A value has been placed on the body that is very different from what God intended. To society, the importance of the body is related to secular values, many of them perverse in nature.

These values play out in many ways: the culture of narcissism and its preoccupation with all things "me"; the high divorce rate and the requirement to stay attractive for the "hunt"; the fascination with youth and beauty that pushes many to have plastic surgery; mass marketing that has created a mania for diets and fitness programs; the requirement to look young in order to compete for jobs in a culture where age is devalued; the dearth of spiritual values, which places more emphasis on having a perfect body; the fix-it mentality that sees the aging body as something that is broken and needs to be fixed; the obsession with sex and its connection to beauty; the celebrity syndrome where growing numbers are fixated on a famous person, usually an actor or actress who is a sex symbol; the pressure on young women to be thin, leading to many eating disorders; and lastly, the non-stop media barrage that endows a pretty face and firm body with value. Anything less is unacceptable.

It's important that we have balance. We must not neglect the body, nor do things that would weaken it, resulting in premature death. But neither must we give it attention beyond what God intended. Clearly, the exaltation of the body that we see nowadays in all its perverse forms is idolatry.

Poor Health

So in this study of the body's importance, we come finally to the greatest cause of premature death — poor health. Some day millions of Christians will stand before God, robbed of years of fruitful living, because they didn't look after their health. They may have run the race and kept the faith, but they will not have finished the course. On Judgment Day, they will see the works and service that they were destined to perform, and they will grieve at the loss.

There are, of course, illnesses and deaths that are unpreventable. But the vast majority of illness in western society is preventable. Some of the prevention takes the form of exercise and discipline. Some of it involves breaking bad habits that have direct links to certain diseases. But sadly, the culprit in most preventable diseases is, quite simply, the western diet.

It is shocking to discover how many people are committing the same dietary sins as their parents, despite the deluge of nutritional information in the last decade. Perhaps it is all too much to assimilate. Many of us are the victims of the propaganda machine issuing almost daily from vested interest groups: Big-Pharma, Big-Medicine, Big-Agra, Big-Business, and even Big-Nutrition.

The Tragic Irony

All the clichés apply and, unfortunately, they are all too true. There **is** a cure for cancer, and it is found in your cupboard. The fourth-leading cause of death in the US is medical error — doctors. There is a reason for the signs in every zoo saying "Don't Feed the Animals." Zookeepers know that if the animals eat our food, they'll get sick, like us. There's not much money to be made in preventing disease, but billions to be made in treating it.

Modern medicine seems convinced that we are all suffering from a pill deficiency, and thus that is their treatment of choice. Doctors treat symptoms, not causes. Most four-year medical programs devote less than thirty hours to nutrition. Nutrition, on the other hand, is the primary topic taught in Veterinary Colleges. The reason is that farmers can't get Medicare for their animals, so they *have* to keep them healthy. If cows were fed Kraft Dinner and Twinkies, we'd have the animal rights people down our throats. But for mere humans, who cares! Or at least that's the way it seems.

We could go on, but it is obvious that to finish our race, we're going to have to take control of our health. To eat the western diet and expect a doctor to pick up the pieces when things fall apart is worse than foolhardy.

It is sinful.

Diabetes

Imagine that you were scheduled to die next Tuesday and someone stepped out of the shadows with the power to offer you a reprieve: You would not die as scheduled, but would, in fact, live another 11.6 years. Think of the implications for your family and loved ones, and think of the eternal consequences for yourself. Think of the service that would still lie ahead for you. Think of the tithes and offerings that you could still send ahead for eleven more years. Think of the additional prayers and acts of kindness that are possible. Think of the worship and growth in godliness. The eternal benefits go on and on.

But why did I choose 11.6 years? Why is that figure significant?

That figure relates to the disease of diabetes. It's the number of fewer years you'll live if you are diagnosed with diabetes after age forty. In just the last ten years, the prevalence of diabetes has increased forty percent and now affects 17 million to 20 million in the US. That represents about two million Christians. Approximately 2,000 people are being diagnosed with type 2 diabetes each day in the US. Type 2 diabetes used to be called "adult-onset" diabetes, but that term has been dropped since type 2 is now being found in children.

It has already been estimated that of the children born in the year 2000, about 35% of them will be diagnosed with diabetes sometime in their life. Fully 50% of the population currently have glucose-handling problems. There are five known risk factors for the disease. But apart from genetics, for non-smoking, non-drinking Christians, it really comes down to two — diet and obesity. And since obesity is caused by bad diet, for *most* of us the equation is pretty simple: diabetes equals bad diet.

Figures That Don't Lie

Let's pause and consider for a moment. About 40% of all deaths are from heart and stroke, 30% are from cancer, and diabetes is skyrocketing. Without even considering all the autoimmune, brain, and neurological diseases, there are three inescapable facts. First, the vast majority of us will die from one or more of these major diseases. Secondly, these diseases are largely preventable. And finally, preventable disease will rob us of vital years that God intended us to have.

We will die before our time.

When Christians die of cancer or heart disease in their late seventies, we tend to think their mission is done and that God has called them home. Somehow this sounds too convenient. However well we may have lived, if we die of heart disease, we are probably dying prematurely. Bill Bright and Derek Prince did a major part of their life's work after they turned eighty. We must never treat these diseases as anything but the enemy of our mission.

The answer is not to feel guilty if we contract these diseases, or judge others that do. The answer is to make changes now, so that if we do contract these ailments, we'll at least have the comfort of knowing that we did our best. That is all we can do in the toxic environment of the 21st century. Like most things in life, there are no guarantees.

It might be beneficial to look at a couple of common nutritional sins before we move on. Some might find the inclusion of this material in a "spiritual" book to be odd. But we have all said at one time or another "my finances are under attack" or "my ministry is under attack" or even "my health is under attack". We know the enemy attacks us. But in the latter case we may not have realized the nature of the attack.

We accept that there is a "world system" run by Satan which is so corrupt that we are commanded to *"love not the world"*. We accept that the enemy is trying to use the public school system to indoctrinate our children, the entertainment world to corrupt our morals, commerce and finance to get us into debt, etc. But we have failed to realize that he is using Big Agra and Big Business to destroy our bodies.

Avoiding "Nutritional" Poisons

The God who made every living thing with a nutrient requirement, also made the satisfying of that need very simple.

Wouldn't you, if you were God? Up until a hundred years ago you didn't have to be smart to eat well. Apart from a few poisonous weeds, it is very difficult to get sick or suffer deficiency from eating natural, unprocessed foods. Wild animals don't die of heart disease, cancer and complications from diabetes. Neither do "lost tribes". But the corporate machine has "fixed" all of that, and now to avoid both poisons and deficiencies, you need to be either lucky or smart.

So let's get smart about a couple of things.

Trans Fats

The diet in 1900 was rich in animal fats from meat, butter, cream, lard, milk and eggs. Heart disease, cancer, and diabetes were virtually unknown. Between 1910 and 1950, deaths from Myocardial Infarction, where a blood clot blocks an artery to the heart, rose from 3,000 to 500,000.

During that forty-year period, people were persuaded to give up their healthy, natural fats for polyunsaturated vegetable oils: namely, liquid vegetable oils, shortenings and margarine. That is really all we need to know. All the so-called "studies" that demonize natural fats as God created them fall somewhere between misguided and fraudulent. The truth is really very simple: according to Stanford University, 75% of the plaque found in arteries is not saturated fat or cholesterol; it is trans fats. So what are trans fats?

To create vegetable oils that are solid at room temperature, a process called hydrogenation was developed. This gave us margarine, and with it, trans fats. Trans fats are corrupted fat molecules that the body must use if it can't find enough natural fat. Recent studies show that the cells in the average person are now 20% trans fats, whereas the figure should be zero. Fries, chips, and other junk food have tested out at a whopping 49% trans fats. These fats are now found in 40% of all packaged and processed foods. On food labels they usually hide under the name "partially-hydrogenated vegetable oil". They impede cell function, lower immunity, and contribute to a host of diseases.

Then there are vegetable cooking oils. When vegetable cooking oils are used in deep-frying or in regular meal preparation, they produce a witch's brew of altered fats that are literally poison. I didn't say they are *like* poison, I said they *are* poison. Some might find that extreme, but not Udo Erasmus, the world's foremost authority on fats and oils. He confirmed this to me in a recent conversation. To turn corn, for instance, into Mazola oil, ten steps are required. Let's look at a few.

The first three are degumming, chemical extraction, and expelling. Then we have deodorizing to get rid of the smell, bleaching to eliminate the gray color, and dyes to create an appealing end-product. Most of this happens at high temperatures. The result is junk oil, devoid of nutrient and full of chemical residues and corrupted fat molecules. It is the equivalent of white bread and white sugar. Heating these oils just adds insult to injury.

Trans fats won't kill you quickly, and you'll never see them listed on a death certificate under "cause of death". But they are an underlying cause or contributing factor in a multitude of diseases. If you have good genes you may beat the odds, but any prudent person who wants to finish the race must avoid these fats.

Look at the wording splashed across the food products in your local supermarket. Last year the rage was "whole wheat", this year "organic", next year "zero trans fat". Big Business knows a good thing when they see it. But the word "zero" as defined by government watchdogs allows for a certain percentage. Don't be misled. Both "whole wheat" and "organic" have now been redefined as well. They are very clever. We just have to be more so.

There is far too much emphasis nowadays placed on heredity — having bad genes. The appeal of this approach is that it makes us all hapless victims who are at the mercy of fate. It discourages personal responsibility. So what is the balance?

Heredity loads the gun, but lifestyle pulls the trigger.

Don't pull the trigger. On bread, use butter; for salad dressing, use extra-virgin olive oil; for cooking, use organic coconut oil. Fifty years ago there was a study done on the health benefits of coconut oil. But **refined** coconut oil was used and, big surprise, the findings were bad news. Many scientists are caught in a time warp and today they still quote that study to discredit coconut oil. They demonize it with the word "saturated". But God gave coconut oil to the Polynesians the same as He gave blubber to the Eskimos. Neither group had any heart disease till they switched to the perverted fats recommended by scientists.

Be Aware

Fake foods and artificial sweeteners are a source of great concern. Aspartame, sold under the brand name, NuraSweet, is a neurotoxin implicated in many diseases. As the lawsuits against aspartame mount, it is being quietly withdrawn. Splenda is the new darling of the fake food/artificial sweetener crowd and it already holds 50% of the sweetener market, but it presents nearly as many problems as aspartame. On food labels it is usually called "sucralose". One other sweetener to be noted is High Fructose Corn Syrup. HFCS now represents 40% of caloric sweeteners added to foods and beverages, and it is the primary sweetener now added to soft drinks. Again, it is a bad news story. The key is to use natural sweeteners like honey, maple syrup, or the natural calorie-free sweetener, stevia.

Then we have MSG, a flavor-enhancing neurotoxin that is added to all fast foods simply because it is addictive — it makes people eat more. But it is also a contributing factor in much disease. We must police ourselves to stay healthy; the government and the marketplace won't do it for us.

Nutritional Summary

As a society we have complicated a very simple matter. The mega-food industry takes most of the nutrients out of the things we buy in the packaged and frozen part of the supermarket and sells them back to us as health food in the pharmacy section. If that was their only crime, our outrage would be justified. But they go further. In order to make this "residue" taste like food, they add a witch's brew of sugar, salt, chemical additives, and bad fats. The result is disease and obesity.

Obesity is currently a plague, and it is a terminal disease in the sense that it'll kill you one way or another. It is a risk factor in virtually every major disease. But obesity has its roots in wrong eating, not in eating too much. When the foods we eat are primarily refined starches, sugars and oils, obesity is almost inevitable.

These foods are poorly utilized by the body so they are generally stored as fat. But because they possess so little nutrient, the vast majority of people now suffer from sub-clinical malnutrition — a deficiency of one or more vitamins or minerals. Thus we have the curious paradox in America of millions of overweight people who are malnourished.

All issues of diet ultimately come down to one simple choice: natural versus processed. The culprits are white bread, white sugar, white rice, white pasta, white eggs, white oil, and white salt. Yes, even white salt. We think of salt as sodium chloride, but sodium chloride is what you get when you process salt. Real salt has the same eighty-four elements that are present in blood plasma. Real salt is a healing force, not something to be avoided. Quality sea salt is vastly superior to regular salt. But even sea salt has to be processed to remove impurities. Crystal salt is the ideal form and is available over the Internet.

Changing your diet doesn't happen overnight. My wife and I have been at it for thirty years. Our intake of processed foods and poisonous additives is minimal, but we also have enough faith and freedom in Christ to eat and enjoy whatever is set before us. And realistically, it's not the occasional nutritional indiscretion that is going to compromise your health, but rather decades of constant abuse.

It can take more time and money to eat properly, but it's false economy to cut corners. Ill health is an expensive proposition both in time and money. You pay now or you pay later. The bottom line is that looking after our bodies is the right thing to do, and our stewardship in this area will impact our judgment.

There is a tendency to say, "It's all too complicated; I'll just trust God." That is not a good idea. *"A wise man sees a danger and avoids it; a fool goes on and is punished"* (Prov.22:3). If we drive on the left hand side of the road in America and trust God, we are foolish; and if we eat poison and trust God, we are also foolish. Every once in a while a cult springs up and drinks poison in a gross misapplication of a well-known scripture verse. And they die — every time. *"Thou shalt not tempt the Lord thy God"* (Matt.4:7 KJV).

The fact is, ignoring health risks under the guise of trusting God hasn't helped the millions of Christians who die every year from cancer, heart disease, and other preventable conditions. To live a long life, we must survive our culture, not embrace it. Nowadays, shopping has gone from a harmless pleasure to a survival game. "How can I outsmart the merchants of death?" is the mindset we need to have as we push-cart our way past the poisonous products with their "low-fat, Vitamin D added" come-ons. "Stick to the outer perimeter of the supermarket" is still one of the best bits of advice you'll ever get.

Spirits of Infirmity

The Bible makes mention of "spirits of infirmity". While I do think it is possible to have a cancer that has its root in the spiritual, I think it a most unlikely source. Blaming cancer on demons does have a certain appeal because it absolves us of responsibility. But the fact is, cancer can be induced at will in lab test animals using the very same things they put in our food, cosmetics, building supplies, and medicine chests. This largely takes it out of the realm of the spiritual and puts it right back where it belongs — in our laps. Satan is far more strategic and high tech than some guy in a red suit caught in a time warp. By corrupting men and having them corrupt the food chain, he gets more bang for his buck.

There is no need to use demons; our diet will do the job.

The Mind-Body Connection

Henry Wright, a Christian minister, has done much work on the mind-body connection. He attributes much disease to negative emotions such as fear, anxiety and stress. No doubt he is correct. These things are sin, and we must acknowledge them as such if we are to walk in health.

There is now solid scientific evidence to prove that our moods, emotions and general outlook have a direct measurable impact on our immune system. The proof comes from psycho-neuro-immunology (PNI), a new medical specialty. In a nutshell, the limbic system of the brain and the central nervous system release certain hormones that fit into receptor sites all over the body, causing them to release various secretions. The quality of these secretions depends on our emotions, beliefs, and prevailing psychological orientation. Since these secretions determine whether the immune system is boosted or weakened, switched on or off, how we think and feel is critical to health. *"A joyful heart is good medicine."*

Negative emotions weaken the immune system and lead to illness. But *recovery* from illness is very much dependant on thoughts, attitudes and emotions as well. In a now classic study, British researcher Stephen Greer interviewed a group of women three months after they had undergone mastectomies to find out how they were coping. He found four distinct types among them. These he categorized respectively as fighting spirit, denial, stoic acceptance, and hopelessness. After five and ten-year follow-ups, it was discovered that 80% of the fighters, but only 20% of the hopeless had survived. These rates had nothing to do with medical prognosis.

God's Provision for Health

The plan of redemption is much more than simply a death on the cross, and its purchasing power is much greater than the saving of our souls. The Greek word *sozo* meaning "to save" appears in scriptures that refer to the saving of the eternal soul, but also in verses referring to our body and even our mind. God wants to save the whole man and He has made provision for it. Why, then, is it so hard to appropriate healing in the body and mind?

At least fifty times I've heard someone ask, "How come there's so much healing in third world countries, but so little here?" In answer, a list of possible reasons is usually offered up. All theories aside, we need to simply obey the scriptures. Even though James 5 links healing to repentance, we seldom offer this as a solution.

What seems absent from the healing line is dialogue. As leaders, we've all had people come to the altar for prayer whose mere appearance should send off warning signals. Many are obese, and yet we don't question their lifestyle or mindset to see if they are in a position to receive healing. It is not unkind to do so. If they are living on white bread and margarine, diet coke and chips, will God heal? If they harbor guilt, anxiety, fear and bitterness, will He heal? Does God heal self-inflicted wounds? I don't know, but I do know this: If He did heal us from self-inflicted wounds, without a change in attitude and behavior, we'd be back in the healing line a year later.

We need wisdom to safely navigate a life that is filled with minefields. The reason I say that is because of the law of sowing of reaping. One of the corollaries states the following: Ignorance that you are sowing will not prevent a harvest. If a man crosses a field with a bag of seed over his shoulder and there is rip in the corner that spreads seed, there will be a harvest. The fact that he is unaware of the rip will not prevent the harvest.

If we sow anger in our children, we will reap a harvest of bitterness. Our ignorance of that fact won't prevent the harvest. If we eat poison disguised as food, we will reap a harvest of disease, though our intentions may have been the best.

Intentions don't count; wisdom does.

In Proverbs 3 we find a landmark verse on longevity: "*How blessed is the man who finds wisdom...long life is in her right hand; and in her left hand are riches and honor.*" The three things that men crave the most, long life, riches and honor, are all found in one thing — wisdom. There are many other verses that take up this refrain. And how do we get wisdom according to Proverbs? By meditating on God's Word. It is true that the meditation itself is "*health to their bones*" (Proverbs 4:22). But wouldn't you rather not get sick in the first place? God's Word is preventative medicine primarily because it makes us wise and teaches us how to live.

Wise people respect their body too much to be dictated to by appetite and ignorance. If food is the life source for their body, they want to know what they are eating. They know that "you *are* what you eat." They observe others and draw conclusions. They know that you have to learn from the mistakes of others, because life is too short to make them all yourself. So they don't just blindly trust doctors but learn for themselves what causes illness. They gain knowledge, develop understanding, and make wise decisions and wise food choices. They are also wise in their refusal to submit to bitterness and fear. They know it rots the bones.

I want to be wise, don't you?

Conclusion to Stewardship

I live in a city that is dominated by one major company — Canfor. This company produces lumber, and they pay a high tariff on all lumber sold to the US, their major market. Thanks to having the most modern sawmills in the world, even with this crushing tariff, Canfor makes a profit. This didn't happen by accident.

Every year, like any other company, the board at Canfor has to decide what part of profits goes into research and development, new plant and equipment, dividends to share-holders, and salaries and bonuses. For ten years, the CEO and board at Canfor have poured money into new tech-nology, and this has turned out to be their lifesaver. They can still turn a profit while older, inefficient mills in the area are going broke.

Corporate stewardship is an awesome responsibility. What's at stake is not just hundreds of employees and thou-sands of shareholders, but the welfare of entire communi-ties. The executives have received a sacred trust, and the decisions they make have to ensure that this great company is around for decades to come. We may think to ourselves, "I sure wouldn't want that responsibility." The fact is, their responsibility pales in comparison to ours.

We are handling an account for the most-high God. We are stewards of resources that determine whether people go to heaven or hell. We are not dealing in bricks and mortar, but eternal souls. We are not dealing with corporate profits, but eternal fruit. We don't retire and turn over the reins; we die and give an account to Him Who reigns. There is no busi-ness in the universe as serious as this. Nowhere else are the stakes this high. This fact alone should add a note of sobriety to everything we do. The opposite of sobriety is not joy; it is foolishness.

Let us be wise and sober stewards of all that has been committed to us.

SEVEN

The Judgment of Character

At one time she was the number one ranked tennis player in the city. She was a brilliant woman and a rising star in the organization where I worked. But life dealt her a cruel blow. While on a special assignment away from friends and family, she suffered a complete mental breakdown. Now, unable to work, she lived alone on a small pension.

Heavy-duty psychiatric drugs were the only thing that stood between her and the "voices". But the drugs came with a cost. They sapped her energy, robbed her of sleep, bloated her body, and kept her imprisoned in that gray apartment. She couldn't so much as cook a meal or walk down the street to the corner. At least once a month she would phone me at the office. I spent hours answering her questions as she struggled to come to a place of faith in Jesus Christ. And finally she did.

Seventeen years — that's how long it took.

But then our relationship changed. Plagued with months of insomnia, it was my turn to crash and burn. Now she was the one encouraging me. I had to take early retirement and relinquish my role as worship leader at church. Apart from that, my life was intact - as intact, that is, as a life can be when suffering the torments of sleep deprivation.

Not so with her. Her best years had been stolen. There would be no husband, no children, no grandchildren, no career, and no dynamic ministry — at least not without a miraculous intervention by God. But to her it didn't matter. She had found the Lord, and that was enough.

From her sparse apartment she would phone me periodically to encourage me. Almost weekly she would write me a letter, and frequently she mailed me books that had inspired her. Her only desire, as she put it, was to serve God and find someone to bless and encourage. I was light-years ahead of her theologically and had been active in ministry for decades, but I was deeply moved whenever we talked.

I was conscious of the fact that I was dealing with a very special person — someone who had lost everything, but found God in a way that few of us do. And in doing so, something had been transformed — her character. She lives a life that most people would find depressing, yet she does it with joy and thanksgiving. I have become acutely aware of how her life is touching the heart of God and of the glory that will one day be hers.

Character

A quick glance at the Beatitudes tells us that the sum total of a person's life is more than just their good deeds, their faithfulness and their sanctification. We are told that the meek will inherit the earth, the merciful shall receive mercy, the peacemakers will be called sons of God, and the humble will be given the kingdom of heaven.

Our character draws a response from God, often an "in kind" response:

>*"With the kind Thou dost show Thyself kind;*
>*With the blameless Thou dost show Thyself blameless*
>*With the pure Thou dost show Thyself pure;*
>*And with the crooked Thou dost show Thyself astute."* (Psalm 18: 25,26)

While it is clear that there is only one judgment, it is also clear that what we *are* is as important as what we have accomplished. All the promises in the book of Revelation are to overcomers. Overcoming is an act, to be sure, but it is much more than that. It is an act that issues out of certain character qualities — qualities like perseverance, long-suffering, and steadfastness. We are told numerous times that he who endures to the end will be saved. Endurance is part and parcel of overcoming, and overcoming is part and parcel of inheriting all things.

We send our good works on ahead, but we take our character with us. Character represents a promise — a promissory note to pay, so to speak. Paul tells us: *"For bodily discipline is only of little profit, but godliness is **profitable** for all things, since it holds **promise** for the present life and **also for the life to come"** (1Tim. 4:8).* So character represents two things: promise and profit. To teach conformity to Christ as a duty and desire is to see only half the picture. The other half is promise and profit. In the life to come we'll be grateful for every earthly trial. Though painful at the time, these trials forge in us a godly character that is eternal in nature.

We are told that " *the trial of our faith...may be found to result in praise and glory and honor at the revelation of Jesus Christ" (1Pet. 1:7).* Think about that. The mere trial of our faith, which is a brief temporal thing, has many benefits. But there are three benefits that are staggering.

At the revelation of Jesus Christ we will receive praise, glory and honor. These may seem like mere words, but a little meditation will allow the full weight of it to sink in. During life God tries us so that the resultant character can be paraded before the host of heaven with accolades of unfathomable esteem. He doesn't have to; He wants to. This is the *"eternal weight of glory"* that Paul elsewhere refers to.

In II Peter we are given a pre-judgment checklist that we do well to consider:

*"For this reason, make every effort to add to your faith, goodness; and to your goodness, knowledge; and to knowledge, self-control; and to self-control, perseverance; and to perseverance, godliness; and to godliness, brotherly kindness; and to brotherly kindness, love…. For if you do these things, you will never fall, and **you will receive a rich welcome into the eternal kingdom of our Lord and Savior Jesus Christ.** (2 Pet. 1: 5-7,11)*

The term *"rich welcome into the eternal kingdom"* is synonymous with a good judgment. Since the judgment precedes the Kingdom, no better phrase describes the glory of receiving your Savior's highest commendation based on your life and your life's work. That rich welcome begins with the praise of the Eternal King and no doubt encompasses the accolades of the heavenly host along with cheers and embraces of fellow saints.

And in this verse, at least, it is tied directly to character qualities.

Love

In the above list, the last entry is love. This is fitting because everything is summed up in love. Since *"God is love,"* it is easy to believe that the most loving people are the most godly people, and hence they will carry the greatest distinction in heaven. We are told in I John that love is the one quality that will give us confidence in the Day of Judgment. That being the case, it behooves us to spend time examining this quality in hopes of coming to a clearer understanding of what love, in fact, is.

"Love is a many-splendored thing." So go the lyrics to an old love song. To separate real love from the shallow, romantic love of the secular world, is not an easy thing. To separate an emotional love for God from an act of the will

228

that embraces the cross, is hard. To separate the love that is a fruit of the Spirit from its counterfeit in fleshly "good works", is difficult. But if we are to grow in love and have confidence on the Day of Judgment, we must look carefully at this most important attribute.

Only of love does God say, "(It) *covers a multitude of sins*" *(I Pet. 4:8)*.

Love is the wild card, so to speak, that trumps even sin itself. On the one hand, it is the thing that we universally crave; on the other, in possessing it, we show that we are disciples of Christ. Therefore, love is something we need to understand.

To begin with, we might ask the question: what is the connection between love and judgment? Interestingly, God made it the barometer of whether or not you dread that day or look forward to it.

We all know the verse: *"Perfect love casts out fear."* It is actually from a passage on the judgment and is meant to teach us something about that subject. Like many verses that are pulled out of context and used almost as a cliché, this one has been misused. Usually when people quote this verse, they mean that if we are experiencing fear, or if we fear Him, we haven't fully accepted God's love. Actually, the verse isn't about God's love at all, and says something very different.

The book of I John deals as much with *our* love as it does with God's love. By making statements like "I can't love; only God can love through me," we reveal an aspect of truth, but we also let ourselves off the hook on a subject where we bear much personal responsibility. So here is the verse in question:

*"God is love, and the one who abides in love, abides in God, and God abides in him. By this love is perfected in us, **so that we may have confidence in***

229

the Day of Judgment; *because as He is, so also are we in this world. There is no fear in love; but perfect love casts out fear, because fear involves punishment and the one who fears is not perfected in love.*" (1Jn. 4:16-18)

This verse talks about the love that has to be perfected **in us,** and if this happens, we will have confidence in the Day of Judgment. If we fear judgment, according to that last line, it's because **we** aren't made perfect in love. So the perfect love that casts out fear isn't God's love; it is ours. This is confirmed in II John 2:5 where we are told: "*But whoever keeps His word, **in him** the love of God has truly been perfected.*"

In I Corinthians 13 we learn that love has qualities: Love is patient, love is kind, etc. In James and John we learn that it is practical: giving help to the poor. In the Gospels we learn that love is holiness and obedience: "*If you love Me, you will keep my commandments.*"

Does God's perfect love cast out fear? I hope not. If it does, there is no hope for the Laodicean church. It's because God's love **is** so perfect that He literally puts the "fear of God" **into** them: "*So because you are lukewarm, and neither hot nor cold, I will spit you out of my mouth.... Those whom I love, I reprove and discipline; be zealous therefore and repent*" (Rev. 3:16,19).

God's perfect love does cast out fear, but it is the fear of everything else *but* Him. Knowing the power of God's love should cause us to trust Him in every circumstance of life, and this should totally eliminate fear. We can't fear both God and Problem X; we can only fear one, and it must be God.

But we are also to fear sin, and lack of love is sin. God mentions several times in scripture the concept of dreading the Day of Judgment, shrinking back from Him at His appearing, lacking confidence on that day, etc. He never rebukes us for this sentiment, as though it was somehow an affront to His perfect love. Quite the contrary. He explains this reaction as a natural consequence of living an unfruitful and unholy life, and then having to face a holy God, who is a consuming fire.

He uses it as a warning.

Like Jesus in This World

So what are we to learn from this passage about judgment? If we take the clause about judgment out of verse 17, it reads like so: *"Love is perfected with us, because as He is, so also are we in this world."* What does it mean to be *like* Jesus in the context of this verse? The gospels tell us.

We see Jesus eating with sinners and ministering to the poor and the needy. We see His absolute rejection of affluence and a comfortable lifestyle. We see His abandonment to His Father's purposes, whatever the cost. We see Him become servant of all, caring nothing for His own needs or the applause of men. We see the ultimate act of love as He is brutally beaten and goes willingly to the cross, to be mocked and cruelly tortured to death.

But then we hear of another cross, one we must carry. We hear of the commission to bring the good news to the nations. We hear of the command to give up all our possessions. We hear of a seed falling into the ground and dying that it might bear much fruit. We hear of a ministry to the sick, to the homeless, to the widows, and to those that are in prison. All involving sacrifice; all involving love; all involving the principle: *"Love is perfected in us, because as He is, so also are we in this world."*

Those familiar with Heidi Baker's story know that she had a powerful call on her life. But she rose above her generation to become a modern day Mother Theresa for a reason. She was aware of her inadequate response to the need she saw everywhere, and she wasn't willing to ignore it. She decried her hardness of heart and beseeched the Lord to teach her to love. And knowing that love wouldn't fall from heaven into her lap, she developed a plan.

While studying in London for two years to obtain her Doctorate in Theology, she went nightly into skid row to feed the poor. It was hard, thankless work. One man whom she fed regularly, cursed her for her kindness. But after many months, when Heidi was attacked by an aggressive lesbian, he came to her rescue and ended up giving his heart to the Lord.

She was learning to love. It didn't just happen and it didn't happen overnight, but in the end, it did, in fact, happen. But it came at great cost. As her love grew, the assignments became more immense, and by degrees she became like Jesus in this world. She became bread for the nations.

Now when you hear her talk, she pines for heaven. She longs to go and be with her Lord, to whom she has committed everything — this from a woman in her forties. But that is what living in love does to you. It casts out fear so that you look forward to meeting God, and Judgment Day creates no apprehension.

God's Response to Our Love
Jesus says something very revealing in John 14.

"He that hath my commandments, and keepeth them, he it is that loveth Me; and he that loveth Me shall be loved of My Father, and I will love him, and will manifest Myself to him." (Jn. 14:21 KJV)

In the next verse Judas asks something very obtuse: *"Lord, how is it that thou wilst manifest thyself unto us, and not unto the world?"(Jn. 14:22 KJV).*

The setting of this discussion was not conducive to a rebuke, or perhaps Our Lord might have given one. After all, Jesus had just covered the issue raised by Judas. He had just *said* that by keeping his commandments, they show that they love Him; if they love Him, they will be loved by His Father and by Jesus; and therefore God will manifest Himself to them. The world doesn't love God or keep His commandments, so they don't qualify for His manifestation.

So, patiently, in the next verse, Jesus repeats what He has just said: "Jesus answered and said to him, *'If anyone loves Me, he will keep my word; and My Father will love him, and We will come to him, and make Our abode with him.' "* *(verse 23)*.

All repetition in scripture is for a reason, and Judas' question becomes the lightning rod for an important declaration. Our Lord is teaching on love and He conveys two significant truths. The first is that love draws a specific response from God. The second is that there is a connection between love and obedience. This second insight is hidden from those who don't understand the text in its original language.

Judas hones in on the first by asking Jesus why He is going to manifest Himself just to them and not to the world. The key word is "manifest". The same Greek word is found in Hebrews 9:24: *"For Christ did not enter a holy place made with hands, a mere copy of the true one, but into heaven itself,* ***now to appear in the presence*** *of God for us."*

The phrase "now to appear in the presence" is the same Greek word as "manifest" in our passage. Think about it. Jesus ascended into heaven and walked directly into the glory of the Father's presence. That is an exact picture of how He wants to manifest himself in our lives. But there is a condition, and this brings us to the second point. His presence is for those who love Him. All sentiment aside, what does that mean?

I was sitting with a group of fourteen church leaders one day, discussing people's experience in worship or lack thereof. I mentioned that the website of a well-known worship leader contained the statement that 65% of Christians have never entered the glorious, manifest presence of God. My comment seemed to fall on deaf ears. There was no "Really?" or "Gee, that's surprising!"

I wondered at that until later in the meeting when we were discussing the question: "Can each of us in this room say that we truly know that God loves us?" That seems like Salvation 101, but for many western Christians the question is not easily answered, and frequently the response is "no".

This group, perhaps because they were leaders, all answered in the affirmative. But almost all described a journey of struggle and pain that had been necessary to bring them to this realization. It was very obvious from their comments that there wasn't much manifest glory in their experience in God, but a growing faith and assurance that He loved them despite their failures. Perhaps this is why they were mute to my earlier observation on worship.

Faith is good, but God promises more to those who love Him — His manifest presence. "Living on faith" without that presence is necessary at times, but as a lifestyle, it is truly a barren existence, and not at all what God intends for us.

Love Defined

So what is this love that is so necessary to the receiving of God's manifest presence? Most of us know that Greek is a more precise language than English. The thing we loosely call *love* has many names in Greek. Within these names are important nuances that are lost in the translation. Things that were very clear to our Lord's listeners are lost on us. And where love is concerned, these things are supremely important.

Many of us have probably had a teaching on *eros, phileo* and *agape*, three of the more common Greek words for love. Even that bit of knowledge is helpful, but we need to apply it to the present discussion. The word used for love throughout the passage we are considering is *agape*.

Strong's concordance defines *agape* love as "a deliberate assent of the will as a matter of principle, duty and propriety". So to put it simply, three things are involved in loving God in the sense of *agape*. We must learn God's principles, our duty, and proper behavior. Then, as an act of our will, we try to live according to the dictates of these three.

How different from the secular view of love. We live in a world where, in deciding how to respond in a situation, most people trust their heart, their emotions, their instincts, and occasionally their upbringing. "If it feels good, do it!" is more than just a 60's slogan; for many, it is a lifestyle. The focus is usually on their selfish need, not someone else's benefit. Does this give us a clue as to the reason for the high divorce rate?

God, on the other hand, expects us to act towards Him out of *agape* love. That is the kind of love where feelings or negative consequences don't even count. Only three things count — principles, duty and propriety. I set my will to act according to these three. We hear people say that they don't want to serve God out of a sense of duty; they only want to serve Him out of love. The statement is meaningless because, love, as we have seen, is *defined* as duty. So the argument has no merit.

Another thing we notice is the way in which the order of two things — love, and keeping God's commandments — is constantly changed. In verse 21 Jesus says, "*He who has my commandments and keeps them, he it is who loves Me.*" But in verse 23 He reverses it and says, "*If anyone loves Me, he will keep My word….*" So which is it? Does loving Him cause us to keep His commandments, or does keeping His commandments cause us to love Him? The question is moot, because the two are the same. The definition of agape love is the same as keeping His commandments. In case we still miss the point, He clearly says in I John 5:3: "***For this is*** *the love of God, that we keep His commandments, and His commandments are not burdensome."*

There is no wiggle room. We can't say we love Him if we don't keep His commandments. The lack of keeping His commandments is why so many people don't experience His presence. His presence connotes passion, intimacy and joy, which are things we justifiably associate with love. But they are the caboose that rides behind the engine of true love, which is an act of the will.

Agape Love Further Defined

With regards to *agape* love, years of tradition have so blunted the force of our Lord's words, that most people miss the point. Subconsciously they think: "I'm a good Christian; I don't steal, I don't kill, I don't commit adultery." But Jesus refers to HIS commandments and HIS word, not the law. And, as we already saw, they fall under three categories — principles, duty and propriety — which equal love.

What interesting words from an old dictionary that nails the three watershed issues in all of behavior! Have you observed that many business people today lack principles? Have you noticed that many men today have forsaken their duty as husbands and fathers? Have you seen the lack of propriety in the way people act today? Their use of profanity, the immodest way in which they dress, and their rampant sexual immorality? So let's take a cursory look at these three in the light of God's Word.

For principles, let's confine ourselves to the Sermon on the Mount. Here we find principles on humility, meekness, mourning, gentleness, mercy, purity, peacemaking, persecution, hungering after righteousness, marriage, divorce, money, fasting, praying, sharing, tithing, serving, lusting, inviting the poor, feeding the hungry, making oaths, loving your enemy, forgiving all wrongs, laying up treasure in heaven, forsaking anxiety, not judging, being a doer of the word, the golden rule, and the fear of sin.

Do we live by these principles?

Next let's take a cursory look at our duty: deny yourself, pick up your cross, follow Him; go into all the world and preach the gospel; seek first the Kingdom of God and His righteousness; be not conformed to this world, but be transformed by the renewing of your mind; present your bodies as a living sacrifice; glorify God in your body; rejoice evermore, in everything give thanks, pray without ceasing; care for widows and orphans; visit the sick and the imprisoned; stir up the gift within you; suffer as a good soldier of Christ.

Do we do our duty?

Thirdly, there is propriety, involving such things as the following: love not the world, nor the things in the world; be holy, for I am holy; do not let immorality or any impurity or greed even be named among you; let all bitterness and wrath and anger and clamor and slander be put away from you; put away the deeds of the flesh, which are immorality, impurity, sensuality, idolatry, sorcery, enmities, strife, jealousy, outbursts of anger, disputes, dissentions, factions, envyings, drunkenness, carousings and things like this.

Do we live proper lives?

These are the things Jesus was referring to when He said: "Keep my commandments. Keep My word. Love Me." All of us, of course, are aware of the importance of obedience. But the thought of love and the Christian faith being reduced to keeping commandments is abhorrent to many. It sounds like legalism or a religion of works. It sounds like the do's and don'ts that caused many to flee dead, traditional religion.

It can be all of those things if done in a wrong spirit, but it isn't even a question of whether these things **should** be done. Our Lord painstakingly repeated this refrain everywhere in the gospels: "If you love Me you, will keep my commandments." But He added a further comment: *"My commandments are not burdensome."*

Unburdensome Commandments

Why are they not burdensome? We hear in the gospels that the Pharisees weighed people down with burdens that they themselves couldn't and wouldn't bear. How are Jesus' commandments different?

First, they come with the power of the Holy Spirit to help you keep them. Still burdensome? Well, consider this then: We have Christ living in us, and it's His life through us that keeps the commandments. Still burdensome? Then look at the next verse in I John 5: *"For whatever is born of God overcomes the world, and this is the victory that has overcome the world – our faith."*

Keeping His commandments in the face of opposition from the world makes us an overcomer. And there is only one thing that gives us this victory — faith. It is the expansion of Colossians 2:6: *"As you therefore have received Christ Jesus the Lord, so walk in Him."*

We started the Christian walk in faith, and we must continue in faith. Everything we do, we do in faith. We need faith initially to make right choices, to obey God, to pay the price. We need faith that, if we do the right thing, He will manifest Himself to us. We need faith that such a manifestation will cause us to love His word, so that obeying it won't be a burden, but a delight.

For many, this is the ultimate faith. For many, His commandments *are* burdensome, because they have yet to enter into the joy of pleasing God. So our journey begins with faith that strengthens love, and culminates in *"faith working through love"*.

Many people assume that the commandments aren't burdensome because we are under grace, and therefore aren't expected to keep them. But Jesus doesn't say this. In Titus we are told that grace has arrived, teaching us to renounce sin. We have Paul's famous dissertation on the foolishness of sinning so that grace can abound.

When we sin, we are to draw near to the throne of grace. This is very comforting, but it will not lessen the burden of His commandments; it just eliminates the condemnation we feel when we break them. Only faith, which produces obedience, which produces love, will enable us to keep His commandments.

Legalism Versus License

There is no way around the requirement to keep His Word if we want to enjoy His presence. And His word has more do's than don'ts. If we don't live by His principles or do our duty, but simply live a life of propriety, we will not be walking in love. And yet this is how many rate their performance: I don't drink, smoke, dance, or gamble, etc. I live a good life.

Whether we realize it or not, having this attitude makes us religious, the very thing many seek to avoid. The struggle between legalism and license has been a source of great angst in the Church over the centuries. One could easily make the case that the greater danger today is license.

It has a curious logic to it, the idea that wherever I find an emphasis on holiness and keeping His commandments, I have discovered religion; wherever I find an emphasis on the Spirit, freedom in the Spirit, and grace versus effort, I have discovered a genuine walk with God. The truth is, we need both. To a mature person they are not incompatible. But to the person in reaction to a legalistic upbringing or, conversely, to the one appalled by carnal charismania, either one of these ditches can seem like the road.

All of this would seem a little perplexing if we didn't have living, breathing examples of these truths in operation. Theories are nice, but do they work? They did for Paul and

King David. Both suffered greatly but had a passion for the Lord and a fixation with obedience. David delighted in the Law and, despite his many failures, was fixated on keeping it. Jesus told us that He did only those things that He saw the Father doing. That was His delight. Paul had the same mindset, but the object of his passion and conformity was the Son. It works! It works for all of us.

You don't need special grace, just a fixation with love and obedience.

Love as Fruit

Having made the case for love as an act of obeying principles, duty and propriety, let me briefly state the other dimension. Love is also a fruit of the Spirit and is the outgrowth of a walk with God. It results in good deeds.

A pastor whose website I visited recently tells of his encounter with death. He had befriended an ex-convict and was driving him to an appointment. Without warning, the ex-con told him to pull into a parking lot, and then plunged a knife into his throat. A wrestle ensued as the pastor fought for his life. However, it was a fight he lost, and in a matter of moments he found himself standing before God.

Unfortunately, it was not a pleasant experience. He discovered, to his dismay, that he had failed the love test. He had been rich in good works, but they were done out of a wrong motive — primarily a sense of religious responsibility. God pronounced vanity and barrenness over his life. He begged for another chance, and his request was granted. Moments later he awoke in the hospital with tubes protruding from his mouth and arms. It took three months for him to recuperate and return to his pastoral duties. When he did, things were very different.

No longer did he rush around meeting needs and carrying out responsibilities in a rote fashion. He made sure that everything he did was in response to God. He now carried out his duties with the unhurried passion of someone who was no longer a servant to need, but a slave to God.

When he visited the sick, instead of marching into the room, he would pause at the door for a moment of prayer. He asked God to do what he could not do. He asked God to fill him with love for the person he was visiting. He said God never failed him, and the result was a new dimension of love that he had never experienced before. We see here the eternal implications of putting our works before our relationship to God. But there are temporal implications as well.

Jack Frost is a man who has a ministry to fallen pastors and church leaders. It is his experience that a high percentage of pastors either fall morally or develop ungodly soul ties to someone of the opposite sex. The primary reason, he says, is a lack of intimacy with God. Many pastors go into the ministry looking for affirmation or seeking to fill a void in their life. They are easy prey to someone who promises to fill that void in a sensual or soulish way. In his view, anyone who becomes a pastor without establishing intimacy with God is an accident waiting to happen.

What is the outcome of spending a life in service if it's not done in love? What is the benefit to the minister, if it wasn't done out of intimacy with God? There is none. How wary we have to be of putting the work of the Lord ahead of the Lord of the work.

But on the other hand, what is the benefit of love without action, intimacy without outgrowth, talk without walk? If we love Jesus, we will keep His commandments. We will live circumspect lives that are focused on meeting the needs of others. These "others" include our brethren in the Church, and that is often where the difficulty comes in.

Loving the Brethern

Most products these days come with an owner's manual. They are written by people we call technical writers. Their work is critical to the safe assembly and operation of every-thing from a TV stand to a nuclear power plant. When it comes to the rules and regulations for a government program or a business plan, technical writers keep everyone on the same page. Got a question or a dispute? No problem — get out the manual.

Apparently that skill didn't exist in the Trinity at the time the Bible was conceived. If the Bible is indeed the Manufacturer's Handbook, as so many suggest, then why can't we put the thing together? Things like the church, for instance. What a mess: so much division; so many pet doctrines. And all of it could have been solved so easily with clear, precise instructions.

Take doctrine, for example. One simple statement could have put to rest the Calvinist/Armenian argument. But instead, we have ample verses to support either view. Or how about spiritual gifts? A simple statement as to the perpe-tuity of spiritual gifts would have ended the cessationist argument. But instead, God left them enough wiggle room. And then there's eschatology. It would have been a simple matter to clearly state the timing and sequence of the rapture, second coming, and millennial kingdom. But instead, there is ambiguity.

However, this lack of clarity is not the most surprising thing. The greater mystery is that the dogmatist never twigs to any of this. It never occurs to him that the Creator of the universe is actually a very good communicator — when He wants to be. It doesn't seem to register with the dogmatist that God could have been much clearer about eternal secu-rity, and that this lack of clarity points to an agenda. So what is the agenda?

Well, for openers, God was much less ambiguous on the point of loving your enemy than He was on the issue of keeping your salvation. That should give us a hint. Maybe loving your enemy demands more certainty, especially if your enemy is the churchman down the street with funny doctrines.

To put the matter simply: It is indisputable that God deliberately uses doctrine, as much for a test, as for a deposit of truth. The test is not: Are we stalwart lovers of truth who refuse to compromise in an age of capitulation? That's a good test for hidden pride. We speak of a different test. The test is this: Will we pay the God-imposed price to bring unity to the Body of Christ? The price of setting aside all non-essential doctrines?

Truthfully, unity can only come through love and *despite* doctrine, not because of it. And on that point, God won't budge. It's His agenda. It could hardly be called a hidden agenda, because it's so apparent to every meek spirit. But to the proud it is indeed a conundrum. But we either fall on the rock, or the Rock falls on us. He is determined to outlast the legalists, the idolaters, the traditionalists and the kingdom builders. He *will* have His glorious Body, it *will* be unified, and it *will* be energized by love. It may just take longer.

God has not chosen the easiest path. Hiring a technical writer would have been much easier, but then the results would always have been suspect. Now, when unity does come, it will come because of love.

Jesus is not coming back till we come "*to the unity of the faith*" by "*forbearing one another in love*", because we are above "*foolish disputations*". I find it curious that prophecy teachers don't report advances in this area the way they do the latest earthquake, false messiah, or move toward the mark of the Beast. Fixating on signs of the coming Antichrist is utterly futile without giving equal time to the growth of Church unity. Christ can't come back till both are accomplished.

In the unfolding of this grand issue, we see the revealing of hearts. Doctrinal meekness, not weakness, becomes but one more tool in the Maker's hands with which to judge.

Because, behind the politics of religion, we see another part of the master plan: a hidden agenda behind the open agenda. This one has nothing to do with the corporate. It is not about the Body and the glorious Bride. It is about you and it is about me.

Where we stand on this matter will have an impact on our eternal destiny. How we perceive this grand debate, and whether or not we respond correctly, will determine if we are a new wine skin or an old one, a kingdom builder or a usurper, a stumbling block or a light. And at the core is love. It is a love for the Body of Christ that causes us to humble ourselves in whatever way, in order to see Jesus come into His inheritance. We will even abandon our pet doctrines, or at least leave them at the feet of Jesus, as we embrace our common unity.

And in doing this we achieve an inheritance for ourselves.

Love's Progression

It all begins with our love for God. Reflecting back on observations from an earlier chapter, we find that a love for God is not the easy thing that it sounds: *"We love Him because He first loved us."* I have no doubt that every born-again, heaven-bound believer loves God. However, as we have seen earlier, intimacy with God comes at great cost. He can be hard to find. *"We happily grope after Him,"* is how Paul describes our pursuit.

Get the picture? We're in a vast room, it's pitch black but we sense His presence. We grope for him — we stagger blindly forward, clutching at some articles, bumping into others, occasionally falling down, all in attempt to find the One that Paul says is *"not far from any of us"*. That is a physical picture of what we experience in the emotional/spiritual realm. To find Him with regularity and to grow to love Him deeply is not the experience of the masses. It is for those who are willing to pay the cost.

Then He says, "*If you love me, you will keep my command-ments,*" thereby introducing love to works. Love for God is not just an emotion or a walk of faith or even a pursuit, but a lifestyle that is lived out in obedience to all of Jesus' commands. Here again, we see the bar raised.

Next we look at our homes and we see the commandment: "*Husbands, love your wives.*" What a strange command! Surely that must be there because many marriages in the Middle East were arranged. No doubt, but even romance-based western marriages have a high failure rate, and the culprit is usually the husband.

Marriage is a great and vital institution, but God consti-tuted it in such a way that it won't work without love. It just has too many challenges. He could have made men and women more alike, and marriage therefore easier, but He didn't because He wanted the strength of marriage to be love, not convenience.

This is true also of the local fellowship. There is tension in any church that has a variety of gifts and callings. Where the leader is pastoral and an assistant leader is prophetic, there will be conflict. Both are equipped differently and view people, ministry, and the needs of the church differently.

The prophet is jealous for the glory of God, and is not content to see people saved and secure — he wants them to be sold out and seeking. This can bring conflict with the pastor. He has the same long-term goals, but is hard-wired to feed, care and protect. These and other tensions are programmed into the five-fold ministries. Again, God hasn't made church life easy — it takes love to make it work.

Then we look at love that attempts to reach out and embrace the lost. It is humorous to hear certain Christians make loud assertions about loving homosexuals. Many don't know a single homosexual, but of course, they love them all. No doubt they are well-meaning, but they are probably deceived about their own hearts. They know that this is the right answer; they are, after all, Christians, and they are supposed to love everyone. But it is definitely easier to love the homosexual you don't know than the spouse that you do.

Many of these people are working on their second or third marriages and are estranged from their own children, but this apparent contradiction doesn't seem to faze them. As Derek Prince once said, "If it's not working at home, don't export it." We don't really have much to say to the homosexual or to the world if we don't love the brethren, beginning with our own families.

Many of us need to begin by loving just one person — our spouse. We need to cry out to God for more love and for the ability to put that love into practice. This may seem like a small thing, but it's a starting point in a process known as "growing in love". From there we may seek to love those with whom we have regular contact, even those that are unpleasant. And the wonderful thing is that we don't have to go looking for them. God has a list for all of us, as part of our training program. It could be a difficult co-worker, a noisy neighbor, an obnoxious relative, etc. The list is endless, and the process can be as hard as you or I want to make it.

As our love grows, we can begin to tackle the unlovables — street people, inmates, and for some of us, politicians. Then, perhaps, we can ultimately move to the sexual deviants who glory in their sin. Finally, we can begin to love our enemies, maybe that person who cheated us, lied to us, or even slandered us.

It is good to love the whole world, but it is best to start with a real, live, breathing, human being. God said if we don't love our brother whom we *have* seen, how can we say we love God whom we have not seen? There is something so uncompromisingly honest in that statement that we should pause every time we read it. If I don't love the brethren, all my pretentious declarations about my love for God are just a noisy gong and a clanging cymbal.

How horrible to discover that too late.

How horrible to be one of the feuding saints who will one day discover that their divisive rancor was but a mirror image of their "love" for God. If we have strife, anger, and hatred toward a brother, and in our prayer and praise time we don't feel conviction, we are deluded. To those who had conflict with a brother, Jesus had one terse instruction: Don't even waste your time bringing your offering; it won't be accepted.

So behind all of God's dealings we find something simple, yet profound; something necessary, yet painful; something unavoidable, yet often resisted. Behind our relationship with God, behind our relationship with the church at large, behind our relationship within the local fellowship, behind our relationship with our spouses, behind our relationship to the world, we find an agenda: love. Love is the agenda.

God has ordered all of life in such a way that nothing in the Kingdom will work without love. He is resolute. He will not compromise. Love stands like a huge barrier in the face of everything that you and I want to accomplish. We can edge around it and give all our money to the poor, but if we don't have love, it amounts to nothing. We can try to buy Him off with sacrifice and have our bodies burnt in the fervor of martyrdom, but if we don't have love, it's all for nothing.

We can end our lives never having given in to the other side, whatever entity that might be — wife, boss, denomination, etc. — but when we *truly* get to the other side, heaven, we'll discover a surprise. It wasn't about slipping through life with our dogma, dignity and defense intact. Just the opposite. It was about surrendering all in the name of love.

In Conclusion

Character will play a large part in our judgment. That is why God will often limit our works to develop our character. When a minister falls morally, he or she is removed for a season. During that time, God, together with those who serve in the role of counsellor, are involved in a work of restoration. This is God's grace. Being taken out of ministry can be humbling and seem counter-productive, but if it produces character, the result will be eternal glory.

As a parent, nothing thrills us more than seeing strong character traits emerge in our children. What parent hasn't rewarded a child for showing courage in the face of great danger? What parent hasn't rewarded a child for diligence in their studies? God is no different. He works daily to develop our character, and His reasons are manifold.

But let us not forget one of the most important: His great delight will be to one day reward openly the character that is at the core of who we are as sons and daughters of God. Much of this character will have been forged in the crucible of suffering. There will be tears of joy for those who have passed these great tests and gone on to receive their inheritance. Let us be faithful to submit to God's dealings, knowing that in the age to come, our character will result in untold blessing.

EIGHT

The Judgment of Good Works

The evangelist was shaken to the core. After all, he'd considered the crusade a major success. His team had flown to a village in Northern Canada and spent a week amongst the natives preaching the gospel. The meetings were packed out and the response was overwhelming. As far as he could ascertain, the whole village had pretty much given their hearts to the Lord. This was virgin territory, not the pickings from an earlier crusade where the residents were simply recommitting or responding to the emotion of the moment.

But after the team had said their farewells and the evangelist was heading for his soon-departing plane, he had an encounter that would be forever etched in his mind. As he threw his luggage on board and proceeded to enter the craft, he was stopped by a voice behind him. He turned to see a man whom he recognized from the crusade. The man's eyes were full of tears and there was anguish in his voice as he spoke. "How long", he asked the evangelist, "have you known about this?"

Taken aback, and slightly confused, he responded, "Known about what?"

"How long have you known about salvation through Jesus Christ?" the man persisted.

Still wondering where the conversation was leading, the evangelist thought back to his own conversion and replied, " Well, for many years, at least thirty."

"Then why didn't you come sooner?" the man demanded. "My wife died last month and now she's in hell. If you had come sooner, she would have known the truth and now she'd be with Jesus."

The evangelist stood there speechless. He had a long list of excuses he could have proffered, but he allowed the Holy Spirit to let him feel the full weight of the tragedy that stood before him. All he could do was embrace the man, grieve at his loss, and quickly take his leave. But he would never forget. He would never forget the urgency of the gospel and the eternal souls that hang in the balance, and he determined to share that story wherever he went.

Good Works

We are men with a mission and, from heaven's point of view, there is no greater mission than spreading the gospel. But any mathematician will tell you there are two sides to every equation. No one gets saved without someone getting paid. God won't let heaven be populated without men being compensated. But the reward side of the equation involves far more than spreading the gospel, as important as that is.

In I Corinthians 3 we find the classic picture of the believers' judgment, involving the metaphor of a building. The foundation is Christ Jesus, and what is built on it is referred to as *work*. *"Each man's work will become evident; for the day will show it."* The Greek word is *ergo*, and literally means *toil*. That should give us an insight into the cost of serving God. The expanded definition of ergo means *deeds* or *works*, and it occurs 171 times in the New Testament. In nearly every case it refers to the righteous acts of the saints. The sheer repetition of this word should impress upon us the importance of good works.

Good works are a generic description of the mission of every believer. We are told in a global sense that we are *"created in Christ Jesus for good works"*. We are further told that *"Jesus went about doing good and healing all that were oppressed of the devil."* As followers of His, there is no higher call than doing good. Throughout the Bible we are told that our works will one day be judged, and this is the picture we see in 1Corinthians 3. This graphic scene is the reason why virtually every book written on the Judgment Seat of Christ focuses on just this one area.

The Judgment of Good Works

But as we have already seen, the believers' judgment encompasses much more than good works. Though I Corinthians 3 gives us a crude picture, it is metaphoric in nature. Our judgment will be as thorough and painstaking as the inspection of any priceless object both for its beauty and its possible flaws.

How thorough will the judgment be? Every act of prayer is a good deed. Every act of praise is a good deed. Every act of kindness is a good deed. Every proper response to God, every inch of growth, every exercise of our faith — all are good deeds. In addition, every thought will be judged, every word will be judged, every test, trial, and temptation will be judged. Perhaps it is sufficient to say that our entire life will be judged. Since the judgment takes place outside our current understanding of time, time constraints as we experience them now will have no meaning

It will also be a day of surprises. We may be shocked by what is revealed about our neighbor, and even more shocked by what is revealed about ourselves. The Bible describes all of our hearts as *"deceitful and wicked"*, and to a certain extent they are unknowable. But the more diligent we are to apply the Word to our lives, the more we *will* know ourselves. The more we examine our motives with the help of the Holy Spirit, the more we *will* know what it is that motivates us. But there is much that must inevitably await the sifting of the Judge Himself because all of our works must be judged under three criteria.

The Three Criteria

Were the works, first of all, done in obedience to God? That which is born of the flesh, is flesh. Secondly, were they done with the right motivation? Paul said that some even preached the *gospel* out of spite! And thirdly, were they done in the power of the Holy Spirit? Were they energized by God and bathed in prayer, or were they simply the result of human effort?

This may seem complicated, but it is necessary. Part of the reason we are told not to judge is because, in our frail humanity, we cannot possibly know the mitigating circumstances that cause others to behave the way they do. If that is true of their misdeeds, it is doubly true of their *good* deeds. Only God knows the true cause and quality of any good deed and, as the righteous Judge, He must expose all false deeds and reward those that are true. Truth and justice demand it.

The Importance of the Criteria

We have remarked several times on our Lord's repetition of the phrase, "the first shall be last." Looking ahead to that day, He gave us advanced warning of one thing we should expect to experience — shock. There are men today who trumpet their works just as the Pharisees did, but the fire of God will test their motivation. Despite their fame in the church world, many well-known Christians will emerge from the judgment with their salvation intact but stripped of any position in the eternal kingdom.

A great many will be shocked in that day. They were prominent and prosperous; they were busy and diligent. Universities, seminaries, and great ministries bore their name, but in the end it was all vanity, and they never even knew it. There will be many such tragedies.

I remember a great missionary teacher talking about a friend of his who was a pastor in Toronto. The man had a knowledge of the Bible that this person rated among the top three of his generation. He was called to be a great evangelist, but for some reason had decided that fulfillment meant being a successful pastor. He labored for decades trying to build a church in Toronto that never got above 200 people.

The missionary confronted him with the fact that he had rejected God's call on his life and was suffering barrenness as a result. But that was the least of the man's worries, as his friend forcefully explained: "Only eternity will reveal how many would have populated heaven had you surrendered to the call, and how much eternal loss will be yours as a result." The man wept bitterly, but that was as far as it went. Three years after that conversation, it was reported that nothing had changed. How tragic. It is God who chooses our works, not us. Fruitfulness and reward come through obedience.

Our Lord's declaration that the first would be last was as much a warning as a prediction, for there will no doubt be exceptions. It must be difficult to be famous and to be among those who are "first" in this life. It must be difficult to do things not to be seen of men, when much of what you do is inevitably seen of men. But many handle the challenge nobly.

I think of a man who is a best-selling author. He had plans to take his considerable royalties to Hollywood and become involved in filmmaking. However, a trip to South Africa changed all of that. In seeing the AIDS epidemic, he was convicted by the Holy Spirit to start an organization to deal with poverty and disease in that country.

When he announced this to his friends and associates, they all advised him against it, especially in consideration of the pressures that his family would endure. This would be the "out" many of us would be looking for. But not him. He had heard from God, and subsequently disengaged himself from several thriving ministries to serve the poor. Standing there on Judgment Day, we will thrill to many such stories. These people are heroes, not unsung heroes, but heroes nevertheless.

But there will also be unsung heroes, because the last shall be first. Those that are last on earth are often people who are hidden away unnoticed both by the world and the church. And yet by faithfully executing their call with purity and in the power of the Holy Spirit, they earn for themselves great prominence in the Kingdom of Heaven. Remarkable, isn't it?

These are often one-talent people who never face the pressures of the high profile. Pride wouldn't be their chief enemy, but, as mentioned earlier, indolence would be the greater threat. It often takes more discipline to perform when no one is watching and little is expected, than the reverse. These people must exercise their calling for an audience of One.

What an honor!

A Prophetic Warning

I doubt any evangelist has been to more cities and venues than Howard Pittman. Pittman is an evangelist to the church, not the world. About thirty years ago he had a death experience and found himself standing before the throne of God, where he was given a message to take to the church. God allowed him to return to earth on one condition — that he would never turn down a request to speak. As a result, he has traveled the globe.

Let me relate the shock he experienced when the issue of works arose. God thundered at him: "What makes you think I would accept the works you did unto your god?!" Pittman was flabbergasted. He had pastored a church in addition to holding down a full-time job. He and his wife had taken in orphans; they had visited the sick and the imprisoned. How could these works possibly have been in vain? God explained to him that they were all done for the kingdom of self. They were done in pride and for self-exaltation, so they were worthless. "They were good deeds; they just weren't Mine."

Those words can either bring despair or resolve. God's purpose in saying them was to save people from despair. Despair is what many will one day feel when they see their works burn up. For most Christians the reason will be simple: They functioned within a religious system and did their works as a duty unto man, and not as service unto God. In the words of Jesus to the Pharisees: "You already have your reward."

To ensure that we don't experience this despair, we need a fresh resolve: henceforth we will only do the works the Father has given us to do. If that requires a little more thought, prayer, and love, then so be it. If that means saying "no" to people who ask us to do things that God clearly hasn't, so be it. We must refuse to be men-pleasers or hyperactive do-gooders. We must resolve to be the embodiment of our Lord's statement, *"I am the vine, you are the branches... apart from Me you can do nothing"* (Jn. 15:5).

But surely that statement is incorrect, for we can do many things apart from God. Yes we can, but nothing that will survive the fire of judgment. I can think of few things more futile than expending great effort to do good works that benefit everyone but us — the doer. **"Apart from Me you can do nothing."**

Nothing that counts, nothing that lasts, nothing that brings glory.

I would rather that this wasn't so. It makes God seem, well, judgmental. I believe it is hard for us to accept God as Judge, except on our own terms. That is undoubtedly why most books on the judgment have been feel-good books. Scriptures and anecdotes are carefully chosen so that both God and man come out smelling like roses.

But can we accept the fact that the God who thunders throughout the scriptures doesn't need a makeover, PR men, and a scriptwriter? Whatever behavior God displays is righteous and just, and helps to define that which is Godlike. We must live by *every* word that proceeds out of the mouth of God, not just the ones that make us feel good.

Pittman has no hesitation in saying these things because he has a mandate, and he got it from the mouth of God. He prefaces everything he says by quoting chapter and verse from the Bible, precisely what God says He will do to people who prophesy falsely in His name. Pittman would have to be the most misguided miscreant on the planet to quote God's judgment against liars and then proceed to lie. I think it is wise to take him at his word.

The Concept of Reward

One Sabbath day Jesus was invited to dinner by a leader of the Pharisees. We have the record of this event in Luke 14. The whole scene was pregnant with speaking points, so Jesus wasted little time. First He healed a man stricken with dropsy and quelled any protest with His "ox in the well" analogy. Then, as He witnessed guests vying for seating, He admonished them for their vanity, concluding with the words: *"for everyone who exalts himself shall be humbled."* Finally, directing His attention to the whole matter of dinner invitations, He turned to the one who invited Him and said the following:

> " When you give a luncheon or a dinner, do not invite your friends or your brothers or your relatives or rich neighbors, lest they also invite you in return, and repayment come to you. But when you give a reception, invite the poor, the crippled, the lame, the blind, and you will be blessed, since they do not have

the means to repay you; for you will be repaid at the resurrection of the righteous." (Luke 14:12-14)

To those standing next to Him, Jesus had one clear message: The greatest rewards for righteousness don't come in this lifetime, but in the age to come. Moreover, when you bless people who cannot repay you, your recompense will come from God. To us this is pretty basic, but to listeners in our Lord's day, it was a revelation. However, it is one thing to know it, but quite another to live it out.

Living It Out

My father-in-law was not a dynamic person. He farmed most of his life, raised eight godly children, and was a grandfather to over thirty. In his early years he did a little church work, but much of his service came after age sixty. At about that time, his wife had an accident, leaving her in a wheel chair, changing both of their lives dramatically. She suffered the pain of disability, but no less of an adjustment was required of him.

He found himself in the role of cook, cleaner, and care-giver. This probably didn't rank with the greatest acts of heroism, but heroic it was. After his wife passed on at age seventy-three, he lived alone in a condo for sixteen years. He spent ample time with family and friends, but that was a small part of his life.

Five mornings a week he would go to a Mennonite mission center where he worked as a volunteer, binding Bibles and other sacred books. He did this faithfully, almost to the day of his death at ninety-one. He could have joined a bridge club and pleased himself for those last years, but he didn't. He gave, receiving nothing back but the friendship of the other volunteers.

If he could come back now, what do you think he would say to us about those last thirty years? He was not an intense man during life, but I know he would be intense now. He has seen heaven, he has seen the reward of the righteous, and he has seen the fruit of giving without receiving back. I know what his message would be. Give, bless, invite, love, show compassion, store up, send on ahead, REDEEM THE TIME, for the reward is more than you can imagine!

Why do I use this example? Because most of us aren't called to lofty ministries. We are called to live the Christian life, which is typified by sacrifice, not citations. Every earthly investor knows the power of a small amount of money, invested over a long period of time at compound interest. That is the Christian life. Prayer, care, financial giving, acts of kindness, etc., done consistently over forty years will reap a great reward. And then God adds the increase, which is much better than compound interest — 30, 60, and 100 fold. What does this mean?

It means that when you sow a good deed here, you reap a harvest in eternity; you are paid back in multiples for everything you do. No farmer would sow a seed if in return he received back just that one seed. But he sows to get multiples, and that is the analogy God uses to describe the return on our good works.

The Race Is Not to the Swift.

We do well to heed the verse which declares that *"the race is not to the swift, but to those who keep on running."* Many start strong but rapidly lose steam. It is not a big thing to start strong. It *is* a big thing to be faithful to our calling — daily, over a lifetime. I have seen many start strong, but despite passion, gifting and initial success, they stumbled, turned back, and squandered decades of their life. The enemy took them out.

As we shall one day see, it is no small thing to enter into all that God has for us in this lifetime. The race we run is a marathon, not a sprint. Those who "do daily" and "die daily" will find great success.

Many people I know in both lay and full-time ministry don't have the word "retirement" in their vocabulary. It is rare for these people to assess their fruit, for they are always moving on to the next phase of their calling. But occasionally during a transition there is a taking stock, if you will.

I remember when I retired from my "day job". In order to make room in our home for changing priorities, papers that had accumulated from decades of ministry had to be sifted through and largely discarded. It was in these papers that I found one small portion of what I hope to receive back from the Lord. It represented twenty years of labor in the teaching and worship-leading ministry: thousands of songs, transparencies, seminar notes, sermon outlines, etc.

Where there are visible remnants of ministry, it is the sheer accumulation that is astounding when measured in years. But it is no less true in the invisible realm of prayer. Our Lord's gift and gratitude for a lifetime of daily prayers will one day shock those who have been faithful.

The Essence of Good Works

Let us look more closely at the essence of good works as God conceived them. To those who were persecuted, Jesus said: *"Be glad in that day, and leap for joy, for behold, your reward is great in heaven" (Luke 6:23).* The Greek word for reward here is "misthos", and it means literally "wages". It is the same word that is used in Luke 10 as part of Jesus' instructions to His disciples as they were sent out: *"And stay in that house eating and drinking...for the laborer is worthy of his wages."*

Clearly, our Lord's use of the word "wages" connotes something earned. Any thought that our eternal rewards are akin to a gratuity from a grateful Father is instantly dismissed. But, we could argue, wages imply entitlement, not grace, and God will be debtor to no man. Surely, He owes us nothing. True. Yet we find examples of great kings in the Bible who gave half their kingdom to a faithful person, though they owed them nothing. The servant, however, is not greater than his master. No earthly kings will be found to be more generous in that Day than the King of Kings.

Sharing the Wealth

But it's more than generosity and it's more than gratitude. Perhaps it is more than the earthly mind can conceive. But we get snippets and inklings. At its core, it relates to the enigma of the Divine Romance — the mystery surrounding our Lord's desire for a bride with whom to share. The word "share" gives us insight into one facet of the extravagant love that God feels.

He wants to share the *"spoil with the strong"*. He wants to share His throne with "overcomers". He wants to share the hidden manna of Revelation 2 and His new name of Revelation 3. He wants to share His joy with those who share His suffering. *"And they shall see His face, and His name shall be upon their foreheads.... And His bondslaves shall serve Him."* Truly, as the axiom goes, everything is better when shared.

But we marvel at the profundity of God creating man, dying for man, and then sharing all that is His with man. No words this side of heaven are adequate either in explanation or in praise. But in the inclusion of details like "names on foreheads" and "bondslaves that serve", we find distinctions, wages, and intimacy.

Sharing Equitably

The finite mind and the dull heart cannot conceive that, like a child counting the days till Christmas, Jesus is counting the days till He can openly pay wages to those that have labored for Him in love. But the idea of recompensing everyone equally would be an offense to the One who spoke the words: " *(Those) who have not soiled their garments, will walk with Me in white."*

It would be an affront to the psalmist who said: *"But God has set apart the godly man for Himself."* It would imply that *"being a man after God's own heart"* brought recognition without recompense. It would make a lie of the promise that *"those who sow abundantly, shall reap abundantly."* It would make an empty statement of our Lord's promise to the persecuted that *"great is your reward in heaven!"* It would give no meaning to His constant repetition of the phrase: *"The first shall be last, and the last shall be first."*

Truly, there will be a first and there will be a last, and there will be everything in between. Just as Jesus has decided to "wear" a resurrected body with nail prints forever to proclaim His love, so shall the saints who suffered be set apart.

In the only graphic picture we have in the New Testament of the believers' judgment, we have this clear statement: *"Now he who plants and he who waters are one; but each shall receive his own wages according to his own labor" (I Cor. 3:8).* As a summary statement of the Christian life, it is marvelous in its simplicity. To serve God and bring in the harvest will require labor. As in all of creation, those who labor will receive wages. To put it in the converse: No labor means no fruit; no fruit means no wages; no wages means no eternal glory.

The Harvest from a Different Perspective

One of the few places that the translators chose to render *misthos* as "wages" rather than "reward" is in John 4:36. Jesus has just told the disciples that harvest time is not four months hence, but right now, even as they speak. He is referring to the harvest of men's souls but doesn't use the term because that is not His focus. Not His focus?! How could the focus of the harvest be anything **but** the souls of men!?

Good question.

That's certainly where we put the focus and maybe that's why we aren't very successful at evangelism. Jesus emphasizes something very different — the other side of the equation.

Jesus says: "*Already he who reaps is receiving wages, and is gathering fruit for life eternal; that he who sows and he who reaps may rejoice together.*" That is one of the most compelling verses in all of scripture. Every time I read it, my pulse quickens. It's the word "already" that grabs my attention first.

In this scene, the disciples were mentally wandering and He brings them to attention with his comment on the harvest. Then He exclaims that "already", even as they are standing there talking, the harvest is taking place and people are receiving their wages! Notice the language. Not a word about lost souls. Not a word about hell and damnation. Not a word about the joy of conversion. The total focus is on **reapers receiving wages and gathering fruit for life eternal**, and **the joy they will experience when sowers and reapers rejoice together in heaven.**

My heart's response is always the same: "Hey wait! Count me in! I don't want to miss out! Where's my share? I want eternal fruit; I want to rejoice with the sowers and reapers around the souls of men." That's exactly the response Jesus wants. He *wants* to pay wages. He wants people to *receive* wages. He wants co-laborers. He doesn't want all the glory or all of the joy to go to Him. He wants to share it. God has bent over backwards to allow men to be full participants in the harvest and to be joint-heirs as a result.

Simple Reward; Ultimate Reward

There is another Greek word that brings out a further nuance in the concept of reward. This word occurs in the banquet scene we looked at in Luke. People who invited the poor were told they were blessed because Jesus would reward them at the resurrection. The word for reward here is *apodidomai*, which means to "give back" or "repay". This has less the connotation of wages for work and more the connotation of blessing for giving. It is not just the crushing sacrifices and exhausting ministry that will receive recompense. Everything we give and do in the name of Jesus will receive repayment. Here we have the cup of water, the small act of kindness, and the cheerful hello to brighten the day of a tired cashier. None will go unnoticed or unpaid.

Then as Bruce Wilkerson notes in his book, <u>A Life God Rewards</u>, there is one final word in the Greek that warrants our attention. The writer says: "*For he who comes to God must believe that He is, and that He is a rewarder of those who diligently seek Him*" (Heb. 11:6). The word here for rewarder is neither *misthos* nor *apodidomai*, but a combination of both. This is the only place in the Bible where you will find it describing a person. God is the misthos-apodidomai — the rewarder who pays back your wages in return.

Isn't it interesting that this compound word, the most forceful word available to describe reward, is used to describe the reward and payback for seeking God Himself? All service for God comes with either wages or repayment, but only seeking God and intimacy with Him brings the compound word, the compound blessing, and the compound reward — God Himself. This is fruit "unto eternal life". This is more than the joy of fellowship on earth, but the reward of glorious union in heaven — the just wage and recompense for seeking Him here.

Other Things That Are Rewarded

We find numerous other things mentioned in the scripture that will bring a reward: fasting, praying, ministering to the brethren, loving our enemies, doing our jobs as onto the Lord, visiting the sick and the imprisoned, helping the poor, receiving a prophet, giving financial offerings, serving as a deacon, etc. The list is almost endless. Do you see the genius of God? He has made a way for every single individual to lead a productive life. And for those who are willing to suffer and overcome, there are yet greater rewards: to rule and reign with Christ.

Then God goes a step further. In my mind's eye I can almost overhear a conversation in the eternal council where the Members of the Triune God are discussing future rewards. The Father brings up the fact that it doesn't seem fair that those gifted as church planters and evangelists should inherit so many souls and receive the rewards that go with them. The Spirit agrees and suggests that the one who simply stays and prays should be given the same reward as the one who goes and sows. This suggestion meets with loud agreement. Finally the Son rounds out the discussion with the recommendation that those who financially support church planters should also share equally in their reward. After all, it's a team effort.

Do you see the grace of God? If you feel like a nobody in the Body of Christ, take heart! Your prayer, praise, offering, and effort come before the throne with the same access and power as that of the greatest apostle. And it will likewise be rewarded the same. Of one thing we can be absolutely sure: we are all called to greatness. That is, we are all called to serve. Serving takes many forms, but we can easily forget that laboring in prayer is service of the highest kind. To presume we are inferior to the greatest apostle or are less accountable is a grave mistake.

Keeping Accounts

But who is keeping account of all of this? Not us, because the scripture says the right hand is not supposed to know what the left is doing. Obviously we can't be told to strive for eternal reward and then be unaware that we're doing so.

But God doesn't want us keeping records. He doesn't want our works to be mechanical. He wants our works to be the outflow of an abundant life. The Bible says, *"We have the mind of Christ."* As we mature and walk in the truth of that scripture, we do naturally what previously was labor and effort. We cease to be self-consciously aware of acting out our righteousness, but instead live out the life of the indwelling Christ. A friend's praise for some little nicety surprises us. We hadn't noticed.

The truth is, even if we wanted to keep records, we couldn't, for the simple reason that we only know in part. God alone sees the total picture. The reason the judgment doesn't take place till after the resurrection is simple: our works continue long after we are dead. If we write a book, for instance, it may be read long after we pass on, and influence people towards righteousness. If we leave descendents, the fruit of their lives and that of their children will continue literally until the resurrection. All of this goes into our account.

At the time of our death we do not know the results of all our prayers, offerings, efforts and influence. We may discover at the judgment that we were one link in a chain that brought a million souls into the kingdom. Oh, the joy that awaits us if we have been diligent and faithful!

I remember an Argentinean evangelist making the following statement: "We justify our lack of results by saying 'God is not into numbers'. Yes He is!! *God is into numbers!* The more souls the better!" It's the same with good works. Volume matters. The fear of legalism and practicing a "religion of works" has caused many to fall into the ditch of inertia. A wiser approach is to keep praying, keep giving, keep witnessing, and keep serving. Examine your heart daily, but let God sort it all out on Judgment Day.

Never forget: *"He who sows sparingly will reap sparingly."*

The Kingdom Script

Keep the goal in mind, which *is*, to quote the title of a famous devotional, "My Utmost for His Highest". His highest comes after the judgment and is related to the kingdom script. God could have chosen any context in which to frame the eternal, but the story is set in a faraway kingdom where you and I have a part to play. In fact, we get to choose our part by the choices we make today. If that sounds confusing, it is because we have never understood our destiny. Our destiny is not some vaporous post-mortem existence, but rather the Kingdom of Heaven and the Kingdom of God.

Those who are looking for the "worker's paradise" won't find it in heaven. Those who are looking for a place where all are equal, where all receive the same wages, and where all hold the same position, will be surprised at life in the kingdom. You and I are not going to the People's Democratic Republic of God. We are going to the Kingdom of God. A kingdom is not a flat structure where supposed equality exists. It is a pyramid structure with a king at the top, princes below the king, and then the nobility followed by commoners. Are there commoners in the Kingdom? We'll have to wait and see, but to be sure there is nobility. It presumably takes the latter to give meaning to the former.

This world is the proving ground for the next world. We are currently in the womb of life; we have yet to experience real life. The purpose of this life is to ascertain who is worthy to attain to the resurrection of the righteous. Having found that company of men and women, God is then in the business of finding faithful servants to staff the many important positions in heaven. God, you might say, is the Human Resources Manager in charge of staffing.

Laying Hold of Eternal Life

The apostle Paul gives Timothy an exhortation that we all need to heed. *"Fight the good fight of faith; lay hold on eternal life to which you were called..."* (1Tim. 6:12). How do you lay hold on something that you already possess? Paul is using an idiom. You and I may already **have** eternal life, but there is a step beyond this that Paul refers to as **laying hold** on eternal life. He explains what this means a few verses later in his instruction to rich people:

> *"Instruct those who are rich in this present world not to be conceited or to fix their hope on the uncertainty of riches, but on God, who richly supplies us with all things to enjoy.*
>
> *Instruct them to do good, to be rich in good works, to be generous and ready to share,*
>
> *Storing up for themselves the treasure of a good foundation for the future, so that they may **lay hold** on eternal life." (1Tim. 6: 18,19)*

In this verse Paul gives us a list of things that the rich must do "so that they may lay hold on eternal life." They are told to do good, be rich in good works, and be generous and ready to share. Although they are told to do four things, it is really just one, and is summarized in the phrase "good works". So laying hold on eternal life means excelling in good works. It is a further elaboration of James' statement that "faith without works is dead." It is a different way of saying "examine yourself to see if you be in the faith." But above all, it is an exhortation to fruitfulness.

Don't go passively into eternity; be aggressive, grab hold of it! Finish the race with a full head of steam! Don't spend your final years in self-indulgence. Go for gold! Good works are a part of every Christian's life, but if we are fixed on the eternal, we will excel all the more.

Paul would later say in II Timothy: *"I have fought the good fight, I have finished the course, I have kept the faith."* But the key is in the next few words: *"in the **future** there* *is laid up for me...*". Paul has already told us that if there were no afterlife, no heaven, and no reward, we might as well party till we die. But since there *is* eternal life, he had a reason to "fight with wild beasts at Ephesus". He had a reason to sacrifice and suffer.

But since salvation is free, Paul's motivation for good works wasn't gaining heaven. From Paul's point of view, just *having* eternal life is not enough; we have to *lay hold* of eternal life. And we see from the above verse that we *lay hold* by *laying up*.

How About Us?

The question then is simply this: Are we laying hold of eternal life? I have been in many services where seemingly every attendee was a believer who already had eternal life. And yet the speaker still gave a gospel message. Perhaps it was to snag a lost soul who may have slipped in under the radar. But more likely it was an expression of wonder and gratitude — a reminder of our great salvation. These reminders are nice, but the emphasis is misplaced.

The emphasis in a salvation message is on the past, whereas the message of **laying hold** is for the present and the future. Yet I have never heard a message on laying hold of eternal life. Somehow the recurrent Bible theme of good works and eternal rewards just seems off topic to so many people. But it is not off topic to God. It is something we are urged to consider. "Fight the good fight; lay hold on eternal life!"

Can you see Judgment Day in your mind's eye? Can you picture someone whose works pass through the judgment virtually unscathed resulting in glory, praise and honor? Can you feel the surge of the crowd around you as they cheer this one who gave so much for your blessed Savior? Can you see that it was all a matter of choice? As others receive their acclaim for making a mountain of works out of a molehill of material, does the point sink in? That could be you; that could be me. And hopefully it will be, for a life of good works is one prayer away, one praise away, and one act of kindness away. Always. It's one moment at a time.

Let us persevere in doing good.

We have discussed the four major areas that will come under judgment, but the whole is greater than the sum of its parts. We can be victorious in those four areas but still fall short in living the Christian life. The Christian life is set apart from every other lifestyle by certain features.

There are many non-believers who are faithful, hard-working, generous souls. They make wise use of their time and money, and lead exemplary lives. On the surface, they stack up pretty well against many believers. But salvation results in more than good works and character. We are born-again into a cosmic battle, and we yield our lives to King Jesus who makes demands that are absolute. These demands give our lives a quality that is very different from that of the agnostic do-gooder.

One of these demands involves a cross. What does this quaint symbol mean to our lives in the world of the twenty-first century? Let us begin with a discussion of this much-neglected subject.

SECTION THREE

Timeless Measures of the Christian Life

The Cross and the Christian Soldier

The Cross

The cross needs a little explanation to a generation who has perhaps never heard a sermon on it. For most people it probably means no more than surrender, commitment, and the Lordship of Jesus Christ. But even these terms don't impact us like they once did. So let us begin with a clear understanding of what the cross is, and move on to its implications for our lives. How we understand the cross, and how well we bear it, will have a great impact on our inheritance.

Jesus said in Luke 14: 27: *"Whoever does not carry his own cross and come after Me cannot be my disciple."* He then moved on to the tower illustration. We know from that illustration that when he says *"cannot be my disciple"*, He means *"won't be able to be my disciple"*.

First, let us be clear on what the cross isn't. It isn't the many hurdles we all face in daily life. It's not "the hand we've been dealt", so to speak. Though we all have personal trials that are unique to us, this is not what Christ was alluding to. As Andrew Murray put it: "Christians need to understand that bearing the cross does not, in the first place, refer to the trials which we call crosses, but to the daily giving up of life, of dying to self, which must mark us as much as it did the Lord." The reason we have to die to self is simple: Self cannot and will not follow Christ.

The cross in Roman times was an instrument of death. It separated those that were nailed to it from the rest of society. Those on the cross had reached the limit of their own possibilities. Whatever their dreams or aspirations had been, they were now unattainable. The implications for our lives are obvious. It has been said that the way of the cross is just as unacceptable to the child of God as the way of salvation is to the lost.

The Offence of the Cross

"Cursed is anyone who dies on a tree"(Gal. 3:13). Paul quotes from a verse in Deuteronomy to remind us that we are redeemed from the curse of the Law because Jesus *"became a curse for us"*. But the idea of a "cursed Messiah" was understandably hard for the Jews to grasp. In our Lord's day crucifixion was a shameful way to die. To suggest to the Jewish authorities that His manner of death was somehow noble, brought the deepest offence.

But this struggle is by no means unique to them. We have seen many Christian ministries fall into derision because they were unwilling to be separated from the world. Many haven't been content to glory in the "foolishness of the gospel" but instead have sought acceptance. Men try in a thousand ways to soften the offence of the cross and thus escape ridicule and persecution. The desire to fit in is human, but capitulation brings offense — to the Lord. It is not a question of whether or not offence will come. The question is who will be offended — the Lord or the world.

I have seen the offence of the cross played out on the world stage on numerous occasions. I enjoy interview shows, and over the years I have seen dozens of high profile ministers interviewed on secular programs. At some point, after the guest minister explains the way of salvation, the interviewer asks the bombshell question: " So are you saying that everyone who doesn't believe like *you do* is going to hell?" The kicker is the "you do". They can't get at Christ, so you become the target. It takes a lot of steel to look the interviewer in the eye and without apology or obfuscation answer a simple "yes".

If the minister says yes, he has committed the most heinous crime of our age. He has been intolerant. And not just that, but also narrow-minded, self-righteous, primitive, anti-inclusive, simplistic, and any number of horrible things. Instantly he has moved from venerated man of the cloth to scoundrel. Why is this? Because of the offence of the cross. There are two reasons why the cross is so offensive.

First, to suggest to autonomous man that he can't choose his own way of salvation is insulting. Explaining that there is one way already determined by God without our consultation is an affront. Secondly, to imply that grace and faith alone are the basis for salvation is an offence to man's pride. He wants to believe that there are good works that he can add to the equation.

The reason most of us get such an easy ride through life is that most people don't know what we believe. Telling them in a way that is neither self-righteous nor apologetic is one of the great challenges of discipleship. The other great challenge is dying to self.

Dying to Self

On the issue of death to self, let me make a couple of basic observations. If the cross was simply overcoming the trials and sufferings that are common to men, then unbelievers can choose the cross as well. They routinely proclaim that how you play the hand you have been dealt is more important than the hand itself. Many unbelievers have overcome great hurdles in life to become successful. If this was truly the cross, then many unbelievers carry it better than we do.

However, the cross is not something we are dealt, but something we **choose** because of our relationship to Christ.

If we're very lucky we get to suffer shame and loss of reputation for His name. We get to experience lost opportunities
and death to personal ambition. Like the grain of wheat, we
get to fall into the ground and die, and thereby bear much
fruit. This the unbeliever cannot do. Only the child of God
can choose this path. This path alone will give us the power
to obey Christ's commands, such as the one to love our
enemies. If you only love your friends and not your enemies,
Jesus has one simple question: "*What do you more than the
pagans?*" This is the defining question.

The cross takes us places even good pagans can't go.

As I write this, a tragic event has just unfolded. A man
who was held in a county jail in Atlanta and on trial for rape
has just killed four people, including a judge. Then he escaped
and forced his way into a young woman's apartment, seeking
temporary refuge. The woman, Ashley Smith, is a Christian,
and over the course of seven hours she talked to the assailant
about her faith. He left his guns lying in the bathroom, and
at several points she could have escaped or even killed him.
The most amazing opportunity came when he asked her to
follow him in her car while he ditched a stolen truck. She did
so, knowing she could just drive away and escape unharmed
if she chose. Yet she allowed the man to get back into her car
and return to her apartment. Why???

Simple: she was a Christian. She was a person who,
despite her own struggles, seemed to grasp a truth that eludes
so many of us: We are not on this earth to serve ourselves.
She feared that if she left the man alone, he would panic and
end up killing other people, and he himself would probably
be killed.

Did you get that? She put her life on the line for a mass
murderer she had only just met and for others that she would
never meet. Why? Because she feared God more than she
feared death. We all die, and she knew her destination was
heaven. But she believed God had put her in this situation

for a purpose, although she herself could not truly understand the scope of the purpose.

She was just doing the right thing. But the watching world was dumbfounded. No unbeliever would do what she had done. None. And the world knew it. It only takes a few genuine disciples to dumbfound the world.

The cross will take you amazing places if you are willing to carry it.

The Cross and the Abundant Life

Few verses have received more attention and sown more confusion than John 10:10, the abundant life verse. In addition to "Abundant Life Seminars", it has no doubt spawned a thousand sermons. If this verse were but one of many on the subject of abundance, I doubt that it would receive much notice at all. But it's the absence of similar statements that give this verse its prominence. You might say that we desperately need it to prove things about the Christian life that aren't elsewhere stated.

By comparison, other weightier subjects have found far less favor. "Bearing your cross", for instance, is a major Bible theme, and yet it has probably generated far fewer sermons than John 10:10. I have never heard mention of a "Cross-Bearing Seminar". Why is that?

The reason we hear so little about the cross and so much about the abundant life is because it is human nature to want abundance. The cross, on the other hand, has little appeal. But God, being infinitely wise, has made the one dependant upon the other. No cross means no abundance. Here is the verse in question: *"The thief comes only to steal, and kill, and destroy; I come that they might have life, and might have it abundantly"* (John 10:10).

The Greek word for life in this verse is *zoe,* which means "vitality", as when we say a person is "full of life". We find the word *zoe* most often joined to the word *eternal,* as in "eternal life", the ultimate vitality. This is the case in John 3:16 where we are told that Jesus came that whoever believes in Him might not perish, but have eternal life. The word for *life* here is *zoe*, the same as in John 10:10.

We know that the promise of John 3:16 is heaven, where eternal life finds its fulfillment. That is also true of the abundant life spoken of in John 10:10. It is in heaven. The Greek word for "perish" in John 3:16 is the same word for "destroy" in John 10:10. The root of the word means "to separate". So both verses speak of the eternal — eternal life with God in heaven, or eternal separation from God in hell. Any application to the physical is purely secondary. The Greek word used for physical life in the scriptures is *psuche* meaning *breath*, and is not found in either of these verses.

Jesus came that we might go to heaven, and that life in heaven should be full of vitality and abundance. We know that heaven entails eternal bliss for all, but abundance is related to reward and will vary greatly from person to person. So there is at least a two-fold reason why our Lord came — to give us eternal life, and to give us abundance in eternity. He gives both, but both in turn require something on our part. To obtain the first requires faith in Christ. The second will cost us our lives.

Who doesn't want abundance in every aspect of their temporal life? That, of course, is the superficial appeal of this verse and the reason it is the text for so many sermons. But by neglecting the primary interpretation, we are steering people away from the eternal to focus on the temporal.

Our Lord's appeal was not to come and live, but to come and die — to die daily. One of the most enduring paradoxes of the Christian faith is that through death comes life. It is hard to mesh the life of temporal abundance with that of the crucified life, especially if we use John 10:10 as our text. The end result is that we often simply avoid teaching the crucified life.

A Better Way

There is a better way. We can teach both the crucified life and the abundant life if we use John 12:24,25 as our text:

> *"I tell you the truth, unless a kernel of wheat falls to the ground and dies, it remains only a single seed. But if it dies, it produces many seeds. The man who loves his life will lose it, while the man who hates his life in this world will keep it for eternal life."* (NIV)

When a seed falls into the ground and dies, it yields a crop. When you and I die to ourselves, our marriage gets better, things go better at work, we squander less money and our finances thereby improve. This abundance comes from the cross, discipleship and death, just as Jesus promised.

But there is yet greater abundance to be had in the mind and spirit, because submission to Christ transforms our character. And perhaps, ultimately, we become bread for the nations. This is the climax to the abundant life and is rooted in the statement: *"Not my will, but Thine be done."* Imagine, if you will, souls coming into the kingdom because of our obedience. That is true abundance.

That is the abundance we need to preach. But our thinking is always too small. Our Lord's next words in this passage settle the issue: *"The man who loves his life will lose it."* The word for life here is *psuche* — physical life. It can't be said too often that Jesus always pits the temporal against the eternal. By focusing people on an abundant life in the temporal realm, we are in danger of having them love their life and try to save it.

The clear teaching of scripture is that we are supposed to lose our life, and for one very important reason: We cannot have an abundant life in heaven if we expend all of our energy trying to have an abundant life on earth.

Happily, through death to self and the crucified life, we can have both. Through death to self we can garner temporal abundance; and in addition, we can have abundant treasure in heaven. Unfortunately, we have a tendency to bypass the cross and the eternal abundance, and focus on something that doesn't work: trying to get abundance by focusing on abundance, teaching on abundance, and praying for abundance. That is putting the cart before the horse. Our focus is to be God, the kingdom, serving, and our eternal estate.

Out of this, abundance must and will come.

The Christian Soldier

Carrying a cross isn't a mystical experience. It will take us some very predictable places. At the very least, it'll take us to war. This is the war for the souls of men that we are all called to. And we don't have to go to the mission field to participate. At any given time in any given war, no more than 10% of a country's manpower is on the front lines. We have what is called the "war effort". Back home, away from the fiercest fighting, men and women are pitching in, building armaments, and supporting the boys in any way they can. These are the factory workers, the medics, the fundraisers, etc. They are no less committed, no less focused.

It's no different from the spiritual war we are in. Most people aren't called to the front line of foreign missions, but we are all called to support the war effort with prayer and finances. And yet, in a sense, there is a front line in every city. In every place where the devil is destroying lives and tormenting souls, there is a battle, and God has called us to be part of that battle even at great personal cost. The apostle Paul said:

"Suffer hardship with me, as a good soldier of Christ Jesus.

> *No soldier in active service entangles himself in the affairs of everyday life, so that he may please the one who enlisted him as a soldier."* (2 Tim. 2:3,4)

Here Paul tells us the one thing that will hinder those in active service: entangling themselves in the affairs of everyday life. Being caught up in worldly affairs renders us ineffective as soldiers. That presents quite a challenge since at every corner we bump into the world and its enticements. But it's a challenge we must overcome or remain soldiers in name only. The expectations of King Jesus are very clear on this point.

He would be incensed if his crack troops were engaged in frivolities or seeking some worldly honor while there was a battle raging. Picture a missionary in the midst of a great harvest who has more interest in his golf score than in souls. It sounds outrageous when expressed in those terms, but how different is it where we live? Are we pleasing the one who enlisted us a soldier, or are we so entangled in worldly affairs that we've forgotten there even is a war?

The Demands of War

I was born during the dying days of World War II. The moviemakers of my youth were obsessed with the war. I've seen dozens of war movies, and the underlying theme is always the same: War is hell; war makes normal life impossible; war alters the future for millions. Everyone wishes they didn't have to fight and sacrifice and give up their dreams and plans. But war makes those kinds of demands. Pursuing a personal agenda is unthinkably vain and selfish when the lives of millions are at stake. It is a life no one would choose, but honorable men accept it as a solemn duty that transcends everything — wives, children, careers and comforts.

The apostle Paul was from a different era, but the essence of war never changes. Spiritual or physical, the demands are the same. What Christian wouldn't want to pursue his own personal ambitions and ignore the war? That would be the most natural desire in the world. But like the men whose names are written on memorials around the world, we just can't do that.

This is the most important war of all, and to "lose our life" in this cause is the most sacred calling on earth. Perhaps it won't cost us our physical life as in martyrdom, but at the very least, it will cost us our self-life. *"We're not our own; we're bought with a price."* There's a call currently going out to all those that are AWOL: "Get back to your regiment. The next great offensive is about to begin."

As an aside, men who forget the battle often succumb to sin. King David taught us that. He even taught us what the main sin is likely to be — lust. Much of the pornography addiction that is sweeping the church is because men aren't on the front lines where they belong. They're away from the battle with idle time on their hands, and they're getting into trouble.

When a Christian falls morally, we often refer to him as a casualty of war. That is sometimes true, but in many cases it is just the opposite. By ignoring the battle, and in particular the battle for the needy, many are falling into perversion.

"Put off evil by doing good" is God's word to His Church.

TEN

Worship and Intimacy

Worship

The catechism that I learned as a child emphasized the role of man in the grand scheme of things. It was, very simply, to bring pleasure to God through worship. It would be many more years, though, before I would discover that worship is more than the rituals we see enacted by various religious groups around the world. Nowadays few believers would confuse the word "worship" with "worship service".

Worship at the very least is a lifestyle, and only incidentally incorporates expressions such as we might see on a Sunday morning. Yet despite a myriad of teachings on the subject, there is much that we have missed about this truly pivotal subject. Worship is at the core of how we relate to God, and so it cannot *but* impact the outcome of our judgment. For this reason we must look carefully at its essence.

Law of First Mention

In Bible hermeneutics there is something we call "the law of first mention". Whenever you want to get at the essence of a doctrine, look for its first mention in scripture. That first usage will tell you something very critical. The first appearance of the word "worship" was not in the place you might expect. No instruments were playing, and there was neither rhapsody nor spiritual fervor. However, something else was present, and that something else will tell us more about the true nature of worship than all the subsequent verses.

The word *worship* first appears in the text describing an incident in the lives of Abraham and Isaac:

> *"Now it came about after these things, that God tested Abraham, and said to him, 'Abraham!' And he said, 'Here I am .'*
>
> *And He said, 'Take now your son, your only son whom you love, Isaac, and go to the land of Moriah; and offer him there as a burnt offering on one of the mountains of which I will tell you.'*
>
> *So Abraham rose early in the morning and saddled his donkey, and took two of his young men with him and Isaac his son; and he split wood for the burnt offering, and arose and went to the place of which God had told him.*
>
> *On the third day Abraham raised his eyes and saw the place from a distance.*
>
> *And Abraham said to his young men, 'Stay here with the donkey and I and the lad will go yonder; and we will* ***worship*** *and return to you.'"* (Gen. 22:1-5)

Here we find Abraham telling his servants that he and the lad were going to go up to worship. What was this act of worship? Human sacrifice.

Imagine you are Abraham. You have a close walk with God; He even calls you friend. You know His nature, His ways and even the things He hates — idolatry and human sacrifice. And yet He's asking you to kill your own son to prove your love. That's analogous to a gang initiation where you have to kill an innocent person to prove your loyalty. Pagan ritual at the command of the most high God! What an offence! But it gets worse.

It isn't just any human sacrifice. You're asked to kill your only son, your most prized possession. And then the final blow: you're asked to kill the seed from which everything you've been promised will come forth. Isaac, the next in line to father countless generations, was to die without offspring. That is analogous to a microbiologist discovering a serum that would save millions, and then being told to destroy it.

At first glance it seems like needless cruelty. But to God, the *"trying of one's faith"* really is more precious than gold that perishes. This is particularly true for those who are singled out for momentous tasks as Abraham was. God is not insecure about offending the mind to reveal the heart. Abraham went through the same screening process we see in John 6. Here the text says Jesus knew which of his disciples were false, and so it remained for Him to ferret them out with phrases like *"eat My flesh"*. It worked. Their hearts were revealed, and they left. Through this test, Abraham's heart was likewise revealed, and God tells us the result: *"Now I know that you fear God."*

I've been asked to do some hard things in my life, but nothing approaching this. Remember, God didn't just take Isaac in a riding accident, but He asked Abraham to sacrifice Isaac willingly. God was after something even more precious than the brokenness of suffering. He was after radical obedience.

So what, based on this story, is the essence of true worship? It is the willingness to put to death the most important thing in your life. It is dying to your hopes and dreams. It is being obedient to Him even after He has deeply offended you. It is radical obedience on every level. In Abraham's case, it also came with the deep trust that *"no good thing will He deny to those who walk uprightly" (Ps. 84:11)*. Abraham knew that God's promises wouldn't end with the death of his son, for the scripture later says, *"He considered that God is able to raise men even from the dead" (Heb. 11:19)*.

True worship, then, can be very costly. It doesn't always come out of a full heart. Sometimes it is simply an act of obedience. And at other times it must be offered in pain. Many have felt hypocritical for worshipping God when their emotions were dull and their hopes decimated. But the opposite is true. Worshipping God in the midst of great pain shows the depth of our faith and touches His heart in a unique way.

In Romans 12 we find worship aptly described as the presentation of our bodies as a living and holy sacrifice. But though worship is primarily a lifestyle, it also has many expressions. Foremost among these expressions is the Hebrew word *shachah*, which means to bow and fall on one's face. But even the *shachah* derives its worth from the sanctity of the believer's life.

Receiving glory from a person who would say the same about any of the idols in his life means less than hearing it from a man who has no idols. Receiving *shachah* from a person who trifles with religion and only dimly perceives God's glory means less than receiving it from a close friend. Abraham was such a man. Abraham had seen God's glory and knew Him intimately; therefore his worship had substance and great significance.

Praise Versus Worship

Worship can be better understood if we contrast it with praise. The distinction is very simple: *God commands praise, but He seeks worshippers.* The Psalms, in particular, are filled with extravagant expressions of praise. We find such an example in Psalm 148:

"*Praise Him all His angels;*
   Praise Him all His hosts;
Praise Him sun and moon;
   Praise Him all stars of light;
   Praise Him highest heaven." (*Psalm 148:2,3*)

Later in that psalm the list grows to include the sea monster, the mountains, the hills, and even the creeping things. All, we are told, must praise God. They are given no choice — it's a command. In Psalm 76 we have the unusual declaration that even the wrath of man will praise Him. And lest we miss the point, we have this final exhortation from Psalm 150: *"Let everything that has breath praise the Lord"* *(Ps. 150:6).*

I remember meeting a fellow, when I first came to town, who impressed me with his intensity. He was a little quirky but very likeable, and since he attended another church, I only saw him on occasion. Evidently he had marital problems although his wife seemed like a gem. One day I heard that he had left his wife and taken up with another woman. My initial reaction was one of sadness. It quickly turned to shock, however, when I encountered the two of them in a restaurant. I was startled to see him publicly embracing her, and I found the moment awkward. He evidently didn't share my discomfort because, without even changing his position, he gave me a hearty greeting.

The next Sunday, who should be in our church but this same fellow. No doubt, I reasoned, he was ashamed to face his own pastor and would sit quietly and observe. But again I was in for a shock. Seemingly oblivious to his surroundings, he had taken a front-row seat and was loudly praising the Lord. When I saw this, I muttered to myself, "You can't do that, you hypocrite!" I was immediately corrected by the Lord. He reminded me of the disciples who shouted "Hosanna!" on His march into Jerusalem. Their love was as fickle as this fellow's. But in answer to an indignant Pharisee, our Lord had this terse comment: *"I tell you that if these become silent, the stones will cry out!"* (Luke 19:40).

The scripture declares that " *the Lord is great and greatly to be praised."* For this reason the Lord accepts praise from everyone and everything. Praise is simply a declaration that

God is great. God doesn't mind even the vilest of sinners saying He's great, because it's true. However, worship is something different altogether.

God is **seeking** worshippers, John 4 tells us. He knows there is coming a day when every knee will bow and every tongue will confess that Jesus Christ is Lord to the glory of God the Father. But now is not that day. In this age, worship is an honor that is only accorded to certain people. You need clean hands and a pure heart. Psalm 101 says: *"He who walks in a blameless way is the one who will minister to Me."*

By that standard we can't tell outwardly who is worshipping in a church service. Though someone may employ all the outward expressions of worship, there may be a great barrier between that person and God. Both Psalm 15 and Psalm 24 ask the same simple question: *"O Lord, who may abide in Thy tent, who may ascend into the hill of the Lord?"* The answer is quite long, but here is the essence: *"He who **walks** with integrity, and **works** righteousness and **speaks** truth in his heart."* This is the kind of person who can approach God in worship and whose life is an act of worship. It involves how we walk, work and speak.

Three times in the scriptures we are exhorted to *"worship the Lord in the beauty of holiness."* This is a requirement, not an add-on. During our Lord's encounter with the Samaritan woman He goes on to say what kind of worshippers the Father was seeking. They are people who will worship in spirit and in truth. All others, we presume, fall short.

We are not discussing salvation, praise, access to the throne, or even prayer. We are talking about being able to meet the basic condition for which we have been created — to worship God. Wouldn't it be sad to hear said of us what our Lord said of Israel: *"This people draw near with their words...but they remove their hearts far from Me"* *(Isa.29:13).*

Worship, then, is even more than radical obedience. It is also communion with God in the spirit and rests on the foundation of truth. It comes out of a pure heart and grows in the knowledge of God.

Faith and the Human Will

Worship, as we have seen, can involve great sacrifice. Many of us may never have an "Abraham experience", but we must all sacrifice. However, unless we learn the nature of this sacrifice we will be hindered in our worship. Jesus addresses this in chapter 17 of Luke's gospel.

In verse 5 the apostles make this request of the Lord: *"Increase our faith!"* Jesus then proceeds to define true faith using the example of the mustard seed. But He still hasn't dealt with their request. They didn't want a definition of faith; they wanted *more* of it. In answer, then, to their desire for more faith, He tells the parable of the unprofitable servant:

> *"But which of you, having a slave ploughing or tending sheep, will say to him when he has come in from the field, 'Come immediately and sit down to eat'?*
>
> *But will he not say to him, 'Prepare something for me to eat, and properly clothe yourself and serve me until I have eaten and drunk; and afterward you will eat and drink'?*
>
> *He does not thank the slave because he did the things which were commanded, does he?*
>
> *So you too, when you do all the things which are commanded, say, 'We are unworthy slaves; we have done only that which we ought to have done.'"* (Luke 17:7-10)

The primary application of this passage is faith, so let's deal with this before we move on to the issue of worship.

When the disciples had asked for more faith, they were making a significant request. Our Lord's response is what we would call "weighty", for it would provide key insight to future disciples on the subject of faith.

It is perhaps for this reason that He is so stern in His answer, which comes in the form of this parable. They thought faith was a matter of **"ask and it shall be given unto you"**(Matt. 7:7), whereas, in fact, it is a **"give and it shall be given unto you"** (Luke 6:38). Some things we are told to ask for; other things only come through great effort — that of giving.

Faith is the currency of the kingdom. Everyone wants more faith. *"Be it done unto you according to your faith,"* our Master said. He also said, *"The just shall live by faith,"* and that without faith it was impossible to please Him. I'm not surprised that there was a Faith Movement, because many of the most powerful scriptures relate to this issue. If we can get this right, then a lot of things will fall into place.

As much as we would like to ask for faith and take delivery of a generous supply, we know it doesn't work that way. At the very minimum, *"faith comes by hearing and hearing by the word of God."* That takes work. The scriptures tell us, as well, that every word, even a word on faith, must be "mixed with faith". That is, it must be believed and put into practice. In the above parable, we have to wait on God before He gives us what we desire. Why is this?

For openers, if we could have faith apart from intimacy with God, we would be far less prone to seek Him and spend time with Him. If faith was simply a principle and operated independently of God, then we could stride about with great arrogance, doing mighty deeds. Since the deeds wouldn't necessarily be of God, we would, in fact, be dangerous.

But faith doesn't come that way. As we minister to God and read His Word, we develop a relationship. Out of that relationship comes confidence that He will do what He said

He would. We take on God's heart and His priorities. We step out with the small faith that we have, and God shows up, blessing us and validating His word. That encourages us to take even bigger steps of faith. This is called growth, and it doesn't come easy. Many times our faith gets us out on a limb, and sometimes God delays His appearing until we are tested and stretched to the limit.

At other times we feel totally inadequate to the task and are amazed as God comes through against all odds. In these cases, God's strength is made perfect in our weakness. If we have achieved a comfort level in ministry, then we are probably falling short of God's best, for He will seldom call us to do anything that we can do easily without Him. Living by faith is truly living on the edge, believing God for ever bigger things.

Because we all like short cuts, having achieved some measure of faith, we are tempted to move to the next level of action without moving to the next level of intimacy. This is where many suffer shipwreck. Pride in our accomplishments creeps in, and subtly we begin to believe we can do it without God. This is the opposite response to what God is looking for.

He tells us that when we have done all that we are supposed to do, we are to say: "*We are unworthy slaves, we have done only that which we ought to have done.*" If God chooses to exalt us, so be it. But let us be wary of believing that our works have earned us some special consideration, or that we can now act independently of God. These verses warn us against such attitudes. Let us now look at how these verses relate to worship.

Worship and the Human Will

You've had a rough day. You've been out ministering for hours and the well is dry, the tank is empty. You stagger into the house and fall into a chair and wait. Wait for what?

Why, for Jesus to come, of course. You've been serving Him all day long, and now you're weary and want to hear joy bells and smell the refreshing scent of His presence. You feel you've earned it.

But Jesus doesn't come. He almost sounds unkind in Luke 17 as He explains the reason. In the modern vernacular, He would say something like this: "Give your head a shake! How many people do you know who would do likewise with a servant? How many masters, who have slaves serving them all day, would wait on their own servants before they have had supper? No, the servant finishes work, fixes his master's supper, and then he is fed." What is the spiritual application?

As tired as we are from serving the Lord, we must minister to Him before He ministers to us. When we begin to praise Him in our weariness, He comes with His glory, anoints our head with oil, and bestows His presence on us.

When we go to church after a hard week, we just want to be ministered to. Yes, God is our focus, but personal blessing is often our goal. It's "fill-up time", and we want the rain from heaven to fall. But that's not how it works. We must lift your hands and open our mouth and declare the praises of the great King. There is protocol to be followed. *"I will enter His gates with thanksgiving in my heart, I will enter His gates with praise"(Ps.100).*

Additionally, God *"inhabits the praises of His people"*, not the feelings of His people. If we are waiting for a pre-determined level of emotion before we start praising, we may wait forever because it may never come. We must offer the sacrifice of praise in our dryness and fatigue.

Why does God do this? In part, He is establishing rank. We need frequent reminders as to which one of us is God and which one of us is not, or, to use the language of the parable, which is the master and which is the servant. He doesn't, of course, do this because of any insecurity on His part, but because of a need on our part.

Our problem is one of will. God has to constantly remind us to engage our will. Yes, He may flood us with His presence at unexpected times, but this is the exception, not the rule. If God's presence came apart from an act of our will, then we would rarely seek Him. Many would be satisfied with the benefits of intimacy even if intimacy itself was absent. But to get the benefits of intimacy, we must **have** intimacy. To get the benefits of **being** in His presence, we must **enter** His presence. *"In His presence is fullness of joy,"* but His presence doesn't drop out of the sky. We must choose His presence and there is a price tag attached. We find the details in Psalm 100.

God must, at all times, stand against self-pity. He must resist inaction born of discouragement. He must teach us the survival skill that glory may not be where we are, but we can bring glory down. He wants us to mature. To do so, we must operate under the spiritual laws that God has established, and one of those laws is the following: *"Draw near to God and He will draw near to you."*

A Royal Priesthood

In several places, the Scriptures refer to us as a royal priesthood. We reign through praise. In every situation there is a battle to see who gets the praise, God or Satan. Are we people who are cast about by the tumult of life, or are we in charge? Praise will often determine the answer. Do we put on the garment of praise for the spirit of heaviness, or is the heaviness energized through the garments of fear and despair? We get to decide.

Church is a sanctuary. Life is what happens to us the rest of the week. It's there, sometimes in the open, sometimes behind the scenes, that we feel the conflict of the cosmic battle for the souls of men. In the power of praise, we can declare that God is on the throne, even in the most difficult circumstances. Regardless of any outward change, that action is itself a victory. It doesn't just bring victory; it *is* victory. It's the victory of our faith that overcomes the world. We all live on bended knee, so to speak. We're either bowing to the god of this world through despair and defeat, or to the King Eternal through praise and worship.

Intimacy

"He who dwells in the secret place will abide in the shadow of the Almighty." (Ps. 91:1)

There's a secret place in God that few people know about. It's not the kind of place you stumble across. You have to know it exists, and you have to be looking for it. It's a place that God has reserved for those who aren't content with the ordinary. Contented people never find this place.

Life is short, and most people try to cram as much as they can into the few years they have. But the modern age can be frustrating. Do we have less time or more time than our ancestors? That is the question that keeps popping up as we view our labor-saving devices but also our more frantic schedules.

The answer, of course, is that we have the same amount of time. In every era there are people who never find time for God. But the opposite is also true. In every era there are people whose passion for God cannot be so easily contained. Mere externals are an annoyance but not a roadblock. They press on.

Some would say it's only a matter of values. We are all familiar with the statement: "You can tell what people value by how they spend their time." Sounds logical, doesn't it? In science it's what we call a logical fallacy. It's totally logical; the only problem is, it's false.

For instance, the average sports game is about three hours long — hockey, football, baseball, etc. Most guys watch at least one a week. It is a rare fellow that will spend that amount of time per week on prayer, Bible reading and seeking God. Ergo, most guys value football more than God. I don't think so. There may be carnality in the church, but it's misleading to view the problem in such a simplistic manner.

If you're still not convinced, then consider this. There are millions of lovely Christian women who spend more time on crossword puzzles, television and visiting over coffee than they do on anything related to their faith or the gospel. Do they really value crossword puzzles more than the Lord? No, they don't. So what's the answer to the riddle?

The Pleasure Principle

The problem is with the wording. The issue is not what we value, but what gives us pleasure or enjoyment. Humans are essentially pleasure-driven in the broadest sense of the word. People take great pleasure in frivolous hobbies, watching sports, family get-togethers, chatting with friends, and even ministry.

Since God created us, He is well aware of our need for pleasure. He even appealed to it in a well-known verse: *"In Thy presence is fullness of joy **(enjoyment)**; in Thy right hand there are **pleasures** forevermore"* (Ps.16:11). Granted, it's a different kind of pleasure but a pleasure nevertheless. But unlike our television sets, God's presence and pleasures don't come with a remote. The most important Being in the universe can't be conjured up at the push of a button; He must be sought. And as we saw earlier, only the most persistent will find Him.

Often people castigate themselves with statements like this: "I know I should spend more time with the Lord. I'm going to make a real effort to do that this year." The word "castigate" gives us some needed insight. People only castigate themselves when they are remiss in doing things that are unpleasant duties. For instance, we say, "I really should exercise more, eat less, keep the place tidier, etc." I wonder how the Lord feels when we lump Him in with all the other things we find tiresome and unpleasant.

But the pleasure principle changes that.

If a husband agreed to have a date once a week with his wife, she would be thrilled. But what if every week, when that time came around, he rolled his eyes, gritted his teeth, and did his duty? She wouldn't be flattered. Being willing to spend time with her is progress, but if he never moves from willing to wanting, and ultimately to taking pleasure in her company, then he falls short. There is a parallel in our relationship to God. We do need to spend more time with Him, but with one ultimate goal: to enjoy Him; to take pleasure in Him.

Taste and See

Taste is something you cultivate. People who don't have taste generally aren't aware of it. They're on the outside looking in at a world they don't understand, but erroneously think they do. When I used to drink wine I could tell the difference between an expensive wine and a cheap one. But those who can't tell the difference think it's all contrived. They call it wine snobbery. They are convinced there *is* no difference. It's the same with fine food, art, automobiles and a thousand other things. We use the word "connoisseur" to describe people who understand the subtle differences.

The word "connoisseur" has a spiritual application as well because we can also develop a taste for the Lord. The scripture says: *"O taste and see that the Lord is good" (Ps. 34:8)*. What a strange statement! What are we to make of it?

Of course we know the Lord is good, but He didn't say "Observe and see that I am good." He said *"Taste* and see that I am good." There are two kinds of people: those that have only observed the Lord's goodness, and those who have also tasted it. Those who have observed the Lord's goodness often proclaim it with great energy. They describe

His faithfulness in providing a financial blessing, health for a sick child, or healing for a broken relationship. This is what testimonies are all about — declaring God's goodness. We can all understand and identify.

But if someone were to say in a meeting, "I tasted the Lord last night and He was good," he might get more than a few quizzical looks. That is the language of the Scriptures, but it's not our language, partly because it's not really our experience. But as well, there really is no language to describe the taste of the Lord. Even a group of mystics couldn't sit around and talk about the Lord for hours in that way. It's too personal, too deep, and too inexpressible. Cultivating a taste for the Lord is very different from observing Him.

The term "mystic" is not meant to be derogatory, although it is often used in that way. The church has had few mystics over the centuries and they've been largely misunderstood and even persecuted. These are people who spend protracted times with the Lord, and their revelations are not always welcomed. But there is something in the experience of the mystic that God has for all of us, and this is what we want to get to. Let me first describe a television interview with a modern day pathfinder.

Experiencing God

The elderly gentleman sat, with head tilted back, before a live TV audience and proceeded to share profound insights into the eternal realm — the realm of God. In a calm voice, with eyes burning, he spoke of an experience in Christ that most would consider unattainable. The force of the man's spirit was palpable. A few feet away sat the host's wife, quietly weeping throughout the entire program.

He went on to describe his search, as a young pastor, for a mentor to show him the pathway into God's presence. Though he searched on three continents, he found none. No one seemed to know. Not disheartened, he pressed on to find

God, and he did. Turning to his host, he began in a simple way to explain the keys he had uncovered in the last forty years.

As the camera panned the studio audience, it was apparent that this elder statesman of the faith had awakened something in the hearts of his listeners. Eyes glistened, even pleaded, and a hush enveloped the set as the man continued.

The program in question was the Benny Hinn show, and the man was Gene Edwards. Gene is a modern-day mystic. He is a noted author, pastor, evangelist and deeper-life minister. I count his book, <u>The Divine Romance,</u> as one of the greatest books ever written.

On the program where Gene Edwards spoke, I noticed something peculiar. Hinn was in awe of the things Gene was saying, and his wife sat weeping the entire time. But, in his response to their comments, there was something in Gene's language and demeanor that were incongruent. He talked about the need to know God in a deep and intimate way, but there was also a kind of cynicism in his tone.

After the interview, I went to my library to get a book by Edwards called <u>The Secret of the Christian Life.</u> The mystery was solved. In the book he describes the many occasions in which he was the main speaker at a conference. At some of these conferences "preachers were ten feet deep and a mile wide". His message to those assembled was that it is possible to know Jesus Christ personally, intimately, and daily. But it needn't stop there. In his own words: "It is possible to step outside of space-time, outside of this realm into the other realm, and there personally know and encounter your Lord, to worship and fellowship with Him there, in another realm."

Edwards concedes that this is a heavy statement, so heavy that it begs to be "challenged, accepted, or at least enquired of". But in twenty-five years, despite being cheered, applauded and amen-ed, not one minister has approached him for guidance on entering that realm. And only once did a layman do so — one lone soul in twenty-five years.

So despite the eagerness of Hinn and his listeners, Edwards was reserved. He'd been preaching this message for twenty-five years and yet had no takers — lots of interest, but no takers. So he wasn't particularly impressed by interest alone. His words are indeed a sad commentary on the dearth of spiritual appetite that has been the church's lot for decades. But it is also a commentary on the human condition.

We love good sermons; we love hearing about the achievements of others. But that is often where it ends. While there may be a longing for more, it is easier and safer to live vicariously through the lives of others. This is even true of the Christ that we see in the gospels. It is easy to marvel at Him, but infinitely harder to follow Him.

Fresh Winds

But that is not where the story ends. It's easy to think, as Elijah did, that we are the only ones who haven't "bowed the knee". But God has a much better view of things. He told Elijah that He had 7,000 who hadn't bowed their knees to Baal (1Kings 19:18). No doubt, there are many today that are experiencing God in a deep way, in the secret place, though perhaps not in the depth of a Jean Guyon or a Gene Edwards. It's dangerous, however, to try to emulate another person's experience in God.

I had a friend once who tried to duplicate Guyon's experiences, and it almost destroyed him. He became mystical in an unhealthy, self-absorbed way, and the failure to achieve Guyon's peace in the face of his own pain, crushed him. We can learn from everyone, but it is the Lord Jesus Christ who is our pattern. He spent many a night with His Father.

Psalm 1 says that if we meditate on God's Word day and night, we will prosper. For many people, that kind of meditation and that kind of prosperity would be a giant step forward. But when we talk about the secret place, we are not talking primarily about scripture meditation or the achieving of a result. The purpose of going into the secret place is just to love the Lord and spend time in His presence. Although our communication with Him there is often without words, the scriptures can be a good vehicle.

Meeting God in this way is transforming and should be the experience of ordinary people, not just mystics. What we need are more people saying, "I spent two hours alone with the Lord last week, and it was wonderful. Or rather, He was wonderful." And thanks to the rise of the prophetic movement, more people are beginning to experience Him in "the other realm". I recently attended a Secret Place conference where there were thousands in attendance. When I heard various speakers recount their experiences, it awakened a hunger in me. And hunger is the key thing, because we can all go there. It's simply believing that God "*is a rewarder of those that diligently seek Him.*"

Understanding His Presence

No one likes to waste time. In our tenacity to find Him, we encounter one misconception in particular that needs to be addressed. One author calls it the "myth of unanointed prayer". He describes the person who is on his knees for an hour and finds it as dry as sawdust. None of his prayers seem to get beyond the ceiling, and it feels like a futile effort. Finally, at the end of his prayer time, he rises to his feet and says to himself, "Boy, that was sure a waste of time." He has just encountered "the myth".

The truth is that emotion is no barometer of whether our time with God was productive. If we pray according to His will, then we will have the things we pray for, even if we lack any sense of anointing.

Being in God's presence is the same way. There are many times when we feel His presence, but there are many times when we don't. The times that we don't are not a waste of time, just as sitting quietly and enjoying your spouse's company is not a waste of time. Being in God's presence is necessary and important, and it bears fruit that other activities can't.

The Power of Routine

There is a power in routine that builds things into the fabric of our relationship with God that isn't available on an ad hoc basis. The basic rule is: If you don't schedule it, it won't happen. That is one thing I learned from my years in an office. We never went to a meeting, however large or small, without our daybook.

We didn't just talk about getting together. No one left the room till we had a time and place, and it was entered into our daybooks. Otherwise it wouldn't happen. We all just had too much on the go. Scheduling God into your life may sound mechanical, but it is a large part of the answer.

Struggling to find time for the eternal God seems laughable, but we all know that it's an issue. I recall reading a book where the author made this statement: "If you examine the lives of most of the great men and women of God, you'll find one consistent pattern in their lives — they all met the Lord early in the morning." As one busy pastor said, "If you want more time with God, you'll have to take it from your sleep."

I'm reminded of David Mainse, host of 100 Huntley Street, a daytime Christian television show. He consistently prayed between five and seven in the morning. I've never known the man to have anything but puffy, half-shut eyes while on camera. He always exuded joy, but the sleepy look just came with the job — the job of meeting God early so that the ministry could be built on prayer, not human effort.

Sobering Statistic

One of the world's most influential teachers on the art of worship-leading is a fellow who grew up in my hometown. On prominent display at his website is this one statement: 65% of Christians have never known what it is to enter the presence of God.

At first glance this statement appears absurd. But is it? Have the vast majority of Christians really entered the presence of God to where they knew they were on holy ground? Probably not. The implication is staggering. Most people live out their entire lives never having experienced the primary thing for which they were created: intimate worship, oneness with God, basking in His glory, being clothed in His presence.

If Sunday morning is the deepest many people get, it does not auger well for their relationship with God. Any worship leader will tell you that the majority of people don't appear to be touching God Sunday mornings, even on the outside, let alone deep in their spirit. The two main hindrances are usually feelings of apathy and unworthiness.

Is it any wonder, then, that the topic of "the secret place" seems strange and surreal to most believers? Is it any surprise that Gene Edwards had no "takers"? Wasn't it even somewhat predictable that a Christian would write a book accusing prominent ministers of encouraging contemplative prayer?

Yes indeed, contemplative prayer! There is such a book, and the author employs the time-tested method of guilt by association. New Age practitioners pray and contemplate "god", so we'd better nip this whole prayer thing in the bud. After all, contemplative prayer can't be right if New Agers do it. It would be funny if it weren't so sad. The author is sincere, but Satan is no gentleman. Misguided zealots are a very effective tool. If books like this one can dissuade even a few people from seeking God, then Satan has achieved his aim.

But as for me and my house, we will seek the Lord.
Even in the secret place.

Conclusion

How we steward our relationship with God will be one
of the key determinants of our inheritance. Out of worship
and the secret place will come the love, joy, peace, strength
and insight we need to successfully wage war, chart our path,
keep our focus, and fight for our families

It is hard to separate worship and intimacy from surrender
and commitment, but it is often in these subtleties that we
find the insights. Being rightly related to God is the most
important issue in life. For this reason we must examine
that relationship from every angle and hopefully add to our
understanding. Let us look briefly, then, at the matter of
surrender.

ELEVEN

Surrender and Commitment

Surrender

I have often heard Christian speakers exhort their television audience to believe God for the impossible. Actually, Christians do this all the time. They believe God for the fruits of commitment and surrender without experiencing either one. Impossible, but nice try.

We often refer to our ultimate submission to God with the term "surrender". Many believers have taken months or even years after their salvation experience to finally say "yes" to God: "OK, it's all yours. My life and everything I have. I surrender all." We do this with great trepidation, fearing that this kind of vulnerability will give God the permission He needs to ruin our lives. We dread the divine "Gotcha!"

Truthfully, if I gave all of myself to God and He gave me back only 10% of Himself, that would be a very lopsided transaction. I would be a huge winner! But He does far more. If we give Him all of us, He will give us all of Him — nothing held back. Think of it. All of God for simply giving back what He already owns by the right of divine creation — my life, a vapor that passes with the morning sun.

Our view of surrender is often so immature. We think surrender is grudgingly giving God the rights that are, in fact, already His. Somehow, we tend to think of God as sitting on the edge of His throne, biting His nails, waiting for our little speech. So finally we give it. Then, when nothing bad happens in the week following our surrender, we heave a sigh, stop looking over our shoulder, and go about our business, thinking to ourselves: "Surrender isn't so bad after all."

Surrender? Our little speech wasn't surrender.

I confess that I've done this and it is, indeed, pathetic. But that is not surrender. Surrender is actively finding the Father's will in every area of life and doing it willingly and with great passion. When things go badly, as they often do, surrender is not questioning Him, but yielding even harder in the darkness of disappointment.

In the romantic movies of my era, when the woman finally surrendered to the male suitor, she didn't sit passively, fearing the worst. She jumped into his arms! Surrender is jumping into the arms of God. But in our fear and confusion, we've turned it into a parody. God does indeed want a willing heart, but in our man-centered universe, our attitude makes God the pleading servant and us the one who confers Lordship. He **is** Lord, and our recognition of that fact adds nothing to His stature.

It is our greatest honor that He consents to being Lord of our lives.

In Psalm 37 we find this statement: *"Delight yourself in the Lord and He will give you the desires of your heart."* When I first read that I thought, "Great, if I can generate some excitement for God, He'll give me whatever I ask for — cars, boats, etc." Pretty carnal, right? Actually, I was ahead of my time. Not long after, a whole movement rose up and taught that the chief result of a relationship with God was getting *things*.

How repugnant.

Later I did a word study on that verse, and here is what it means: "Make yourself soft and malleable, and God will give you more of Himself." You see, *more of Him* is the "heart's desire" of every Christian who allows himself to become putty in God's hands. Being putty in God's hands is the picture of surrender. That's as good as it gets for a true seeker.

You start out looking for mere blessings, and you end up finding God Himself.

Commitment

Have you ever been in a service where there was an altar call for people to get serious with God? People stream forward, hands outstretched, voices shouting loud repentance. But nothing changes, and six months later there's another altar call. They all go forward again.

Why is there seldom change? Because we have never gotten to the place where we really comprehend our true condition. In a Christian world of suffocating mediocrity, we have never appreciated God's total call on our lives. Therefore we are never truly broken, never aware of our desolate and bankrupt condition. We know something is wrong, and in response we go to the altar, but the inner man is scarcely moved by the process. But even if we are moved, we are still lost as to how to channel our new resolve.

Altar calls can be a good thing in the sense that they clearly identify a need in our lives. They can be bad if the assumption is that, by simply going to the altar, we are addressing the need.

Recommitment

Then there are the altar calls for people to "recommit their lives to Christ". All sentiment aside, what does it mean to "recommit our lives"? It means we will try once again to meet the western standard of faithful church attendance and Bible reading. We will stop drinking, smoking and gambling. We might even give up one night a week to seek out fellowship.

And all of this makes us "committed" or "recommitted", and earns us the loud praises of our contemporaries.

But is this the real thing, or is it just one more trip on the merry-go-round of mediocrity? I would simply ask the following: Are recommitted Christians now disciples of Christ? Are they indifferent to the charms and affronts of their culture as they pursue their calling to love the Lord with all their heart and minister to a dying world?

It seems almost unkind to frame it that way. It is easier to treat commitment as a nebulous concept that can't be defined. Or if it *can* be defined, it is ungracious to do so, lest we offend those who are complacent. It *does* seem more civilized to simply refer to every believer as one who has "committed his life to Christ", even if it depreciates the term.

The problem is that if church leaders never teach commitment or model it in their lives, multitudes will assume that they themselves are committed. That puts both leaders and followers in jeopardy on Judgment Day.

Struggles of a New Believer

As a new believer, I used to look down my nose at pew warmers, churchianity, and cheap grace. But I underestimated the power of the culture, both Christian and secular, to mould our thinking and lower our expectations of ourselves. Commitment, I discovered, is a daily battle, and it doesn't necessarily get easier with age.

Logically, commitment should take on a deeper and more expansive meaning as we grow in God. But the opposite often happens. As we move on in life, we discover many more things that demand our attention, and we can end up progressively committing less to God. We may be unaware that it is happening, or feel tricked and trapped. But the result is the same — deception. Deceived into living a life that seems full, where everything we do seems necessary, and yet having little room for God. This is lamentable because of the ripple effect it has on others.

When people get saved, their life is a clean slate except for the mark sin has left on it. Everything that will now be written on their lives will largely come through two sources — the Lord and His Word, and the Body of Christ and her teachings. It pains me when I see young Christians move out of their radicalism and take on the language, conformity and sectarianism of the church.

You may have heard the charge that older Christians patronize new converts by saying, "Don't worry, the excitement will pass. You'll settle down like the rest of us." I have never heard that said, and I think it rarely happens. I think what actually happens is that older Christians encourage young believers with their words but not with their lives. Young Christians interpret the Scriptures in terms of what they see in the lives of older, more mature Christians. If they see a lack of sacrifice, they will soon stop serving. If they see indifference to prayer, they will go easy on themselves. If they see lives of ease and affluence, they will gradually adopt that lifestyle.

Tragically, they can wake up ten years later and discover they have become comfortable Christians, and not even know how it happened.

The Need to be Honest

Perhaps it's not pleasant to make these observations, but they need to be made. For some, to return to church and give up blatant sin is indeed progress. But it's the designation of "committed" that gives them the false assurance that they are indeed followers of Christ.

We hear of the assurance of salvation that people are given in large crusades when nothing more than a trip to the altar has taken place. It's a good first step, but for most it's just the beginning of a process that, in time, will result in true salvation with confirming works that follow.

In like manner, we overuse the term "committed" to describe a person who has simply understood some of the responsibilities of sonship. All he is committed to is moving ever so slightly inside the door of salvation. Unfortunately, when he does that, he may find it crowded, for that is where many of us are standing.

What then is commitment? Firstly, it is a continuum; and secondly, it has many expressions. The Lord Jesus modeled the ultimate commitment. The apostle Paul told us to follow him as he followed Christ. We couldn't find two finer examples than Jesus and Paul.

Or perhaps it's more practical to think of the most committed person we know. His calling may be vastly different from our own, but with a bit of thought we can readily identify the elements that make him committed. We can begin to model these things. That is what discipleship is.

Perhaps it requires a daily act to remind us of our commitment. Every morning Bill Bright got out of bed, got on his knees, and surrendered afresh to the Lord.

Or take the comment of a prophet I know. "Every morning," he said, "hell should be on tiptoes as you lie there in your bed. When you begin to stir and your eyes open, there should be a chorus of terrified screams from the watching demons. 'Oh no, he's awake!'" Hell fears a committed Christian. Our names are written in heaven, but are they known in hell?

Getting Committed

The random thoughts contained in the last few paragraphs may be of help, but to truly understand commitment we need to go to the words of the Master Himself. In the gospels we often find Jesus making abrupt, in-your-face comments that really need no interpretation. *They simply need to be heard and obeyed.* This segues very nicely into our topic. We have already taught on the cross, so let us approach this matter of commitment from a different angle. We'll do this by tying into one of our Lord's favorite topics: obeying His word and doing His will.

Doers of the Word

The greatest man who ever lived ended the greatest discourse ever given with the following words:

> *"Therefore every one who hears these words of Mine and acts upon them, may be compared to a wise man who built his house upon the rock.*
>
> *"And the rain descended, and the floods came and the winds blew, and burst against that house; and yet it did not fall for it had been founded upon the rock.*
>
> *"And everyone who hears these words of Mine, and does not act upon them, will be like a foolish man, who built his house upon the sand.*
>
> *"And the rain descended, and the floods came, and the wind blew, and burst against the house; and it fell, and great was its fall." (Matt. 7:24-27)*

Powerful words, powerful concept. I have a friend who can turn almost any prayer and exhortation into another opportunity to drive home this point. No matter what the context, he'll suddenly exclaim, "And Lord, let us be doers of the word, and not hearers only." Always good for an "amen!"

The Lord had the same fixation. At one point in the gospel, a certain woman, caught up in the ecstasy of the moment, blurted out, *"Blessed is the womb that bore You, and the breasts at which You nursed" (Luke 11:27).* A harmless statement, but Jesus couldn't let it pass: *"But," He said,*

"On the contrary, blessed are those who hear the Word of God, and observe it."

Jesus knew the tendency of the crowd to swoon over His persona, His miracles, His teachings, and even His parentage, but neglect one small thing — to actually do what He said. Jesus didn't like gushy sentimentality, even where His mother was concerned. I think telling people they couldn't follow Him unless they hate their own mother, makes the point. He was stern. That's the impression that is given. He placed hearing and doing far above sentimentality.

He knew the tendency of men to venerate the great Man's mother while ignoring the great Man's message. Men love ceremony; they love putting people on pedestals; they love fawning over celebrity. It's obedience they have a problem with.

A little later on, someone came to Jesus and said:

" 'Behold, Your mother and Your brothers are standing outside seeking to speak to You.'
But He answered the one who was telling Him and said, 'Who is My mother and who are My brothers?'
And stretching out His hand toward His disciples, He said, 'Behold, My mother and my brothers!
For whoever shall do the will of My Father who is in heaven, he is My brother and sister and mother.'
" (Matt. 12:47-50)

Something in our affable nature bristles at the seeming rudeness. "Give it a rest, Jesus. Lighten up! I think you've made your point. Say 'Hi' to your mom." No, He wouldn't. And He was even willing to allow the inference that His family wasn't doing the will of His Father — all in the interest of making a point. And so, what an important point it must have been, requiring as it did, such persistent referencing.

Later, with more than a hint of impatience, He brings closure to the issue with one seminal question: *"And why do you call Me, 'Lord, Lord,' and do not do what I say?"* (Luke 6:46). Translation: What could be more absurd than saying Jesus is Lord and then not doing what He says?

Above all else then, obedience is what defines a committed Christian.

Deception

In his letter, James addresses the issue of hearing without doing as well. *"But prove yourselves doers of the word and not merely hearers, who delude themselves" (James 1:22).*

Here we have the word "delusion" or "deception". So what is this deception that people who hear, but don't do, fall into? It is that by simply **hearing** we are changed and become different. "Ah," we say to ourselves, "Now I get it; now I see. How come I didn't see that before?" We go away deceived, thinking that something profound has happened in our lives when all we did was hear a good teaching. James compares this to looking in a mirror.

"For if any one is a hearer of the Word and not a doer, he is like a man who looks at his natural face in a mirror; for once he has looked at himself and gone away, he has immediately forgotten what kind of person he was." (James 1:23,24)

The Word throws the spotlight on our soul and character the way a mirror reflects our appearance. People who look at themselves in the mirror in the morning don't forget what they look like. They just put their imperfections out of mind as they get on with their day.

The same is true of hearing the Word. It only has temporary benefit in its capacity as an illuminator. How many people can remember Sunday's sermon a day later, let alone the following week? Whereas applying the Word, or doing the Word, causes a change in our character, and the benefit is life-long. It is similar to the life-principal of "use it or lose it".

Observations on the Problem

Some people blame the church for the way we move from teaching to teaching before people have a life-changing grasp of even lesson one. I remember Juan Carlos Ortiz years ago addressing this problem. He was correct in his observation that we approach no other area of life in such a random manner. But practical alternatives are not easily arrived at, and I'm sure the one suggested by him was more wishful thinking than a serious solution.

He recommended that we should learn and apply every truth before we move on to the next one. If it takes three months of continuous repetition, so be it. Unfortunately, I'm still working on something I heard in a seminar thirty years ago, so perhaps these things are better left in the hands of the Holy Spirit.

Others are less kind. I remember a prophet saying that there is a symbiotic relationship between the pastors and the congregants. The pastor's role is to preach and the congregant's role is to listen. As long as no one expects big changes, the tithes keep coming in, the pastor gets paid, and everyone is happy.

He said that no pastor can preach for more than two years without repeating himself, but many people attend the same church for decades. So, to keep things afloat, we all maintain the pretense that change is still possible. Of course it truly is, this prophet went on to say, but probably not in that environment. In his mind, people need to get out of the nest, move on, and experience this life they've been hearing and reading about.

These are valid points, but they don't have universal application. I know people in ministry who have a tremendous burden to see people grow and mature. But the onus is on the sheep as well as the shepherds. It's the sheep that have to persevere in being doers of the Word. No one can do it for them. The issue is commitment. We have to be committed enough to read the Word of God for ourselves and obey it, whatever the cost.

Building Life Through Commitment

But let's return to the passage we started with in Matthew chapter 7, for Jesus was not just talking about deception, but destruction. Here we have two men building identical houses, one on sand and one on rock. The person building on sand was a hearer while the one building on rock was both a hearer and a doer.

As one person put it, "What is life, after all, but a building up of character, habits, memories and expectations? Like stone on stone, we add one thing to another in building the house of our lives. Everyone wants to build something secure. People, even good people who are not saved, appear to build well, and feel, undoubtedly, that their house is well and wisely built on money, friends, health, successful business practices — all of which are commendable in themselves, but disastrous without a rock foundation."

However, there are others who build their houses differently. "They do so by daily adding to their service, their knowledge of God, their victory over faults, their joys and hopes, till their life becomes a palace fit for God."

I know people like this.

It is evident, then, that the parable compares the building practices of the believer and the unbeliever: one builds on the foundation, Christ Jesus, the other does not. So we know that the foundation is the critical thing. But that doesn't mean that what we build on that foundation has no importance. It has great importance. Leading a fruitful life and being able to stand in the Day of Judgment, is dependent on *hearing and doing* versus *hearing only.*

Receiving the Word

God's word comes to us in various ways. We can observe godly behavior in the life of someone we respect, and this can have a life-changing effect. I learned much of my child-rearing practices during a short one-year period where I observed a pastor raising his three young children. We are all living testaments, either modeling or not modeling the Word of God for others to follow. We are to exhort one other unto good works. And while words can be effective, it's really how much of the Word that is operative in our lives that influences people.

Then there is the hearing of the Word through the teaching of others. At one time I was negligent in the area of prayer, particularly with my wife. I recall sitting in my home one day, reading various Christian periodicals. I scanned several articles and noted with interest three scriptures. These scriptures were somewhat obscure, but for some reason they caught my attention. Giving it no further thought, I went downstairs to my study and flipped on a ministry update tape from a famous preacher.

In the first five minutes of the tape he quoted exactly three scriptures, the identical three scriptures I had just read. The hair stood up on the back of my neck. God had my attention and I knew that whatever followed on this tape was a direct message for me. The message was on the power of praying with your spouse. The scripture says that if two of us agree as touching anything, it shall be done. The most powerful agreement on earth is the "one flesh" agreement of a husband and wife. This agreement has more authority than any other type of prayer.

The minister's wife also spoke on this audiotape and went on to stress this point. She said her husband was the famous one, the one that touched millions of lives, but she was the one that was constantly under demonic attack in the health area. She wondered why until she understood the power of spousal prayer. Together she and her husband could launch prayers with power that was not available when they prayed separately. One could put a thousand to flight, but two, ten thousand. It was for this reason that the enemy sought to destroy her: to break the power of that agreement.

When I heard this, I resolved on the spot to be a doer of this Word. From that day onward, my wife and I have prayed together daily with few exceptions. Only heaven will show what setbacks would have befallen us, had we not been faithful to act on this Word.

Finally, there is no substitute for simply reading the Bible under the guidance of the Holy Spirit. We refer to the written word of God as the *logos*. We should meditate on the *logos* and commit it to memory. But when the Spirit quickens a passage, we have the *rhema*. God is speaking to us, directly and personally. There are groups of Christians who deny that God speaks today in prophecy as He once did, but no one doubts that He speaks to us through His Word.

In Conclusion

As Christians, we face one overarching choice. The choice is between radical Christianity and cultural Christianity, New Testament Christianity versus Western Christianity. How can we tell the difference? With the Bible as our plumb line, it should be simple. But we read the Bible through the lens of our culture, guided by the lifestyles of those around us, and influenced greatly by the preaching we hear.

For this reason, it is very difficult for any of us to rise above the spiritual level of our generation. Jesus speaks about hearing and doing, but hearing in itself is a challenge. When you read certain passages often enough without doing what they say, then you are no longer *hearing* them. To move back into "hearing mode" takes a unique orientation, which is somewhat challenging. That orientation is simply this: I must read the Bible asking the Holy Spirit to take the scales off my eyes and show me things that I am commanded to do but am not yet doing. And then the final step is obedience — simply doing what the Bible says.

For those that are truly serious, I would recommend the following: Get away for three days and do a fast. Take a red-letter edition of the Bible with you and only read the red letters — the words of Jesus. Do it over and over for twelve hours a day. You just may encounter a Jesus and a radical lifestyle that you have never seen before. This is the real Jesus, not the cultural one, and it is the real Jesus that you will one day meet.

I say none of this to discourage us, but simply to make us aware of why Jesus spent so much time on this subject. He knew how difficult it was to *do* the Word and also the implications of not doing it. "Committing our lives to Jesus" is a nebulous phrase; it really doesn't mean anything. Being committed to Jesus as a doer of His word and a doer of His will is meaningful and measurable.

Judgment Day is about things that can be measured.

I want to measure up, don't you?

TWELVE

Caring for the Poor

Most of us are familiar with the famous quote from Francis of Assisi: "Preach the gospel at all times; if necessary use words." The gospel without words: What does it look like? To answer that question, let us ask another: What is the irreducible minimum of Christianity? If we reduced Christianity to its minimum component, what would we find? The answer may be a little surprising. Let me paint the picture.

The setting is Palestine about thirty years into the life of our Lord. The prophetic clock has struck the hour, and a man named John emerges from years of seclusion. He's never performed a single recorded miracle, but he has the purity and purpose that shakes kingdoms. And the kingdoms of this world were being shaken.

It's important to note that John begins to preach his message of repentance near the city of Jericho. During the reign of Herod, Jericho had gained a position of economic and political importance within a decadent society. Here, in this city of wealth and luxury, were both the hippodrome and amphitheatre. It was Las Vegas North — a resort for the idle rich — a place where they gave themselves to amusements, riotous living, and an abandonment to sexual pleasures.

Only one man stood as a rebuke to this manner of life — John the Baptist. His Spartan lifestyle and solitary wanderings had forged a character that was indifferent to the opinions of men, fearless in the face of controversy.

John's words along with the sheer force of his personality held his audience in morbid suspense. When John mentions an axe, a root, and a fire, they need no further explanations, no more analogies. They get the picture.

"What shall we do?" they cry.

John opens his mouth and begins to speak: " Forgive your debtors, honor God with your tithe, be diligent to keep the law, and be sure to observe the holy feasts." No, he doesn't say that. Nor does he say: "Repent, turn from your sins, believe on Him who is to come; the Kingdom of God is in your midst!"

The answer, when it finally comes, isn't deep or theological. *"And he answered and said to them, 'Let the man who has two tunics share with him who has none; and let him who has food do likewise.'"* (Luke 3:11).

What, that's it?

Yes, that's it. John was already preaching a baptism for the repentance of sins, but that doesn't answer the more practical question: "What shall we do?" It gives no clue as to the nature of *"fruit meet for repentance"*. This simple instruction was a start, you could say.

What we have here, then, is basic instruction on Christian or kingdom living. At its most rudimentary expression, it's looking after those less fortunate than ourselves, but not, as we see, out our excess. He didn't say if you have extra tunics. He said if you have two. The implication for food is the same. Keep what you need, give the rest away. It's a radical way to define the coming kingdom, and yet it's so practical that even a hardened unbeliever could appreciate it.

Who, for instance, is the most admired figure of the recent past? In a kinder age, before ministers came under attack, Billy Graham usually garnered this accolade. But for the decade preceding her death, it was a nun who worked in the streets of Calcutta, known to the world as Mother Theresa. When people visualize the ultimate Christian expression, it is always someone who has committed his life to the poor. That is the highest thing that man can conceptualize.

I once had a fellow say to me concerning the obnoxious behaviour of a professing Christian: "I don't even believe in God and I'm more of a Christian than he is." So in this person's mind, and perhaps in the mind of many, the term "Christian" means less a creed and more a lifestyle, the highest expression being benevolence.

At the large government office where I worked, there were fund raising events every Christmas. The staff wanted to give to the less fortunate. Some years we raised several thousand dollars, and it was always given to the same organization — the Salvation Army. I've had more than one person tell me that if they ever did start attending church, it would be a church like the Salvation Army. Translation: a church with substance; one that cares for people.

People despise a gospel that is all words and no action, do they not? They despise a gospel that condemns but doesn't lift up, that challenges but doesn't encourage, that points the way, but isn't willing to lift a finger to help.

Jay Bakker, son of Jim Bakker, tells of an experience he had while ministering to skateboarders and druggies in a major city. He lived amongst them and identified with their circumstances in an effort to win them. He said sometimes people from upscale churches would drive into skaters' territory in their expensive cars. They would come to a halt, roll down their windows, shout some scripture verses at the skaters, and then roar off. They wouldn't so much as dirty the soles of their feet.

Repugnant!

Such is the gospel when it's preached simply to ease the conscience of the messenger, and not to build a bridge to the lost.

Promises and Perils

There is much lip service given to caring for the poor, but in practice many of us fall short. To encourage us in this regard, God has given us many promises in the Scriptures such as this one found in Proverbs 19: " *He who is gracious to a poor man lends to the Lord, and He will repay Him for his good deed" (Prov. 19:17).*

There are few promises in the Bible that parallel the ones found in Psalm 41 for those who consider the poor.

> *"How blessed is he who considers the poor;*
> *The Lord will deliver him in a day of trouble.*
> *And he shall be called blessed upon the earth;*
> *And do not give him over to the desire of his enemies.*
> *The Lord will sustain him upon his sickbed;*
> *In his illness, thou dost restore him to health."*
> *(Ps. 41:1-3)*

The same promises are found in Isaiah 58 and a myriad of other places. Helping the poor seems to be the one activity that God promises to bless in every conceivable way.

But the reverse is true as well. Woe to those who exploit or abuse the poor. I remember an incident from the summer that I got saved. I was searching for God at the time, trying, through books and meetings, to make some sense of it all. I was the houseguest of a wealthy friend named Bill Graham (no relation to the famous evangelist). Bill was nouveau riche. He had made millions in real estate and had recently purchased the mansion of the previous mayor of Vancouver. Sitting by the pool at Bill's home, one would never guess that he lived in a metropolis, since all that was visible were trees and lawn.

Life was good. We would dine almost nightly at major restaurants. I remember one night, sitting in the dining room of one of Vancouver's finest hotels. We were part way through our elaborate meal when Bill looked up and with the smuggest of grins said, "I wonder what the poor are doing tonight." My blood ran cold at that statement.

Something inside me recoiled. Bereft of God though I was, I knew you didn't mock the poor. Things seemed to start unraveling for Bill shortly after that, and in three years he was broke. Was there a connection? We'll never know, but scripture makes it plain that Bill committed an indiscretion of the most serious kind.

> "He who mocks the poor reproaches His maker;
> He who rejoices at calamity will not go unpunished." (Prov. 17:5)

> "He who shuts his ear to the cry of the poor
> Will also cry himself and not be answered."
> (Prov. 21:13)

Notice that you don't have to outright abuse the poor to incur God's disfavor; just ignoring their cries is sufficient.

Some of us are in desperate need of a reality check. Many of us have forgotten our spiritual heritage and are vague on the reasons we were called to salvation. In general, affluent westerners have an entitlement mentality that needs to change if we are to serve the poor. A brief look at our past may help.

Origins of the Church

The apostle Paul was less than flattering in his description of the new church, but he gives us some badly needed insight:

> "For consider your calling brethren, that there were not many wise according to the flesh, not many mighty, not many noble." (1 Cor. 1:26)

Not many wise, not many mighty, not many noble — yes, basically, that would be us. So why has God chosen to build His church with such an inauspicious group of people? Paul tells us in the following verses:

"But God has chosen the foolish things of the world to shame the wise, and God has chosen the weak things of the world to shame the things which are strong, and the base things of the world and the despised, God has chosen the things that are not, that He might nullify the things that are, that no man should boast before God." (I Cor. 1:27-29)

So there you have it. So much for any thought that we were chosen because of any innate nobility on our part. God basically chose you and me to get back at the establishment. He wanted to prove to the proud, who wouldn't come to the banquet in Matthew 22, what He could do with a bunch of misfits. He did this so "that no man should boast". A boastful Christian is an oxymoron. There's nothing to boast about except God's grace.

A little deflating, isn't it?

To the proud in heart it is, but to someone who is poor in spirit and knows that apart from God's grace he deserves hell, it's strangely comforting. No image to live up to, no airs to put on; just simply following Christ. How do you think the Lord feels when the church tries to imitate the very crowd that He rejected? I think He feels the same pain He did when Israel wanted to be like the nations. They wanted a king. Being chosen of God and having Him as King wasn't enough.

Our Time in History

The problem is that we don't see ourselves as ignoble and unsophisticated. Most of us have good jobs, respectability, and lives that seem full and desirable. What escapes our notice is that we are the beneficiaries of generational blessings. These have come to us from godly forefathers who built a country that honored God and punished sin. Since about 1970 that has changed, and two centuries of spiritual capital has been largely dissipated. Just one generation, that's all it took.

When we look at our culture, it seems inescapable that we have not been good stewards of the blessings we have been given. God will not be mocked; what we sow we will reap, and that without partiality. The "without partiality" is the hard part. There have been no affluent people in history who did not think that they deserved their affluence, or who believed it could ever end. "It can't happen here," is forever the cry of the proud and the decadent. But if we don't repent, it will happen here — the financial humbling and, with it, the simpler lifestyle.

Our other struggle is with our time and place in history. How would you like to be born into the most prosperous fifty years in human history and end up on the most prosperous continent? Well, let's give ourselves a pat on the back, because such was our fate. Do you think it might distort our view of reality? It's unavoidable. So that's why it is somewhat confusing to hear James say:

> *"Listen my beloved brethren, did not God choose the poor of this world to be rich in faith and heirs of the kingdom which He promised to those who love Him?"(James 2:5)*

It's confusing because, as stated, that has not been our experience in the western world. It's hard to comprehend, but more people are brought to Christ in Africa on a weekend than in America in a decade, and most of them are poor. A couple of years ago, for instance, Rheinhard Bonke had a crusade in Africa where, in one meeting alone, over a million were saved. We'll never know how many Christians there are in China, but the figure is at least sixty million. That's twice the population of Canada, and yes, they're mostly poor.

The fact is, we are an anomaly, us rich Christians. James said, in the verse above, that He gave the kingdom to the poor, a group that He further defines with the phrase, *"to those who would love Him"*. There we have a key. The gospel is most successful when it's sown amongst the poor and downtrodden because they really need good news. Like those who are forgiven much and love much, the poor tend to have a gratitude that expresses itself in an undivided heart.

God is particularly offended when believers are partial to the rich. James launches into a diatribe against the rich in chapter one of his epistle. You can sense the outrage when he says that being partial to the rich, while ignoring the poor, is sin. Then in the same breath, he proceeds to talk about the sins of adultery and murder. He's not just having a bad day, but is expressing the heart of God in this matter. We find the reason in the Old Testament.

God says in Deuteronomy 10:19 that Israel is to help widows, orphans and aliens, *"for you were aliens in Egypt."* He further says concerning the release of slaves, that they were not to let them go empty-handed, for *"you shall remember that you were a slave in the land of Egypt" (Deut. 15:15)*. There is a direct connection in these verses to our own lot. As believers, we were all slaves once to sin and are now aliens in this world. So as aliens and former slaves, we are expected to have an abundance of mercy towards the poor and those that are slaves to sin, the two groups that Jesus spent a lot of time with.

There's a safeguard, as well, in remembering the poor. The root of all sin is pride and self-exaltation. When a person has no care for the poor, he can be led away from truth and into sin — even gross sin. This was Sodom's problem. Sexual perversion was not the initial sin, but instead the result of a more basic sin.

> *"Behold, this was the guilt of your sister Sodom: she and her daughters had arrogance, abundant food, and careless ease, **but she did not help the poor and the needy.***
>
> *Thus they were haughty and committed abominations before Me. Therefore I removed them when I saw it." (Ezek.16:49,50)*

This is always the pattern, and we see it today. Abundant food and careless ease lead to arrogance and a self-centeredness that shows no concern for the poor. This, in turn, opens a person to temptations of the worst kind, including sexual perversion. It seems odd to see the sin of neglecting the needy right up there with sexual perversion, but it gives us an insight into God's value system.

Structure of the Kingdom

It is interesting to note how the kingdom of God is structured. Jesus Himself said, *"Let him who is greatest be servant of all."* We find in the book of Ephesians a list of the five-fold ministers: apostles, prophets, evangelists, pastors and teachers. The church is founded on the apostles and the prophets, with the apostolic order being the first among equals.

It is interesting, then, that the apostolic ministry should find itself first in service but last in privilege. This is how Paul describes the lot of the apostle:

> *"For I think that God has exhibited us apostles last of all, as men condemned to death; because we have become a spectacle to the world, both to angels and to men.*

We are fools for Christ's sake, but you are prudent in Christ; we are weak, but you are strong; you are distinguished, but we are without honor.

To this present hour we are both hungry and thirsty, and are poorly clothed, and are roughly treated and are homeless;

And we toil, working with our own hands; when we are reviled, we bless; when we are persecuted, we endure; when we are slandered, we try to conciliate; we have become as the scum of the world, the dregs of all things, even until now." (1 Cor. 4:9-13)

Let's see — the apostles were hungry, thirsty, poorly clothed, roughly treated, homeless, the dregs of society and the scum of the earth. Who does that sound like? Why, it sounds like the poor. And not just the poor, but the poorest of the poor. There aren't many people anywhere that have it this bad. And yet these are God's most precious servants.

God has truly turned everything on its head. The first shall be last and the last shall be first. Why are men of such stature willing to abase themselves for the sake of the gospel? Apart from their love for God, there is only one answer, and it is found throughout scripture:

"But remember the former days, when, after being enlightened, you endured a great conflict of sufferings, partly, by being made a public spectacle through reproaches and tribulations, and partly by becoming sharers with those who were so treated,

*For you showed sympathy to the prisoners, and accepted joyfully the seizure of your property, **knowing that you have for yourselves a better possession and an abiding one." (Heb. 10:32-35)***

So there it is — the *"better possession"*, the one that abides. What is this possession? It is *"the city which has foundations whose architect and builder is God."* These saints may look pretty motley to us, but the scripture says, *"God is not ashamed to be called their God, for He has prepared a city for them."*

People like this don't really care much for this world. They see the vanity of it all and they aspire to something much better — the eternal city. The last thing we should do is feel sorry for them. Their suffering has propelled them into unimaginable glory. That is, after all, what Paul meant when he said: *"For I consider that the sufferings of this present time are not worthy to be compared with the glory that is to be revealed to us" (Rom. 8:18).*

Paul uses the pronoun "us", but this verse doesn't have universal application. He was talking about himself and his fellow workers. He wasn't talking about the sufferings that are common to man. He wasn't talking about the *"labor and sorrow"* that is endemic to earthly life. No, he was talking about something more.

What, for instance, do many of us suffer that the unsaved person next door doesn't suffer? Probably nothing. The gospel has only brought us benefits. He was talking about suffering for the sake of the gospel. That suffering wasn't just the experience of first century apostles. It goes on today wherever there is the clash of the two kingdoms. The inner cities of this world are full of Christian workers who pay a genuine price to minister to the poor.

Poverty and Godliness

As we look at the issue of suffering and poverty, we must make one thing clear. In no place does the Bible equate poverty with godliness. While suffering performs a powerful work in us and we are to suffer for Christ, we are nowhere encouraged to initiate suffering as something that ingratiates us with God.

During church history there have been periods where people have debased themselves physically, and confused it with holiness. Every Catholic priest takes a vow of poverty and chastity, but it certainly does not make them any holier. Often quite the opposite. The law and the traditions of men have the effect of awakening and empowering sin, not taming it.

God has the right to test us in the financial area at any time, but His love for the poor is not inconsistent with His desire to bless His children financially, and thereby make them a source of blessing to others.

Are we feeling distant from God? Perhaps it's because there is no care for the poor in our lives. The bottom line for all of us is found in Jeremiah chapter 22 where God makes the following statement:

> *"Did not your father eat and drink,*
> *And do justice and righteousness?*
> *Then it was well with him.*
> *He pled the cause of the afflicted and needy;*
> *Then it was well.*
> **Is that not what it means to know Me?** (Jer. 22:15,16)

That scripture makes it plain. If we truly want to know God better, we know where to find Him. Job did. That's what made him such a great king and greatly loved of God. In defense of his righteousness, Job gives a long list of his charitable acts, but two verses will suffice:

> *"Because I delivered the poor who cried for help,*
> *And the orphan, who had no helper,*

The blessing of the one ready to perish came upon me,
    And I made the widow's heart sing for joy." (Job 29:12,13)

When God wants to do something significant He finds a person. Leaders, and leadership in general, have a huge impact on the spiritual tone that is set in any generation. For this reason I rejoice at some of the things that have occurred in the past decade. We have significant international leaders that have launched major ministries to help the poor and alleviate pestilence and disease. This augers well for the church and sets an example for all of us as to where our priorities should lie.

Most passionate Christians long for a flesh-and-blood encounter with Jesus Christ during their stay on earth. That is a desire that God will honor. Jesus tells us very plainly that we can meet Him as often as we want, but that He will come to us in disguise. In Matthew 25, He tells us what the disguise is: "*I was hungry and you gave Me something to eat.... Truly I say to you, to the extent that you did it to one of these brothers of Mine, even the least of them, you did it to Me.*"

So in ministering to the poor, we are ministering to Jesus. In so doing, we encounter the living God here on earth, and earn His eternal gratitude in heaven.

It is a win-win proposition.

SECTION FOUR

Inheritance in the Eternal Kingdom

THIRTEEN

The Reward of the Righteous

Heaven

Montel was well meaning, but you could tell he didn't get it. His topic was crystal meth and his guest was a pretty, young drug user. She was a normal kid with a normal background who thought she would take meth "just one time" at the urging of a friend. It was instant nirvana. "Everything felt beautiful," she said. "I had boundless energy. I felt a power and peace I'd never known. I knew then that I would take this drug for the rest of my life."

The producer, wanting an Oprah-like climax, offered the young woman a free trip to a treatment center as the audience cheered. But she turned him down cold. She had just finished a fourteen-day "run". She'd been high and sleepless for fourteen days, and now, twenty-four hours later with only a few hours rest, she was on live television. A slight agitation was the only indicator that her body and mind were in exhaustion and withdrawal. With a giggle and a half smirk she stood her ground despite several appeals; she wanted nothing to do with treatment. She had found nirvana and she wasn't about to give it up so quickly.

Another "lamb to the slaughter", we might all agree. But in this woman's comments we hear something that is seldom mentioned concerning drug abuse. We rightly identify the causes of drug use as peer pressure, low self-esteem, escapism, etc. But one of the core issues is never mentioned: Drugs bring "heaven" to earth. Heroin addicts have a saying:

"If God created anything better than heroin, He kept it for Himself." Those who have experienced the rush and euphoria of a heroin high can't fathom anything better.

But there *is* something better, and God has not kept it for Himself. He longs to share it with the redeemed. It is heaven. *"Precious in the sight of the Lord, is the death of His Godly ones" (Ps. 116:15).* They get heaven: not a counterfeit, but the real thing.

One of the hardest things about being a recovering addict is knowing that "heaven" is one toke, one needle, or one hit away. That is an awful burden to bear. In a world full of disappointments, difficulties, heartbreak and outright boredom, it's hard to live with the knowledge that you can experience bliss for a mere twenty dollars. Once you cross that line and experience the euphoria, earth never feels the same again.

Taking drugs is an attempt to visit heaven without going through the Door, Christ Jesus, and is, in effect, climbing over the wall. Any blessing is a stolen blessing and there is hell to pay. At some point every user has to pay the piper as he begins the descent into "the hell of drug addiction".

If you have ever taken drugs or have seen the depravity that an addict will resort to in order to get high, you can appreciate that there is another dimension of pleasure that is beyond the natural and outside of the permissible. I've been in a place of worship when, in the rarified air of the Lord's presence, the euphoria has been like a drug high with the added ingredients of glory, purity, and oneness with my Maker.

And yet this is still earth, absent the manifold presence of God, absent the holy city with streets of gold. Heaven will indeed be a place of unimaginable glory. It gives me joy to talk about the reward of the righteous, and it all begins with a place called Heaven.

Heaven is more than eternal bliss; it is more than seeing God face-to-face. It is the place that satisfies every human longing. Drugs, and indeed every other escape mechanism, are often attempts to dull the pain of two particular impulses that can never be satisfied this side of heaven.

Mark Buchanan describes these two impulses eloquently in his book, <u>Things Unseen</u>. The first impulse is to go beyond. "We seek novelty. We hunger for new beginnings. We crave discovery, conquest, adventure — to find that which has yet never been seen." But we have a second impulse — the impulse to go home. "We cherish the familiar. We long for the way we were. We seek safety, domesticity, serenity — to find again what we've lost." Why won't we be bored in heaven? Because in heaven these two impulses will be perfectly joined. We can't even guess what that will feel like. But for those of us that are both stifled and at the same time insecure, it will be — well, it will be Heaven!

Because heaven is our real home, we will never feel truly at home on this earth. Unfortunately, we can't see heaven, and that can be a problem. We have to hold heaven in our hearts lest we misspend our lives in the futile effort of trying to create heaven on earth.

In the natural, things that are close always look bigger and more real than those that are far away. That telephone pole on the horizon looks like a toothpick compared to the road sign we just passed. But we know it's an illusion. At some point we'll arrive at that pole and it will dominate our view. That is how we must look at heaven. Heaven is infinitely more imposing than any manmade structure. It is infinitely more real than any temporal reality.

But knowing that is one thing; living it out is quite another.

Joint-heirs with Jesus

Heaven is our most obvious inheritance, but not our greatest one. Our greatest inheritance is God Himself. The sons of Zadok, who did not go astray, received the same promise that earlier in Numbers had been given to all Levites: "And *it shall be with regard to an inheritance for them, that I am their inheritance; and you shall give them no possession in Israel — I am their possession*" (Ezek. 44:28).

This is the ultimate reward of the faithful. Although it is spiritual in essence, it continues into the natural: "*They shall eat the grain offering, the sin offering, the guilt offering; and every devoted thing in Israel shall be theirs.*" They get God first of all, and then they share in all that is His. Though all New Testament saints are priests and have access to God's throne, this Old Testament promise is, in some way, a shadow and type of the coming Kingdom. From the concept of "seating" in the Kingdom, we know that we are all granted both intimacy *and* honor, but it varies according to our service. Not everyone has an equal share.

In Romans we are told: "*The Spirit Himself bears witness with our spirit that we are children of God, and if children, heirs also, heirs of God and joint-heirs with Christ, if indeed we suffer with Him in order that we may also be glorified with Him*"(Rom. 8:17).

That we are heirs of God is grace. Every child of God, irrespective of works, has an eternal abode. Being a joint-heir with Jesus, however, is something more. It involves deeds. This is made apparent by the "if" clause which Paul adds. He distinguishes the heirs of God from the joint-heirs of Christ with the word "suffer". Suffering is at the core of being a joint-heir with Christ.

Additionally, being a joint-heir doesn't mean being an *equal* heir. In human affairs, the will of a wealthy person may contain many heirs — joint-heirs, if you will. But the bequests will be as varied as the esteem accorded each person. The chief beneficiary may receive millions, a favorite nephew thousands, and a distant cousin a keepsake like a piece of furniture or jewelry.

But while an earthly benefactor can reward anyone he pleases, God is committed to paying wages. We know that God will reward the simplest acts of kindness. But the phrase, "great is your reward in heaven," is one our Lord reserved for things like persecution, sacrifice, and servanthood.

The word for "suffer" in the above verse in Romans is *supasko,* and is only found in one other place: *"And if one member suffers, all members suffer"* (1 Cor. 12:26). At issue is not just suffering, but shared suffering, and not necessarily only the physical kind. If a fellow parishioner suffers ill health, we are not required to flagellate ourselves in order to feel his pain. But we *are* required to carry his pain. We are required to share in each other's sufferings, whatever they may be.

Likewise, to be glorified with Jesus, we must share His sufferings. This is referred to elsewhere by Paul as *"the fellowship of His sufferings"*. While some are called to martyrdom and may suffer torments for the sake of the gospel, this is not what is meant by this verse. Suffering is inevitable to anyone who is serving God and is a threat to the kingdom of darkness. Every servant of God has had frequent temptations to turn back, abandon his ministry, take the easy road, and yield to sin. It may not be pain or persecution, but it is still suffering, and it can be acute. This suffering comes with every ministry and is present at every *level* of ministry.

It is important to honor men and women with international callings and powerful annointings. But we err in assuming that along with fame comes a buffer zone where they enjoy God's special blessing and protection. Quite the opposite, in fact. "The higher the levels, the bigger the devils."

One day while watching Ken Copeland's program, I heard him utter this statement: "I'd quit right now, but I'm afraid I'd go to hell." That is an exact quote from America's greatest faith preacher. There is no free ride for the famous. We all suffer pain and discouragement. The great apostle Paul said that he "*despaired of life itself*". But in these sufferings we share something very precious with the One known as the Man of Sorrows — fellowship.

So we are heirs of God, and can choose to be joint-heirs with Jesus. Though every human being suffers, only believers have the privilege of suffering for Christ and sharing in His inheritance. That gives rise to a question: What is Jesus going to inherit that can be jointly ours? In Psalm 2, God the Father says to His Son: "*Ask of Me and I will surely give the nations as Thine **inheritance**, and the very ends of the earth as Thy possessions.*" Here we have a reiteration of the fact that part of our inheritance, like that of the Lord's, is people. As joint-heirs, we will play a special role in the administration of the nations.

Paul concludes the passage on suffering with a message of hope: "*For I consider that the sufferings of this present time are not worthy to be compared with the glory that is to be revealed to us*" (Rom. 8:18). And if that is not specific enough, he gives us this promise: "*If we suffer with Him, we shall also reign with Him*" (2Tim. 2:12).

We Will Be Like Him

The apostle John says in 1John. 3:2: "*Beloved, now we are children of God, and it has not appeared as yet what we shall be. We know that when He appears, we shall be like Him, because we shall see Him as He is.*" We are children of God and as great as that is, it is only stage one; stage two hasn't happened yet. In stage two we meet Christ and are transformed into His likeness. We do grow in Christ-like-ness here on earth, and will be rewarded by God accordingly. But only in heaven will we be "like" Him in the full sense of that word. When we get to heaven, we aren't just going to be new and improved. We are not just going to be *us* minus the baggage. We are going to be like Christ. That is a mind-boggling thought. We know that we are **not** going to be deity. But you and I are going to enter into a condition described as "like Him" which is much more than sinless perfection. Although this is one of the greatest rewards of the righteous, it is practically indefinable.

We cannot understand what the state of "like Him" will be, and can only use weak earth-bound phrases that are so limiting: unimaginable glory, transcendent oneness, beautiful holiness, etc. None of this really expands our knowledge, but comparisons come to mind. We are the caterpillar that will one day be the butterfly. Paul alludes to this metamorphosis in 1Corinthians 15 where, in a discussion of bodies, he talks about the glory of the earthly and the glory of the heavenly.

But that change, although glorious, is external in nature. The "like Him" change goes much deeper. It is many mysteries wrapped into one. As the bride of Christ, we will be "one flesh" with our Husband. He is also the first-born of many brethren, so we share His lineage. We are also one spirit with Him because *"the one who joins himself to the Lord is one spirit with Him."* We are also **"in Christ"**, symbolized by Noah's Ark — the big ark. But there is also **"Christ in us, the hope of glory"**, symbolized by the Ark of the Covenant — the little ark.

Us in Christ, Christ in us; one flesh with the Lord, one spirit with God; the first-born of many brethren. When you put all the pieces together, it starts to sound a bit outrageous. Many Christians do not realize their position in Christ, but how unintelligible we would quickly become if we tried to communicate the full reality. The full reality can't be understood, much less communicated.

Why did God write this story line into the gospel narrative? Isn't it enough just to be saved, to go to heaven, to enjoy the Lord, and to rule and reign with Christ? Yes it is, but God always does exceedingly, abundantly, above all we could think or ask. Only a madman with messianic delusions would have the gall to ask to be like God. But without our even asking, God includes it in the benefit package. *We will be like Him.*

Why is there a "because" in the verse in John? Why is it *because* we see Him as He is, that we will be like Him? It could just be a reference to the transforming power of heaven, but it seems that God included this detail for a reason. It appears that grace is needed to complete the sanctification that began on earth. When we finally stand in His presence, something in that profound encounter will do the final work. We will be transformed into His likeness.

He That Overcomes

Life, as the saying goes, is a battle. You either beat it, or it beats you. On skid row are the empty shells of men and women who have been beaten by life. For the Christian there is double jeopardy. Like our unbelieving neighbors, we are prone to being defeated by the circumstances of life — its trials, its treacheries, and its tragedies. But we can also be defeated by life's allurements — its prestige, its positions and its possessions. These things the world calls success. Though people may say the best things in life are free, they, in large part, expend their lives trying to attain the other.

So we have to beware of both success and failure. When Jesus said, "*I have overcome the world*" (John 16:33), He was talking about both the good and the bad, both the seductive offerings of Satan and the angry railings of men. The world, then, comes at us from both sides: on the one hand, to berate us into compromise and idolatry; and on the other, to beat us into defeat and despair.

In either case, surrender on our part constitutes being overcome — a very ignominious term. Both of these eventualities are described with one of the vilest words in language — vomit. The one who has escaped the defilements of the world and then has once again become ensnared is likened to a "*dog returning to its vomit*".

Conversely, to the believer in Christ who has all the refinements and yet has been totally captured by the world, Jesus says, *"I will vomit you out of my mouth."* We might prefer a more delicate term, but we'd be in danger of missing the point. The point is that people make trades that are both onerous and odious. They exchange the glory of God for creeping insects, the blessing of God for gratuitous lust, and the fellowship of God for worldly honor.

Jesus leaves us no wiggle room. The well-manicured man in the pin-stripe suit who fawns over the world is no better than the drunkard in the gutter. To God, they've both been overcome and are equally deplorable. That's not the stuff of great sermons, but it's nevertheless true. Our aversion to this truth is understandable. We're human. We love shadings, mixtures, and compromises. They appeal to our high sense of etiquette and reasonableness. We don't like words like "vomit" or phrases like "brood of vipers" or accusations like "your father the devil". They seem raw and a trifle uncivilized. It's not the kind of poetic parlance we'd expect from a great man and a great spiritual leader.

The false gods who came to us disguised as eastern gurus had a huge impact in the 1960's. Superficially, there was an attraction. They babbled about peace and appealed to our sense of propriety. But with their saccharine smiles, flabby morals, and singsong voices, they are the antithesis of the God of the Bible. It is the God of the Bible and His Word that will ultimately judge us. We need the unvarnished truth about what He thinks.

We know that we have overcome the world by our faith (1Jn.5:4), that we are not to be overcome by evil but to overcome evil with good (Rom. 12:21), and that we are to reign in life through Christ Jesus (Rom.5:17). Logic itself dictates that if we didn't overcome and reign in this life, we certainly wouldn't be qualified to reign in the next one. So there is much at stake in how we use the grace that is allotted to us for the purposes of maintaining a victorious Christian walk.

I marvel in particular at Christian women who, despite poverty, unfaithful husbands, wayward children, and a host of other problems, are still positive, cheerful and able to encourage others. These are indeed overcomers. The thrones of heaven will be populated with such as these.

As an aside, the concept of overcoming explains much of the testing we experience on earth. You can't be an overcomer unless you have something to overcome. Don't be surprised at your fiery trials, Peter tells us in I Peter 4:12. Don't think them strange. Without them you couldn't be an overcomer.

The importance Jesus places on overcoming is evident both in the language and space He gives to the subject. We find both passion and urgency in passages where He discusses it. But equally compelling are the sublime promises He offers to those who overcome.

> "To him who overcomes I will grant to eat of the tree of life, which is in the Paradise of God." (Rev. 2:7)

> "He who overcomes shall not be hurt by the second death." (Rev. 2:11)

> "To him who overcomes, to him I will give some of the hidden manna, and I will give him a white stone, and a new name written on the stone which no one knows but he who receives it." (Rev. 2:17)

> "And he who overcomes, and he who keeps My deeds until the end, to him I will give authority over the nations, and he shall rule them with a rod of iron, as the vessels of the potter are broken to pieces, as I also have received authority from My Father; and I will give him the morning star." (Rev. 2:26-28)

"He who overcomes shall thus be clothed in white garments; and I will not erase his name from the book of life, and I will confess his name before My Father, and before His angels." (Rev. 3:5)

"He who overcomes, I will make him a pillar in the temple of My God, and he will not go out from it any more; and I will write upon him the name of My God, and the name of the city of My God, the new Jerusalem, which comes down out of heaven from My God, and My new name."(Rev. 3:12)

"He who overcomes, I will grant to him to sit down with Me on My throne, as I also overcame and sat down with My Father on His throne." (Rev. 3:21)

These verses are meant to hold our fascination. How different many lives would be if there were seminars on overcoming where we were taught this subject with the same intensity that we are taught earthly prosperity. What if, instead of endless teachings on investments, finance and money, the verses above were taught for what they are — the true reward of the righteous that, unlike the baubles and bangles of earth, will still have meaning millennia from now.

Promises to Overcomers

If we look at what is promised to the overcomers of the seven churches and the seven church ages, there is a lot of overlap. So much so, that, with few exceptions, it is safe to say that all overcomers will inherit the same promises. The most common promise is salvation, as indicated in the following phrases: "not hurt by the second death"; "white stone"; "not erase his name from the book of life"; "I will confess his name before My Father"; "eat of the tree of life"; and "clothed in white garments".

Then there are promises that refer to ruling and reigning: "sit on a throne"; "pillar in the temple"; and "authority over the nations". And finally there are promises concerning our relationship with the Lord: "hidden manna"; "a new name"; "the Morning Star" (Jesus); "the names of God"; "the Lord's new name"; and "the name of the City of God"(the New Jerusalem).

It cannot be said too strongly that God would never have put these promises in His Word unless we needed them. They are for our benefit. Many have noted that the reading of the Book of Revelation, unlike the other books, comes with a distinct blessing: *"Blessed is he who reads and those who hear the words of the prophecy, and heed the things which are written in it; for the time is near" (Rev. 1:3).* But as this verse states, the blessing doesn't come from just reading it, but rather from both reading and heeding.

In the letters to the churches we are told again and again to heed: *"He who has an ear, let him hear what the Spirit says to the churches. To him who overcomes, to him I will give…."* So what is the primary blessing that comes to those who read this Book? It is discovering what it is we have to overcome, and the promises that are ours if we do so. This knowledge can tip the scale in the struggles of life. We will look at this momentarily, but before we do, let us consider once more the church letter that has the greatest application to our own day.

The Laodicean Age

The sin of the Laodicean church is summed up by our Lord in one word - lukewarmness. It is a church with such ease and affluence that it declares unabashedly: *"I am rich and have need of nothing."* On a scale of one to ten, they would score a zero on hungering and thirsting after righteousness. In their eyes, they have need of nothing, but in the Lord's eyes they are wretched, miserable, poor, blind and naked. How could two people see things so differently? Because one judges carnally and the other spiritually.

Our Lord's answer to their condition is to *"buy from Me"*. That is an unusual command because normally we are told to ask. In only three places in scripture are we told to buy. What is it they are to buy? The answer is substantial: *"...gold refined by fire, that you may become rich, and white garments, that you may clothe yourself, and that the shame of your nakedness may not be revealed, and eyesalve to anoint your eyes that you may see" (Rev. 3:18).*

First, they are told to buy gold refined by fire. Here the Lord uses the classic illustration of purification through suffering. Secondly, they are told to buy white garments representing the righteous acts of the saints. They had been leading selfish lives and their works were found wanting. Lastly, they are told to buy eyesalve that their spiritual eyes might be opened. God's Word had been supplanted by culture and reasoning. In summary, we see the Lord addressing the three problem areas of sin, selfishness and unsound doctrine. But more to the point, He is dealing with a stronghold — pride and deception.

No one truly considers himself a Laodicean Christian. By definition, all such people are deceived about their true condition; they think they are rich and have need of nothing. Being unaware that you are backslidden makes repentance unlikely. And yet they are commanded to repent and to do so with *zeal*. Difficult? Yes, but the Lord promises He will get their attention: *"Those whom I love, I reprove and discipline; be zealous therefore and repent."*

Then the mood shifts. And in one of the greatest pictures of humility recorded anywhere in literature, we have a portrayal of the great King, waiting to be invited in by an arrogant, lukewarm slave who has repented. Like the prodigal son, the Laodiceans don't just get their relationship back, He also lavishes them with great wealth. *"He who overcomes, I will grant to him to sit down with Me on My throne, **as I also overcame** and sat down with My Father on His throne."*

The Laodicean believers who overcome are promised thrones. But what is it they have to overcome? For the answer to that question we have to look at what Jesus had to overcome. In Hebrews 12 we have wording similar to the above passage, and here Jesus tells us what He had to overcome: *"Who for the joy set before Him, endured the cross, despising the shame, and has sat down at the right hand of the throne of God."*

In Revelation 3, Jesus says that He *overcame* and **sat on His Father's throne**. In Hebrews 12, it says He *endured the cross* and **sat on His Father's throne.** So if the laws of logic apply, overcoming equals enduring the cross. It was embracing the cross that made Jesus an overcomer. It will be the same for us. The Laodicean sin was that they forgot the cross. They lived crossless lives, identified with the world and its affluence, and in their blindness thought they were okay.

What is this blindness? It's the ability to read the scriptures and filter out all references to self-denial and death to the world. It further manifests itself in pride — pride in physical as well as spiritual riches. How could they think they were spiritually rich? Easy — they had big buildings, nice choirs, ten-piece worship bands, well-paid pastors, nice missions programs, and prestige in the community.

But there is an antidote to spiritual blindness — suffering. It would take suffering for them to see their lukewarmness, wean them from their comforts, and restore their hunger for Him. That is happening now in the lives of many people, and thank God it is.

Now we want to look briefly at the opposite scenario. Not everyone in our day is lukewarm, but we can say with certainty that everyone struggles.

Holding Fast

In speaking to the church at Thyatira, Jesus says the following:

"Nevertheless what you have, hold fast until I come.

And he who overcomes, and he who keeps My deeds until the end, to him I will give authority over the nations, and He shall rule them with a rod of iron, as the vessels of the potter are broken to pieces, as I also have received authority from My Father; and I will give him the morning star." (Rev. 2:25-28)

Even though this was written to a specific church, like all the scriptures, it was written for our instruction. Good advice to one group of Christians has application to all. There are some important insights in this passage that will help us and they need to be noted.

There are believers who have run the race well, but for some reason, whether suffering, infirmity, temptation, perhaps even old age, they are struggling. Though the end is in sight and the prize in view, they are tempted to give up. Others have lost the victory, given in to apathy, and are simply trying to get the most out of life before the Lord calls them home. If that is the situation you find yourself in, take heart. Our Lord's instruction to the people at Thyatira was to "hold fast" until He comes.

He then defines that term as encompassing two things: overcoming, and keeping His deeds until the end. Overcoming, in this case, means overcoming whatever sin, temptation, obstacle, or infirmity will cause you to capitulate, turn back, or give in. To resist these things is to overcome, but something more is required if we are to prevail — keeping His deeds until the end. We must be faithful.

Promises Instead of Comfort

Jesus, as is often the case, offers little comfort but makes a promise instead. *No doubt He knows that we need the promise more than we need the comfort.* Comfort is focused inward, whereas promises are focused upward. Comfort consoles us in the temporal, whereas promises point us to the eternal. This is important. In His letter to the Ephesian church, Jesus takes a similar tack. He tells them they will be cast into prison and have ten days of suffering before they die. He offers no comfort but instead a promise — the crown of life for those who prevail. We need to know what is at stake more than we need to be given comfort. And what is at stake is huge.

There are two amazing promises for those who hold fast. The first is that He will give them authority over the nations. This is a direct reference to the millennial reign, and shows that ruling and reigning with Christ has conditions attached to it. It is obvious that those who do not hold fast or endure to the end, will not qualify for this honor. This first promise seems sublime until we look at the second. *"And I will give him the morning star."* Later we find out who the morning star is: Jesus.

In Revelation 22:16 Jesus says, *"I am the root and the offspring of David, the bright morning star."* So Jesus crowns this passage and the promise to overcomers with a gift offering — Himself. Hopefully, at this point, you don't need to question why Jesus would offer an incentive that clearly all believers in heaven will enjoy. Despite our limited understanding, we can be assured that Jesus will "give" Himself in differing measures to each of us according to our faithfulness.

Jesus as Elder Brother

Jesus has many roles with respect to the redeemed. The manner in which He expresses Himself to us in Scripture will be governed by the role He is assuming. This is key to understanding why Jesus so frequently offers promises instead of comfort. In the passage we are considering, after Jesus says He will give the Thyatirans authority over the nations, He adds *"...as I also have received authority from My Father."* Why did Jesus receive authority from His Father, and why does He feel it necessary to point this out?

We looked at the answer earlier: *"He who overcomes, I will grant to him to sit down with Me on My throne, as I also overcame and sat down with My Father on His throne"* (Rev. 3:21). Jesus received authority from His Father because He was an overcomer. But in the inclusion of this detail, there is insight into our own situation, and this is the reason He points it out.

Here we see Jesus in the role of elder brother, the first born of many sons. As our forerunner, He learned obedience through the things He suffered. But He overcame. He compares His journey to our own, and along with it, the reward. Here it is imperative that we understand our position with respect to the ministry of Jesus Christ. We must realize that, though He is God, He offers us two unique roles according to the scriptures: we are co-laborers together with Christ, and joint-heirs with Jesus.

Jesus labored to enter into His inheritance, and now out of unimaginable grace, He offers us the same thing. The qualification for being a joint-heir is the work of being a co-laborer, which involves suffering. The Christian life is a labor of love but fraught with difficulty. It will take the cross to successfully navigate it. The blessing of the Book of Revelation is in discovering the reward for those who do.

Thrones and Dominions

Of the rewards for overcomers mentioned in scripture, two have special prominence. These are thrones and dominion; ruling and reigning; to sit on a throne and to have authority over the nations. We know that these positions are among the highest rank in heaven and are only promised to overcomers. By continually referencing them, the Lord makes it plain that these are to be greatly sought.

Have you ever admired someone and wanted to be their right-hand man? Have you ever esteemed an employer, a pastor or an official so much you wanted to serve as their assistant? That's the essence of ruling. It's not about egos and power trips, like it is here on earth. All of that is gone once we cross over: no sin, no base motives. So let's not be falsely humble about not wanting to rule in the eternal kingdom. Jesus said it was something worth giving your life for.

To many of us, ruling and reigning with Christ may sound like work. To the carnal mind, looking after New York for a thousand years certainly doesn't sound like a reward. On earth the word "politics" has a negative connotation, and it is hard to comprehend rulership without the attendant politics. But we need to see it through the eyes of faith. Present paradigms are inadequate to explain the future reality. We only need to understand two things: Firstly, every reward bestowed by God is a good thing. Secondly, administrating the Kingdom for the God we love will bring joy that has no earthly counterpart.

The Allotted Portion
What else does God put into the mix for those who love Him? We have an interesting statement in Daniel 12:

"Now at that time Michael, the great prince who stands guard over the sons of your people, will arise. And there will be a time of distress such as never occurred since there was a nation until that time; and at that time your people, everyone who is found written in the book, will be rescued.

And many of those who sleep in the dust of the ground will awake, these to everlasting life, but the others to disgrace and everlasting contempt.

And those who have insight will shine brightly like the brightness of the expanse of heaven, and

*those who lead the many to righteousness like the
stars forever and ever." (Dan.12:1-3)*

Notice, first of all, that in heaven redeemed men will all
emit a light according to the glory of their eternal bodies.
This glory will be directly proportional to their service to
Christ on earth. Jesus makes reference to this in the gospel
of Matthew: *"Then the righteous will shine forth as the sun
in the kingdom of their Father. He who has ears to hear, let
him hear"* (Matt. 13:43). "He who has ears to hear" is like "a
word to the wise is sufficient." Jesus is not going to belabor
it. If we're wise, we'll get the point.

Secondly, Daniel divides all believers into two broad
groups — those who have insight, and those who lead
many to righteousness. It seems like there are introverts and
extraverts, those who study and those who take action, the
inward journey and the outward expression, gaining insight
and winning souls, the great commandment and the great
commission. It appears that all spiritual activity from meditation to handing out tracts fits into one of those broad categories. One is basically inward and the other outward. God has
a specific role for each of the two major personality types.

Lastly, notice in this same chapter God's firm directive
to Daniel: *"But as for you, go your way to the end; then you
will enter into rest and rise again for your allotted portion at
the end of the age"* (Dan. 12:13). Notice the words, "allotted
portion". We should salivate as we read this phrase, for that
is what God has for each one of us. Every servant of God
has an allotted portion waiting for him in heaven. God has
determined from the foundations of the world what that will
be. The question is, will we attain to it?

Daniel obviously did, but will you and I?

The Reward of Crowns
There are five different crowns mentioned in scripture:

1) The crown of life — the martyr's crown;
2) The crown of gory — the elder or pastor's crown;
3) The crown of rejoicing — the soul winner's crown;
4) The crown of righteousness — the crown for those who love His appearing;
5) The crown incorruptible — the victor's crown.

To the natural mind these may seem odd, perhaps even frivolous. But let us be careful of despising what the Lord has so carefully prepared for those who love Him. In Revelation 4 we have a precious scene in heaven where the twenty-four elders cast their crowns at the Lord's feet. Not surprisingly, this scene has figured strongly in the lyrics of hymn writers. It is a visible expression of the sentiment that all glory belongs to the Lamb.

But even if the sole purpose of obtaining a crown is to cast it at the feet of Jesus, isn't that a distinction worth having? But, of course, that is not the sole purpose. The whole concept of reward is that **we** are the beneficiaries. Crowns may be an archaic symbol in the twenty-first century, but their true value will one day be made manifest.

The Judgment of Leaders

When viewing the list of crowns, one could justifiably ask the following question: How is it then, that leaders receive special crowns? Not everyone can be a pastor or an elder; they must be called of God. Isn't that a kind of favoritism? Yes, it is. Spiritual leaders are favored with both the blessings and the difficulties of their calling.

In Hebrews 13 we find the following statement: *"Obey your leaders, and submit to them; for they keep watch over your souls, as those that will give an account."* This watching at the very least involves protection, nurturing, and teaching. Some take this calling very seriously, and will receive the blessings that come with faithfulness. Only true spiritual leaders really understand the sacrifices that result from a commitment to shepherd a flock in a godly fashion. Most have never given the crown a thought, but neither would they be surprised that there is one.

However, there are doubtless many leaders who have been negligent. Or worse, they have been opportunists. They have seen leadership in terms of benefits and have used the position for gain. The crowns are only for those who serve well. Those who don't serve well will be surprised at the weight God puts on something they didn't take seriously or misused in a carnal way. There will be a tremendous accounting.

In Paul's final charge to the church at Ephesus, he acquits himself with the following statement: *"Therefore I testify to you this day, that I am innocent of the blood of all men. For I did not shrink from declaring to you the whole purpose of God"* (Acts 20:26,27). As leaders, we must likewise presume that to be innocent of the blood of all men, we must also declare the whole purpose of God. This statement flies in the face of the "happy hour" mentality, which sees no evil and only preaches a positive message. The whole purpose of God will encompass the whole Word of God. One of the purposes of God is that no believer face judgment unprepared. Paul was faithful to warn his spiritual charges about Judgment Day.

Before we move on to the parable of the Lamb's Supper, it would be advantageous to use the technique of contrast to more fully understand the issue of inheritance. Jesus, for instance, didn't just teach on the fruitful life; He employed contrast in the parable of the sower to show us three things that would cause us to lose the fruit of our labor, and therefore our reward as well. We can learn from the mistakes of others. We can learn from what the Bible has to say about lost inheritance. It is not negative to do so, but it *is* sobering.

So let us consider the issue of despising our inheritance in order to more fully understand what it will take to secure it.

FOURTEEN

The Esau Principle - Despising Our Inheritance

" *See to it...that there be no immoral or godless person like Esau who sold his own birthright for a bowl of stew" (Heb. 12:16).* Is there any more pathetic verse in the Bible than this one? Here you have the implied contrast — the shrewd, conniving Jacob whom God loved, and the immoral, godless Esau whom God hated. But why is making a bad trade in a moment of weakness, so immoral and godless? For the answer we have to look at the nature of Esau's offence.

Esau committed an atrocious act in God's eyes. He traded something priceless for something worthless. He sold his birthright for a bowl of stew. From time immemorial, a man's firstborn son was given privileges above those of his younger brothers. These included a double portion of the inheritance as well as certain blessings and distinctions.

The text in Genesis is brief, but it tells us all we need to know: *"Once when Jacob was cooking some stew, Esau came in from the open country famished. He said to Jacob, 'Quick, let me have some of that red stew! I'm famished!'"* (Gen. 25: 29.30).

The fact that Esau was walking and talking destroys the famine argument. Thanks to television, we have all seen the face of famine. Esau was simply hungry. Plus, there is no evidence that he couldn't have made himself something to eat, for there were foodstuffs in the house.

So it seems like it was the smell of fresh stew and not hunger per sae that caused him to capitulate. In other words, he gave away his birthright to satisfy not hunger, **but instant gratification**. He justified it by saying that his inheritance was worth nothing to him dead.

A man of honor, who understood true value, would rather have died than surrender to such ridiculous terms. At the very least, he would have grabbed something from the pantry or found himself some edible weeds and bark. He would never have given in to impulse. Jesus faced the same temptation, and after forty days without food He truly was starving. However, unlike Esau, He responded to Satan's offer of bread with the contempt it deserved.

I will always remember Ern Baxter's comment on the collapse of the healing movement in the fifties. Under the weight of moral failures and deceptive practices, the anointing finally lifted from these once great men of God. "What bothered me," said Baxter with pain in his voice, "is that they sold the anointing so cheaply." They traded the power and glory of the most high God for a one-night stand, a romp in the sack with an adulteress. They moved in the power gifts and saw thousands healed, yet they treated the anointing as having less worth than a night with a harlot. They threw it away for instant gratification.

God hates that attitude. If they had at least been shrewd enough to trade it for riches, God may have felt less insulted, less offended, less violated. But such are men when, in their darkened imaginations, they are unable to distinguish between copper and gold. And like Esau, they don't even seem to care!! Live for the moment, whatever the cost. How vain, how foolish, and how horribly expensive on Judgment Day.

Temptations of the Latter Years

Something happens to us as we age. Though there are promises of entering the afterlife with youthful vigor, for most of us this is not the case. Often men weaken, not only physically, but in their moral resolve as well. Things that they have worked for their entire lives can be casually thrown away. More than one man has said something like the following: "I've served the Lord all my life; now with the years I have left, I want to have some fun." Then they cast off restraint and begin doing the very things they have preached against all their lives, with no thought of the consequences. They evidently feel they've earned the right to sin. They consider it time off for good behavior. But "time off" from the path of life has devastating consequences.

What they fail to understand is that throughout their many years of service they have been laying up something pure and undefiled in heaven. By not valuing it, they have ended up despising it. They prefer a voucher for sin to the glories of the eternal Kingdom. And for their foolishness, they lose everything. How very sad.

At other times men resist sin and wrong choices, knowing that if they are not weary in well-doing, they will one day reap. But sometimes when victory is the closest, they flag and suffer great loss. The man who set up the first franchise of Christian counseling centers in America had marital problems for decades. By all accounts, his wife was indeed a difficult person. But she apparently wanted the marriage to work and resisted the idea of divorce.

Finally, after years of struggle, the man gave up and filed for divorce, knowing very clearly what the cost would be. Soon after, he began to pay that cost. He embarked on a trip across America to shut down all the centers that were part of the great ministry he had built. I could tell many such stories, but you and I will one day hear them all. Standing in that great assembly, our hearts will be broken one last time at the futility of what men have traded for the glory of God.

Train-Wreck Syndrome

All of us, to some degree, suffer from "train-wreck syndrome". We are drawn to the sirens and flashing lights that signal an accident. Few of us can avert our eyes as we pass a mangled death scene on the highway. Many slow down to gaze with morbid fascination at the devastation before them.

My personal fascination has nothing to do with train wrecks, earthquake devastation, or even the destruction wrought by a Tsunami. What cuts me to the core is seeing men and women throw away their inheritance. To me, that is devastation of the highest order. I feel a pain that is deeper and more profound than that caused by physical death. The fact is, we all live forever, and so death is not the end, nor is it *the* great tragedy. *The* great tragedy is the inability to distinguish between the sacred and the profane.

Looking at Our Own Lives

While it is instructive to look at the failures of other men, it is more profitable to look at our own. How much of *our* inheritance is being squandered? What future blessings do *we* trade for the temporal pleasures of this world? God has predestined both our works and our rewards, but it takes the one to garner the other. If we don't prize our inheritance, it is unlikely we'll meet the conditions to receive it. We can sell it very cheaply and not just to satisfy appetites like lust.

How many hours, weeks and lifetimes have been frittered away with mindless distractions because believers never discovered their purpose? I suspect Esau is not an aberration. He represents multitudes who will one day discover to their dismay that they, too, traded their inheritance cheaply.

The Invitation

The Pain of Wasted Lives

Have you ever had a friend or a relative who had a wayward son or daughter? They didn't value a good name and righteous standards, but were constantly in trouble with the law. They may have dropped out of high school and, though brilliant, they couldn't even hold a job.

Have you seen the pain these parents experience as they see the child they love wasting their life? They see all that unrealized potential squandered on drugs and booze. Perhaps their child has even stolen from them to support their habit. Maybe in the need of the moment they sold Mom's $5,000 ring for one hit of cocaine — the epitome of perverted values. It's been known to happen.

If you understand how these parents feel, then you have some inkling of how God feels when we waste our lives. Many carnal things that we call noble pursuits, He regards no differently than a drunkard's dissipation. There is a scripture that is poorly understood because of the inconsistent translation of a Greek word into the English. These verses will tell us much about God's attitude toward wasted lives.

> "Then Jesus said to his disciples, 'If any one wishes to come after Me, let him deny himself, and take up his cross, and follow Me.
>
> For whoever wishes to save his life shall lose it; but whoever loses his life for My sake shall find it.
>
> For what will a man be profited, if he gains the whole world, and forfeits his soul? Or what will a man give in exchange for his soul?
>
> For the Son of Man is going to come in the glory of His Father with His angels; and will then recompense every man according to his deeds.'" (Matt. 16: 25-27)

361

In this passage the same Greek word that is translated "life" in verse 25 ("save his life/lose his life") is incorrectly translated "soul" in verse 26 ("lose his own *soul"*). Using "soul" gives the impression that verse 26 applies to an unbeliever who is highly successful but is going to hell. However, this entire passage deals with the believers' judgment, and the word "soul" should have been translated "life" as in the other two cases.

So what is Jesus trying to tell us in this passage? Very simply, that if you try to save your life, you'll lose it — waste it, that is. If you don't die to self and embrace the cross, you won't be able to fulfill the destiny God has for you. If you "save your life", you will be self-centered and perhaps have an easy life, but in the end you'll be the loser. At the judgment you'll be recompensed according to your deeds, and your deeds will reveal that your life was wasted.

However, if you lose your life for the Lord's sake, you'll find it. It will have value; it won't be wasted. You'll also lead a more meaningful life, but the emphasis here is on eternal benefit. "Losing your life" may involve hard choices. You may miss temporal opportunities for riches and honor because of your faithfulness to the Lord and the gospel. Make no mistake: there is a price to serve God. If you willingly lose your life, then you'll fulfill your destiny and you'll have great reward.

Finally, to drive home the point, Jesus takes the most extreme example. He says that even if a man is the most successful person on the planet, his success is of no benefit to him if he wastes his life. If he totally abandons the crucified life and lives strictly for his own ambitions, he will receive nothing on Judgment Day. And then Jesus adds: *"Or what can a man give in exchange for his life?"*

That last question is a haunting reminder that there is going to be great sorrow on Judgment Day. When a person stands before God and discovers that he has wasted his entire life, he would give anything to have it back. But it's over. His eternal destiny is set. It cannot be changed, and all the tears will avail nothing.

We must bear in mind that pain in this life is inevitable. Jesus said that if we bear fruit, He would prune us so that we bear more fruit. In other words He will cut us, and cutting hurts. This has several applications, but pruning usually represents the trials we undergo that make us stronger. However, if a branch produces no fruit, it is cut as well, and the result is loss.

So if we produce, we are cut, and if we *don't* produce, we are also cut. There is the pain of discipline or the pain of regret — we choose. The pain of discipline is a "now" pain, but it produces an eternal harvest. The pain of regret is what you feel when you stand before God and see that you have wasted your life. The result is great loss.

It's a terrible thing to waste a human life. Have you ever wondered why God despises the sluggard? The proverbs are full of His scorn and contempt for these individuals. In God's eyes, there is only one thing worse than a person who misspends his life pursuing vain temporal things: it is the one who does nothing at all with his life. God delights in activity, and is the most creative and industrious Being in the universe. Life is a precious gift, and He is deeply offended at the sight of someone despising his life through indolence.

Trivial Pursuit

God's chief competition is the world. In a superficial sense, the world seems to have a lot to offer, and much of it appears harmless. It *is* harmless and that is part of the problem. A while back the Reader's Digest published an article where the author listed the top 100 things he wanted to do before he died, and recommended others do the same. Now, years later, these lists can be found everywhere on the Internet. The lists are, in large part, absurd, and are a graphic illustration of how misguided people are in what they see as important. But as Christians, we must be wary lest we too be persuaded to waste our time on temporal, frivolous goals.

I'm reminded of a quote I saw once under the plastic desk pad of a co-worker, a quote I have seen several times elsewhere. It goes something like this: "If I could live my life over again, I'd be far less serious. I'd play more hooky, eat more ice-cream, watch more sunsets, climb more mountains, take more risks, laugh more, travel more, stay out more, stay up more, live in the moment, etc." To be sure, this has a euphoric, if somewhat infantile, appeal to it. Reckless abandon is actually how some people live their lives, but unless it is reckless abandon for Jesus, they seldom make it to heaven. And if they do, their mountain climbing skills don't garner them much reward.

The life well-lived is the life of a servant. This is what Jesus modeled and taught. He never presented it as glamorous, intensely gripping, or superficially satisfying to the senses. He often pictured it as difficult and sacrificial, but the compensations are many — love, joy, peace, fulfillment, and ultimately, eternal profit. This is the measure of a man's life: Was it profitable? Was it fruitful? Was it expended for God? Did it benefit people? If we invest our lives in the things that perish, we face the mockery of both God and men.

Few of us have understood that God is a mocker. Psalm 2 says He laughs at the nations, He scoffs at them, He holds them in derision. But individuals, not just nations, are the target of His mockery.

God as Mocker

In Psalm 52 we find the following verses:

> *"But God will break you down forever;*
> *He will snatch you up, and tear you away form*
> *your tent,*

And uproot you from the land of the living.
And the righteous will see and fear,
And will laugh at him, saying,
  'Behold, the man who would not make God his
refuge,
  But trusted in the abundance of his riches,
  And was strong in his evil desire.' "

In both the Old and New Testament we are told to love even our enemies. In fact, David, who wrote Psalm 52, said that he was in sackcloth and ashes when his enemies were in pain. So why in this Psalm does he mock them? Quite simply, because God mocks them. God does so for three reasons: they didn't make God their refuge, they trusted in the abundance of riches, and they were strong in their evil desire. Or, as the NIV puts it, they *"grew strong by destroying others"*. In other words, they lived for the temporal and felt very secure, with no need for God and certainly no fear of Him.

We gain insight into the intensity of God's emotions by the language He uses to describe their death. The violence depicted in the phrases "snatch up", "tear away" and "uproot" show the suddenness and the contempt with which He destroys their lives. It is very reminiscent of the New Testament farmer who was going to build bigger barns to contain his bounty. God had other plans. That very day his soul was required of Him. Anyone who trusts in riches and ignores the One who gave them, does so at his peril. The response of the righteous in Psalm 52 is twofold. Their first response is fear. As at the deaths of Ananias and Saphira, the fear response to God's judgment is totally appropriate. We should be afraid lest we be guilty of something that would incite similar wrath.

Their second response is to laugh and mock the man who would not make God his refuge but trusted in riches. In a sense it's prideful to mock the unregenerate, because "there but for the grace of God go I." But on the other hand, a life given over to dissipation and temporal pleasures cries out for mockery.

We pray for the ungodly while they are alive, but after they are dead, their lives are worthy of scorn. I remember a famous actor who openly mocked Christianity as a farce and an empty superstition. This man was a legendary alcoholic and womanizer who lived in excess with no thought for his eternal soul. Shortly after making this statement, he died of an alcohol-related disease. I couldn't help but think: "Behold the man who would not make God his refuge, and was strong in his evil desire."

At other times we fear. John Lennon bragged openly on one of his album covers of his distaste for religion. He believed in nothing but himself, and he had no hesitation in announcing this to the world. I remember the last day of John Lennon's life. He had just emerged from years of seclusion and had given a radio interview. In it he talked with giddy excitement about the future. He had the next twenty years planned, but it all ended that day. I remember the shudder that went through my body when I learned of his death. "Behold the man who would not make God his refuge, but trusted in the abundance of his riches."

The Prodigal Son

There is one aspect of the Prodigal Son parable that is never mentioned. When the older brother complained that no calf had ever been given to him for a celebration with his friends, the father replies, "*You are always with me and everything I have is yours.*" That answer has always seemed rather lame to me. My mental response has always been: "Gee thanks, Dad. But how about the fatted calf?"

What the son is forgetting, and we often miss, is that you can't both *spend* your inheritance and still *have* your inheritance. The father expected his sons to work during their lifetimes for an inheritance that would come after his death. The prodigal son, though still a son and blessed by his father, had already spent his inheritance. But the older brother still had his. The calf signified grace, and the older brother should not have mistaken grace for inheritance. He should have rejoiced at his father's mercy. Many of us face the same challenge because we tend to focus more on blessing than inheritance.

There can be jealousy in the church when God blesses a returning backslider seemingly more than a faithful servant. There will always be more excitement over the one that has been lost than over the ninety-nine that were not. But it is simply grace. The wasted years can never be reclaimed; the inheritance has been squandered. The joy of the return will, on Judgment Day, be overshadowed by the sorrow at the loss.

In Ezekiel 44, the priests who fell away were restored, but their sentence was hard: They could minister to the people, but they could not minister to God. Ministry unto God was strictly for those who hadn't fallen away. Backsliding carries a price tag. Does this mean that backslidden believers can't minister to God in heaven? I believe they can, but not with the intimacy of those who serve before His throne.

A Metaphor

I have heard every possible description of heaven from those who claim personal revelation. One person claims he was caught up in the spirit and shown three heavens. The first is for people who are born again, but lived selfish, fruitless lives. The second is for committed Christians who garnered reward through considerable effort on earth. The third, where God's throne is, is for bondslaves and martyrs — those who gave everything. They will be the aristocracy of heaven. I don't know if this is true, but whatever the reality, this metaphor captures something of the distinctions that exist in heaven — distinctions based on service on earth.

Everyone understands the concept of a trade. At some amusement parks you purchase tickets that can be used for any ride or event. But with these tickets comes the knowledge that with every spent ticket something is being traded: the future. You cannot use later what has been spent now.

Life is like that. Time and money, for instance, are two simple things that once spent, are gone forever. We need frequent reminders that every day we are involved in a trade — the giving of finite resources, either for things that perish with this world, or things that endure unto life eternal. Let us be good traders and not despise our inheritance.

FIFTEEN

The Invitation – a Parable

Awards Day and the Lamb's Supper

Perhaps the greatest understatement of all time is recorded in Revelation 19 where we find these words: *"Blessed are those who are invited to the marriage supper of the Lamb" (Rev. 19:9)*. The word "blessed" conveys so little of the honor and bliss that will be the companion of those who are present at this momentous event. Take the marriage of an earthly king and multiply it by a billion, and you would just be reaching the outskirts of what we will experience.

A sports illustration may help us in our understanding of the events that transpire at the awards ceremony in heaven and at the marriage supper of the Lamb.

In hockey, winning the Olympic Gold medal requires endurance and total commitment. By the time the final game is played, many players have missing teeth and facial stitches. They have paid a huge price for victory! So with the final whistle and the announcement of the winner, the arena erupts.

At center ice there is bedlam, with a group hug, hoots of joy, and ecstatic grins. In the middle of the hug is the coach, the goalie, and some of the key players who made the victory possible. In the next ring of the hug are less important, but still critical, players. They likewise have made huge contributions, and savor the victory as much as anyone.

But at the outer perimeter of the group we see something very different. Here we witness players awkwardly clasping those in front of them, trying to appear jubilant. But their enthusiasm seems wooden and forced. Their eyes are vacant and glassy. They are trying too hard to show excitement, and it is painfully obvious to the onlookers.

Who are these players? They are the ones who were on the team but contributed nothing to the victory. They will get medals, but they know they have done nothing to earn them. They were simply members of the team. For them it is a hollow victory; for them it is painful to be around the genuine joy of those who have paid the price for the triumph. They have mixed emotions. They are participants in the greatest celebration imaginable, and yet they feel set apart, like observers at someone else's party.

But there is another group of players that aren't even in the victory circle. These are the players who are highly gifted and had been expected to lead the team. Yet because of selfishness and poor effort, their talent was wasted. They had been benched. So the team had to win without them. What dejection they feel, what self-contempt, what grief for having let the team down!

Immediately following the game, an Olympic Dinner is held for the players in gratitude for what they have done for their country. The dinner is sponsored by the government and in attendance is the King. All those who were critical to the victory are celebrated and given seats of honor. You can see in the face of the King how much their sacrifices have meant. In return, the players are jubilant. The honor they are given has made all their hard work and suffering worthwhile.

But at the far end of the table the mood is different. The food is just as good and the players can clearly see the King, but they know that they have done little to deserve the honor of the occasion. And now it was too late. The game is over, and the seating is fixed.

The Wedding Feast from One Vantage Point

Gradually this Olympic banquet scene fades into another banquet scene — the marriage supper of the Lamb. And you're sitting there, near the far end. The table is probably at least a hundred miles long and yet you can see the Lamb quite clearly. In fact, you see everyone clearly. You can also hear the Lamb's voice and, what is truly marvelous, you can feel His love, even after the way you disappointed Him. But you wonder what it would be like up closer to Him. You wonder what the people near Him are experiencing. You'll never know. You have joy, you have bliss, but about the other...you'll just never know.

Then you see someone you know sitting quite near the throne. It is someone from your church and you're in shock. Sure, you had admired him because he was a godly man. He seemed to labor tirelessly, but you had assumed that that was his calling. He was, after all, a very gifted man, and you knew well the scripture: *"To whom much is given, much is required."* But you made the mistake of thinking the opposite was true as well.

You had thought that being average meant getting a free ride. You got to enjoy life while gifted people like him had to do all the work. You rejoiced at your good fortune, but in your rejoicing you forgot to do the simple things, like pray. You also forgot to serve, and you even forgot to worship. It seems, in fact, that you forgot to do everything that required work, effort, and sacrifice. In thinking God required little, you ended up giving Him nothing. And now that is what you were receiving back from Him — nothing. It really was true that those who sowed sparingly also reaped sparingly.

And then comes the second shock. Turning your attention back to the head of the table you spy a woman you have known for years. On earth she had never attracted much attention, being very much a behind-the-scenes type of person. But as you think about her life, the reason for her seating becomes painfully clear. She was a servant and you were not. She was a teaching assistant in a Christian school and poured her life into others. She did all the little things that added up to the one big thing: love. She loved people, and her love changed many lives, especially those of her students. Why hadn't you seen this before? How had you missed it?!

You had heard about the believers' judgment once or twice, but it just seemed like words. It went over your head. You had thought if you were a decent person and lived right, everything would work out okay. In that way you weren't really much different from many of those in hell, for that is what they had believed as well.

Thank God for the blood of Jesus, you think, through a swell of tears. Like those seated near you, you are grateful just to be there. The judgment was severe. It seemed to last at least as long as your life. Nevertheless, when the full accounting was over, He wiped away your tears, embraced you, and reassured you of His love.

And you have that same love for Him. The joy that you had sung about while on earth is now your constant companion. And yet you realize if you had your life to live over again, you would live it very differently.

A Second Vantage Point

Then the scene shifts again, and now you find yourself seated near the throne. "Why me?" you ask as you note your placement. You had never given Judgment Day much thought, but you had been taught from childhood that the crowning achievement of one's life was to hear "Well done, good and faithful servant." You knew that this meant a life of obedience. But still, you were surprised at the Lord's exuberant response to what had been, after all, a rather ordinary life.

But you also knew that there had been key decisions that had shaped your destiny. While on earth, you had been aware of the choices you faced, and how they would set the course for your life. One was the decision to go into the ministry. You had felt called, but certainly not equipped. But laying aside your fears and doubts, you plunged in, and God had been there to meet you and walk with you every step of the way.

Then there was the time you faced a revolt within your church leadership over some moral issues. You knew you had to take a stand, but there was a great amount of gossip and confusion surrounding certain people's actions, including your own. It was all you could do to hold your ground and let the Lord vindicate you. At the time you knew all too well the effect your actions would have on your future ministry. A compromise at this point would have meant peace, but the price would have been your integrity.

Thank God you hadn't compromised, you exclaim inwardly with a rush of emotion, tears welling up in your eyes. So much growth, so many souls, so much ministry had come from the release of the Spirit. How close you had come to missing that.

And then there was the betrayal you had suffered at the hands of a father in the faith. There was also the tragedy in your son's life and your own illness. At each point you had to fight bitterness, doubt and depression. But with each difficulty, the grace was there if you wanted it, and you did want it. You had seen others do well for decades, but then shrink back because of deep offense or great affliction. With God's grace you had determined that you would never succumb to discouragement, and by His grace you didn't. But it all seems strangely foreign now.

Indeed, every trial and every temptation seemed so difficult at the time, but Paul was right. They really *"weren't worthy to be compared to the coming glory"*. That is the universal observation of the people around the banquet table. How trivial those trials seem from this side of the veil.

Many are feeling the sting of being fooled and defrauded of glory by things so inconsequential that they can barely remember them. Others are feeling the way one does when a split second decision avoids an accident. They look back on right choices they made by the skin-of-their-teeth, and now, like the near-accident victim, they are shuddering at what might have been.

Now they are seated at the King's table; they have come through it; they are in heaven. All the hard decisions are behind them. That which was written in Isaiah 25 has finally come to pass: *"And the Lord of hosts will prepare a lavish banquet for all peoples on this mountain; a banquet of aged wine, choice pieces with marrow, and refined aged wine"*(verse 6). Accomplished also is His promise in verse 8: *"He will swallow up death for all time, and the Lord God will wipe tears away from all faces."* And the response from the dinner guests is exactly as prophesied: *"Behold, this is our God for whom we have waited that He might save us. This is the Lord for whom we have waited; let us rejoice and be glad in His salvation"* (verse 9).

Yes indeed: let us rejoice and be glad in His salvation!

The Grand Irony of Life

Let us move beyond the banquet scene and elaborate on what I call "the grand irony of life". How strange that this incredibly short thing called life affects the next billion years. I have always wondered at Abraham's comment in Luke 16. There we have the story of the rich man and Lazarus. The rich man was in Hades, and seeing Abraham afar off with Lazarus in his bosom, asked for a drop of water to cool his tongue.

To his request Abraham replied: *"Child, remember that during your life you received your good things, and likewise Lazarus bad things; but now he is being comforted here, and you are in agony."* Notice the chilling way in which Abraham refers to the man as "child", and the absence of any venom in his answer, as if he were talking to an old friend.

But it is the answer itself that is even more chilling. During their brief life, one was rich, the other was poor; one had good things, the other bad; one had nothing to give, the other seemingly *gave* nothing. The sentence for this brief period of suffering or splendor was so profound — eternal bliss or eternal agony.

It all seems so out of proportion. If life was a thousand years, it might make *some* sense. Surely it would seem a *little* less lopsided if we had a thousand years to decide for Christ, to pull our life together, and to accumulate good works. But we don't. We have seventy or eighty years to determine our placement in the eternal ages.

Life is like parenting in that you have one brief crack at it, one chance to get it right. Any detour or major failing can have severe consequences. The unavoidable truth is that we have precious little time to waste. There is no time to achieve all of our selfish ambitions before we commit our life to Christ, and no time to waste on frivolities after we do.

The labor of those who applied themselves to single-mindedly serving God without waffling or wavering will one day astound us. Most will be obscure people *"of whom the world was not worthy"*. And yet what they leave behind will set them apart. I find a recent example from the Arts to be most illuminating.

The Unknown Soldier

As we approached the new millennium, various intellectual bodies sought to identify the man of the millennium: the most significant figure of the last thousand years. This was no easy task, with so many luminaries that would warrant consideration: Galileo, Luther, Einstein, Guttenberg, Washington, etc. The winner was surprising — the bard from

Stratford, William Shakespeare. Why surprising? Because almost nothing is known about the man.

We know that he was born because we have his birth certificate. We know that he was married because we have his marriage certificate. We have a couple of reviews of his plays, so we believe that he in fact wrote them. But we know little else. It is only what he left behind — his works — that give him the fame and honor that he possesses. And not just honor, but honor above anyone in the past thousand years.

That's the way it will be on Judgment Day. There will be people about whom we know nothing, but from whose lives came fruit that multiplied and resounded down through the ages. They found God and made Him their untiring passion, and in so doing they moved heaven and shook the earth.

The voracious readers among us occasionally hear of a person who won an entire village, which later impacted a region, and in due course changed a nation. But of the true leaven of the gospel that permeates the earth we know so little. But everything is recorded, and that record is just as tangible as the Shakespearean volumes in any library.

It is hard to judge before the time, and that is why God told us not to. Mozart was a world famous violinist by the age of seven. Bach was not nearly as prodigious. Yet today few would disagree that Bach is the greater of the two. But it often takes the collective wisdom of many centuries for men to judge true worth, and even then they are often wrong. If judging something like music is difficult, how much more so the matters of the heart. But God suffers from no such limitation. He knows the end from the beginning, and the ultimate worth of everything.

One day, so will we.

The Moment of Truth

The Marriage Feast of the Lamb has yet to occur. But it will. As long as we are alive, our seating has yet to be established. So for us there is still time and opportunity. We can still affect the outcome of that great day. Some of us may only need to make minor adjustments. For others, it may require a total rethinking of their Christian faith and priorities. Fear, as we have seen earlier, is a good motivator. It compels us to honestly ask: How do I feel about facing God with the record as it currently stands?

No weightier question exists.

The Great Mystery

"Will there be remorse in heaven over lost reward, and will there be envy and rancor towards those who have achieved great honor?" That was the question posed to me recently by a friend. Heaven is a place of eternal bliss ruled by a just God. God's justice differs from the courts on earth in that it is perfect. Because it is perfect, everyone will accept it. Once the tears are wiped away, and people have their assignments, however small, they will perform them with absolute joy for the God they love.

The unnerving part is that they will never know what they are missing, and in a place of perfect joy, they won't care. They will honor those who are above them in rank. The reason I say *unnerving* is because only on earth do we have the capacity to care whether we have special access to the King, or just some routine function. This teaching is meant to awaken something in our souls that cries, "I want more!"

"I want more and I'm willing to pay the price!"

Just because a person is happy to be least in the Kingdom doesn't mean that he isn't missing something or Someone. Think of your favorite food. There was probably a time when you'd have chosen Kraft Dinner. Just because a child is happy with Kraft Dinner doesn't mean he isn't missing something. But a child doesn't care that he is missing "indescribable culinary delights". He hasn't experienced them, nor has his taste been cultivated. But as an adult, you care. The idea of going back is unthinkable. The idea of ordering Kraft Dinner in the finest restaurant in the world is unthinkable.

But not to a child.

I have used the most prosaic and pedestrian of all analogies to describe something so sublime that it *cannot* be described. In heaven, there will be levels of joy, ecstasy, and worship that are directly proportional to our assignments and our intimacy with God. Here on earth that knowledge is strictly for the spiritually hungry, and cannot be understood by those who simply want eternal bliss.

Which are you? Which am I?

In Conclusion

The knowledge that there is a judgment has always been a benefit in my relationship with God. For one thing, it discourages sin and allows for unbroken fellowship, thereby fostering intimacy. But I've also been aware of God's responsibility to me.

If I discipline my son and he still ruins his life, then I'm acquitted. I've done what I could. However, if I don't discipline him and he fails, then I'm culpable. I have not carried out my responsibility. I'm partly to blame. It's no different with God. All failures in this life impact the life to come, and God is very cognizant of that fact. He's aware of His responsibility as Father.

But the other side of the coin is also true. If I stand before God some day and witness others being honored while I receive nothing, I have a right to ask why. If others had opportunities for overcoming that I never had, then something is amiss. Truthfully, I never had a chance to gain those rewards.

God is at work in our lives in both respects. He disciplines us to save us from the eternal harm we might do to ourselves. But He also provides us with opportunities for eternal gain. In particular He offers us Himself, but it is we who determine the level of intimacy we enjoy. One of the most enduring maxims is that we are as close to God as we want to be. These dynamics knit us to God in a deep way, because these are issues that truly transcend time.

The believers' judgment is something we rarely hear about. In Hebrews 6, the author included divine judgment in his list of the basics. The inference is that judgment is foundational and should be learned and understood by every new convert. Our accountability to God, our home in heaven, and the unseen world in general, are frequent themes in scripture.

Paul summarized the manner in which we should view the world in the following words: *"We look not at the things which are seen, but the things which are not seen; for the things which are seen are temporal, but the things which are not seen are eternal"* (2 Cor. 4:18).

Here we have the great test. Do we really believe that the other world is more real than this one? Do we really believe that physical life is a brief period where the great challenge is to commune intimately with the unseen God? Do we really believe that our life comes from God and should be given back to Him without reserve? Do we really believe that this magnificent obsession is worth every effort, every sacrifice, and every tear?

The apostle John recorded the answer given by those who had crossed over: *"Worthy is the Lamb."*

To Contact the Author

Email address: michaeldavidson@shaw.ca

Home Address: Michael Davidson
259 Pioneer Ave.
Prince George B.C.
Canada
V2M 4L9